Discipleship Training Program
Workbook 8

Fourth Semester

Fourth Quarter

Classes 92 - 105

Arthur Bailey
Arthur Bailey Ministries
PO Box 49744
Charlotte, NC 28277
PJ Langhoff (Ed.)
Second Edition
ISBN: 978-1-5057221-9-2
Library of Congress Control Number: 2015900605

Welcome to
House Of Israel
Discipleship Training Program

At House Of Israel, it is our goal to reach, to preach, and to teach men and women to become disciples of the Kingdom of YeHoVaH. One method we use to accomplish this goal is through comprehensive and dynamic training classes. We are certain that upon completion of our Discipleship Training Program, you will have a better understanding of discipleship, and become empowered to more effectively study and communicate the Word of YeHoVaH.

If at any time you have questions or concerns about this program, please feel free to contact us by phone, by email through our web sites, or by mail. We invite you and your family and friends to attend and to participate in our services at House Of Israel in Charlotte, at one of our satellites, or through any of our online sites. We provide programs through the internet, in print, and on television stations around the world.

Shalom!

Dr. Arthur Bailey

Mailing Address
Arthur Bailey Ministries
PO Box 49744
Charlotte, NC 28277

Office Phone Number
888-899-1479

Web Site Addresses
www.ArthurBaileyMinistries.com
Discipleship101.tv
Leadership101.tv

Fellowship Location
House Of Israel
1334 Hill Rd.
Charlotte, NC 28210

Fellowship Hours
Thursdays @ 7pm ET
Saturdays @ 11am ET

Table Of Contents

Fourth Semester
Fourth Quarter

Discipleship Training Program Workbook 8

Fourth Semester

Fourth Quarter

Classes 92 - 105

Discipleship Training Class 92

Messiah-Centered Principle (part 12)

Objectives:

As a Discipleship student, at the end of this class you will be able to:

- Define prophetic information about Yeshua's names and titles
- Name the prophetic words in the *Psalms* relating to Yeshua

We are going to be picking up where we left off last lesson and that is Messiah in the prophets. Then we are going to pick up on Messiah in the *Psalms* as we are looking at the Messiah-Centric principle, known in Christian circles as the Christ- or Christo-Centric principle. We are going to be looking at this and taking our time, because there is a lot of ground to cover on this particular subject.

We have noted that the Messiah-Centric principle is that principle by which scripture is interpreted in relation to its center — Messiah. In Christian circles they call him "Christ." Looking at this particular principle, we started out with the understanding that after his resurrection, Yeshua appeared to two disciples on the road to Emmaus. On this particular road, he shared or he listened to these disciples sharing with him about all the things that had taken place in Jerusalem (as if he didn't know).

Once he got to a place where he began to share with them, the Bible says that he opened up their eyes. He began to teach them all the things that were written about him in the law, in the prophets and in the *Psalms*. From the Torah, from Moses (the law), from the prophets and from the *Psalms*, Yeshua was able to communicate with these disciples. They were fully convinced that he was who he was and that he had risen from the dead.

The disciples began to share about the Messiah with the Hebrew community, the Jewish community and those who were believers in the Almighty but who had not received the Messiah. Peter, James, John and Sha'ul, as well as Priscilla, Aquila and Apollos all shared with the first century Hebrew community. They shared from the law, from the *Psalms* and from the prophets. They were able to convince these individuals that Yeshua was the Messiah of whom Moses spoke.

This is important because for the first 100 years or so, we know that there was no written New Testament. The first letter, the first gospel account of the gospels was around 50 to 52 A.D. So we have several years before there is even one letter; before there is one written account of what Messiah did (the gospel record). Then there is the book of *Acts*. We know that these brothers preached Messiah from the Tanakh or from the Old Testament. All that was referring to "the scriptures" in the New Testament was referring to the Tanakh, the Old Testament, the law, the prophets, the *Psalms* or the writings.

We know that for the first century, they preached Messiah from the law, the *Psalms* and from the prophets. We as believers today should be able to convince non-believers in Messiah (especially the Hebrew community, the Jewish community). We are able to communicate that this Messiah Yeshua is "the Prophet," "the Messiah" and the "son of David" whom Moses prophesied. This is whom David wrote about and whom the prophets prophesied about (that he is the Messiah).

Well, how are we going to do that? We do that by understanding Messiah in the Tanakh. We have looked at the Messiah in the Torah. We looked at him from *Genesis, Exodus, Leviticus, Numbers* and *Deuteronomy.* Then we started looking at Messiah in the prophets and we are still there. Then we are going to look at Messiah in the *Psalms.*

Messiah in the Prophets, continued

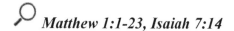 *Matthew 1:1-23, Isaiah 7:14*

Let's look at specific verses in *Matthew.* We know that the genealogy is important in order to be able to trace the lineage of Yeshua, because it is important for individuals to know that Yeshua was of the line of David.

Throughout the gospels, you will find that individuals refer to him as the "son of David."

Matthew 1:17-23

Now here the angel appears to Joseph and refers to him as a son of David, because he was of the household of David and David was of the household of Judah.

(Matthew 1:21) *"And she shall bring forth a son, and thou shalt call his name* JESUS: *for he shall save his people from their sins."*

As we look at verse 21 and the following verses, we are going to see what seem to be contradictory remarks. He says, "You shall call his name Yeshua." It goes on in verse 22, referring to the prophet. We need to know by "the prophet," what prophet are we talking about? That is because if we don't know what prophet he is talking about, how can you justify that a prophet said this?

Unfortunately too many people read their Bibles without researching what is being said, like the Bereans do; to make sure that what is being said is actually what is written.

The phrase *"...which was spoken of YeHoVaH by the prophet"* has two implications. The prophet said these words, but the prophet was speaking on behalf of YeHoVaH, so the words that the prophet was speaking were actually YeHoVaH's words.

This is important, especially when we begin to talk about the law. Most people think that because Moses wrote the law, then it is the Law of Moses.

But Moses received the instructions and wrote them down, so they were not Moses' words. They were YeHoVaH's words, given to Moses. Moses was the scribe or the one who wrote down what YeHoVaH gave him. The people falsely associate or attribute the law to Moses instead of to YeHoVaH.

When the prophet Jeremiah speaks or the prophet Isaiah speaks or any prophets speak on behalf of the Almighty, it is not the prophets' words. It is YeHoVaH's words, spoken to the prophet. The prophet is simply the mouthpiece that YeHoVaH chooses to use. When we see, *"as spoken of YeHoVaH by the prophet,"* what prophet is he speaking about and where is it?

(Matthew 1:23) "Behold, a virgin shall be with child, and shall bring forth a son, and they shall call his name Emmanuel, which being interpreted is, God with us."

We have some clues here as to what to look for, but wait a minute. First of all, the angel says to Miriam, "You are to call his name Yeshua." But the prophet says they are to call his name Emmanuel, which being interpreted is "El with us."

It is important for us to see this, because we use the term "Emmanuel" meaning "God with us" or "El with us." When we look at this — I gave you the reference as to what *Matthew* is referring to here and it is from *Isaiah 7:14.*

(Isaiah 7:14) "Therefore the Lord himself shall give you a sign; Behold, a virgin shall conceive, and bear a son, and shall call his name Immanuel."

It is interesting that here it is L-o-r-d, YeHoVaH, Adonai himself shall give you a sign. This is what *Isaiah* says, so *Isaiah* says that his name should be Emmanuel/Immanuel. Well, Immanuel is not a name. When the word is being used, understand what Immanuel means. Immanuel means "with us is El" or "El is with us." That is what it means. "God is with us."

When we look at what *Isaiah* says, the word here, "Immanuel" is from the Hebrew.

H6005 — *Immanuw'el*, im-maw-noo-ale; from **H5973** and **H410** with a pronominal suffix inserted; with us (is) God; Immanuel, a type name of Isaiah's son:--Immanuel.

It is a combination of 5973 and 410 — those are Strong's numbers. In other words, when the angel says his name will be Yeshua; the prophet said that through Yeshua, God will be with us. El will be with us. We are going to look at something else the prophet said.

⌕ *Isaiah 9:6-7*

The prophet Isaiah is writing. No prophet seems to write more about the Messiah than Isaiah. Isaiah says a lot that is quoted. And people, when it comes down to looking at the prophet to find the Messiah, *Isaiah* is the book from which most people spend most of their time identifying the Messiah.

In this passage the prophet is about to identify that this is a son and that there are some unique characteristics about this particular individual.

First, the government shall be upon his shoulder. It is not talking about Washington, D.C. or the county seat or the capital of some country. What it is talking about is the Kingdom; that he will govern the Kingdom of YeHoVaH. Now the Kingdom of YeHoVaH will be an external place, but currently it is an internal state. In other words, the Kingdom of YeHoVaH is in us. The Holy Spirit is within us. Our body is the temple of the Holy Spirit. And the Holy Spirit, which is the Almighty — YeHoVaH is Spirit dwelling in us and governing (or is supposed to).

Supposed to — so this is where the fruit of the Spirit: self-control, self-governed appears. In other words, we are supposed to be controlled by the Spirit of the Almighty who dwells in us through Yeshua. Therefore the Kingdom of YeHoVaH is within us. But the Kingdom of YeHoVaH shall be external when the King comes and establishes his reign here in the earth realm.

Let's look at some of these other characteristics.

Notice what happens here. You will see words and commas. In other words, he is going to be called a lot of things. One of the names he is going to be called is "Wonderful." In some denominations, they say that he should be called "Wonderful Counselor." They are totally ignoring the comma between "Wonderful" and "Counselor." Of course we know that commas were not part of the language, so we could say "the Wonderful Counselor the Mighty God the Everlasting Father the Prince of Peace" as one long phrase. But the fact is that he is going to be called "Wonderful." He is going to be called "Counselor." He is going to be called "the Mighty God." He is going to be called "the Everlasting Father." He is going to be called "the Prince of Peace."

What is interesting is that we can get our mind around some of these statements. This is the prophet speaking. We know that Yeshua had no children. We are not his children, so how is his name going to be called "the Everlasting Father?" These are things that I believe are going to be revealed in time to those who have eyes to see and ears to hear.

Understand something. We have no problem identifying him as "Wonderful." "Oh, he is wonderful." We have no problem identifying him as "the One who gives Counsel." "Oh, he is a wonderful counselor." We have no problem calling him, "Oh, he is the Prince of Peace, Sar Shalom." But then when it comes down to "the Mighty God" and "the Everlasting Father," that is when theology kicks in. Religion kicks in and disputations kick in.

I say when people want to have those kinds of conversations, that you need to take that up with *Isaiah*. I did not write this.

He will be called all of these things by different people. Some people will only refer to him as the Prince of Peace. Some people will only refer to him as "the Counselor" and some "Wonderful," but *Isaiah* says that he will be called all of these.

Let's literally break down these words to try to get an understanding of what *Isaiah* is communicating through the use of these particular Hebrew words.

The word for "wonderful" is *pele* or "miraculous." I don't have a problem identifying his birth as being miraculous. There was no human male, no physical earthly human being impregnating Miriam. This was (as some would say) an immaculate conception. As far as we know and I believe, he is a miracle. That is the word that is being used here. He will be called a miracle, wonderful.

The second statement here is the word "counselor" or *ya'ats*. This is a primitive root word meaning "to advise." It is one who advises, resolves or one who takes advice. Of course he takes advise from only one. That is from the Almighty himself. He said, "My words are not my own. I speak those words that have been given to me to speak." It means one who consults, one who counsels or guides. We can see that this word "counselor" is *ya-ats*.

Then there is this challenging statement, "the Mighty One" or "the Mighty God." We see the word *gibbowr*, warrior. It is negatively used as "a tyrant." Some people in the world would certainly refer to him as a tyrant, because it is as if he doesn't want you to do anything or have any fun. He just wants to control you. But that is not the case. He is a mighty man or a mighty one.

Then there is the word "El." It means "strength" or "mighty." It also refers to the Almighty. It is used as a deity. In this particular case it is YeHoVaH or El or Elohim or as we say, "God." This is a mighty one, one who has power, who is full of power or one who is strong.

Then there is "the Everlasting." This word by implication means that it has no end. It is without end. It is in perpetuity, everlasting, eternal, perpetual. He is the Mighty, Almighty, the Everlasting. Here it is the word "Father" (ab) and this is to be chief. The Chief One.

He is the Prince, "Sar." That is the head person, captain, chief, general, governor, prince, master or ruler.

And of course there is the word "shalowm." The thing about this word "shalowm/shalom" that I love so much is that it has many meanings. Most people refer to "shalowm" simply as "peace." "Shalom brother. Peace be unto you." "Shabbat Shalom." They would say, "Sabbath peace." The word "shalom" has so many more definitions than simply "peace," because it is the thing that attributes peace to us. We are at peace when all is well. We are at peace when we are happy. We are at peace when our welfare is good. I am not saying that we are "on welfare." Welfare is not a negative term. It is just how people use terminologies. We are at peace when we are healthy. We are at peace when we have prosperity. We have our needs met. This word "peace" has to deal with being in good health, perfect health. It is when things around us are peaceable, when we feel safe or when we are whole.

When I use the word "shalom," it encompasses all of these words. Yeshua shall be called the Prince of Wealth or Health, the Prince of Prosperity, the Prince of Being Well, the Prince of Being at Peace and at Rest and Safe and Whole. All of these words are who the Prince of Shalom encompasses or is.

These words are all referring to Yeshua.

Hebraic words from *Isaiah 9:6-7:*

Wonderful	H6382 — pele, peh-leh; from H6381; a miracle:--marvelous, wonder(-ful, -fully)
Counselor	H3289 — ya'ats, yaw-ats'; a primitive root; to advise; reflexively, to deliberate or resolve:--advertise, take advice, advise (well), consult (give, take) counsel (-lor), determine, devise, guide, purpose.
The Mighty One or The Mighty God	H1368 *gibbowr*, ghib-bore'; *gibbor*; intensive from the same as H1397; powerful; by implication, warrior, tyrant:--champion, chief, excel, giant, man, mighty (man, one), strong (man), valiant man. H410 el, ale; shortened from 352; strength; as adjective, mighty; especially the Almighty (but also used of any deity):--God, god, goodly, great, idol, might(y) one, power, strong. Compare names in "-el."
Everlasting Father	H5703 — *'ad*, ad; from H5710; properly, a (peremptory) terminus, i.e. (by implication) duration, in the sense of advance or perpetuity (substantially as a noun, either with or without a preposition):--eternity, ever (-lasting, -more) old, perpetually, + world <u>without</u> <u>end</u>. H1 — ab', awb; a primitive word; Father, in a literal and immediate, or figurative and remote application):--chief, (fore-) Father (-less), patrimony, principal.
Prince of Peace	H8269 — *sar*, sar; from H8323; a head person (of any rank or class):--captain (that had rule), chief (captain), general, governor, keeper, lord ((-task-)) master, prince (-ipal), ruler, steward H7965 — *shalowm*, shaw-lome'; or ulov; shalom, shawlome'; from H7999; safe, i.e. (figuratively) well, happy, friendly; also (abstractly) welfare, i.e. health, prosperity, peace:--do, familiar, far, favour, + friend, great, (good) health, (perfect, such as be at) peace (-able, -ably), prosper (-ity, -ous), rest, safe (-ty), welfare, (all is, be) well, wholly.

In ***Isaiah 9:7*** it says:

(Isaiah 9:7) *"Of the increase of his government and peace there shall be no end..."*

He will continue to conquer. In other words when he comes, the whole goal is to get the entire inhabitants of the world to worship the one true El.

That is what it started out as and that is how it shall end up. When you look at the fact that Yeshua/YeHoVaH sent Moshe into Egypt to tell Pharaoh to let the people go, it was not so that the people could be free to do their own thing.

Now of course, that is part of being freed, because once you are free, you are now free to make your own decisions. There is no one making decisions for you. You are free to make your own decisions. Until you are free, you can't make decisions on your own.

Like for instance, a child who lives under their parents' roof is not free. They are under the tutelage of their parents until they are able to be on their own and make their own decisions without their parents having to bankroll their decisions. If somebody is bankrolling your decision-making, then you are not free. This is what the *Proverbs* writer says: that the borrower is a slave to the lender. If you owe people money, you are not free. If you are in debt, you are not free. If you live under someone else's roof that is not yours, you are not free. It is like being (in some cases) — hopefully your home is not like a prison. But prisoners don't decide what they are going to do or what they are going to eat or when they get up.

When you are in the military, you are not free. You are the property of the U.S. government.

The bottom line is that when YeHoVaH sent Moses to tell Pharaoh to let the people go, he said it was so that they may come and worship him. That was the purpose of setting the people free. That is the same purpose today. Whom the Son sets free is free indeed. Now the question is, what are you going to do with your freedom?

Either you are going to come under the Master, or you are going to choose a master to serve. Either way you make the choice. No man can serve two masters. And so:

(Isaiah 9:7) *"Of the increase of His government and peace there shall be no end, upon the throne of David and upon his kingdom, to order it and to establish it with judgment and with justice from henceforth even forever. The zeal of YeHoVaH of hosts will perform this."*

We see that *Isaiah* is identifying Yeshua as the one who is going to sit upon the throne of David. He is the one who will be called Wonderful. He will be called Counselor. He will be called Prince of Peace. He will be called Mighty God. He will be called Everlasting Father. He will be called the Son of David. He will be called *the Prophet, the Messiah.*

Then there is the entire book of *Isaiah 53.*

 Isaiah 53

This is extremely powerful. I just want to have us go through it. It is a pretty short chapter, so it shouldn't take long.

(Isaiah 53:1) *"Who hath believed our report? and to whom is the arm of YeHoVaH revealed?"*

This is so important. When we begin to talk about the report that we are going to believe, this takes on so many facets, especially as I am dealing with believers. I mean, dealing with unbelievers is one thing, because now I have to get an unbeliever to a place where they believe that all things really are possible.

I should not have to convince a believer that healing belongs to them. A believer should already believe that. If a believer doesn't believe that, then the believer doesn't believe the report of the Almighty. His report says that by the stripes of Messiah you were healed.

Just because the healing has not manifested is not cause to not believe that by his stripes you were healed. You see, by his stripes you were also saved. Salvation has not manifested as it shall be manifest to those who endure to the end. Those who endure to the end shall be saved. The key is what do you believe? Because if you don't believe in healing, what is the point of me praying for you to be healed? What is the point of anybody praying for you to be healed?

There are people who say that they are believers, but they don't believe in healing. I had a fellow call me at 7:30 in the morning and it is really sad. He left a voice mail at 7:30 in the morning. He was haranguing me about not answering the phone. He was calling me a fraud and saying how it is all a bunch of lies. Now, I am thinking to myself, "This fellow is up at 7:30 in the morning, calling our number and surprised that no one answered the phone." Call your bank at 7:30 in the morning and see if they answer.

The point is that it is 7:30 in the morning. So at 8 o'clock I called him back. I said to him, "You know, what was the purpose of your message?" And he wants to preach to me. You are watching our program at 7:30. You are calling on the phone. Why are you calling? This is a number you call to receive prayer. So he spouts off with "You all are a bunch of frauds." I started talking to him and here is what I heard. This man watches Christian TV. He accumulates all of this nonsense and decides he is going to call us and dump.

I called him back and I asked him, "What was the purpose of your call? Did you want something? Is there a way we can minister to you?" And then he says, "Yes. I want you to pray. I want you to pray for our Father." He says, "I want you to pray, not TO our Father. I want you to pray for our Father. You know, God has feelings." He wanted me to pray for God. I said, "Sir, obviously you have us confused with all of these other ministries that you have been listening to.

That is because the things that you are saying about this ministry; on none of our programs have those statements ever been made. This tells me that you have been listening to other ministries. You decide to call this ministry to dump on us. I need to let you know that we are not those ministries and we are not like those ministries. I am taking the time to call you back, like we said we would do, to understand is there any way we can pray for you and I would encourage you to listen."

He says, "Well, what time do you come on?" We gave him our program dates, the times they come on. He says, "Okay. I am going to listen and I am going to record them this time, word for word." I said, "Well sir, do that" because all I want him to do is to listen to the programs. He is going to find (just like so many others) that when you listen to the program with your preconceived ideas of what you are going to hear, you will only find that what you are hearing is not what you thought you were going to hear. Now what are you going to do?

Again, this man is listening and he is hearing all those reports from all of those individuals. He decides that he is going to come and dump it on my doorstep.

Now, this is the way many believers are, because they have been disappointed. Now they come and say,

"I want you to pray for me."

"What do you want me to pray for?"

"Well, I want you to pray that God will heal me."

"Do you believe in healing?"

"Well, I believe he can heal and I've been prayed for" (and blah-blah-blah) "and I've not been healed and if he wants to heal me, he'll heal me. It is in his time."

"Okay."

Whose report are you believing? You see, that's not faith talking. *Isaiah* says:

(Isaiah 53:1-3) "Who hath believed our report? and to whom is the arm of YeHoVaH revealed? For he shall grow up before him as a tender plant, and as a root out of a dry ground: he hath no form nor comeliness; and when we shall see him, there is no beauty that we should desire him. He is despised and rejected of men; a man of sorrows, and acquainted with grief: and we hid as it were our faces from him; he was despised, and we esteemed him not."

This is describing the Messiah. Why is he a man of sorrows? It is because he looked at the people who had all of this religious activity going on. He wept because they were a people without a shepherd. They were blind people following blind guides. They had no life in them. They were full of traditions and religions based upon what they had been taught by those who were responsible for teaching Israel.

It is the same situation we are in today. You have all of these teachers, all of these preachers, even preachers in L.A. and Georgia, Atlanta preachers and all of these ministers who are not preparing people. There are people out there that I believe whose heart is in the right place, but they just have the wrong message. The reason why I know they are out there is because I was one of them.

My heart has always been to serve and to please my Father and because of that I am where I am today. But there was a long stretch of my ministry where I had the right part. I had the zeal for YeHoVaH, but it was not according to the knowledge, the truth, so I was preaching a message with all of my heart. I believed in the message that I was preaching, I just had the wrong message. It was not that I wasn't sincere and that I wasn't trying to please my Father in heaven. I

believed and I can tell when I come into contact with them. There are ministers out there who are so serious about wanting to please the Almighty. They just have the wrong message.

There are people out there in these places. Their desire is to serve, as they know him, God, with all of their heart, with all of their mind and with all of their strength. They are doing what the preachers are telling them to do, just as the people in Yeshua's day were doing what the religious leaders were telling them to do. They trusted the religious leaders who were supposed to have this relationship with the Almighty, to tell them what the Almighty says. Because the guides had the wrong message and were blind, they were communicating the wrong message to the people and the blind were leading the blind.

I was blind. I was blind, but now I see. Halleluyah!

Now it is a matter of helping to remove the blinders from the eyes of other people out there who are genuinely, sincerely desiring to know the Almighty. That is why we have to have the television programs. That is why we have to be on the Internet. That is why we have to be on *YouTube*. That is why we have to be on every venue and use every means of communicating the true gospel of the Kingdom. It is because when those sincere, genuine people hear the truth, something within them is going to be stirred, just like something in me was stirred and just like something in you was stirred.

That stirring stirred you to step up and to search and to look for the Almighty in places that you had not looked before and to search your Bible. You came to realize that okay, I have inherited lies. The people who have been teaching me some of these lies were not intentionally trying to deceive me. They were simply teaching me what they knew.

Unfortunately, they had the wrong message.

Yeshua knew, so he had compassion. He had compassion for the people. Now there were people who did not care and people who wanted to quiet him and to silence him. There were people who did not mind having the wrong message. They wanted to continue to perpetuate that wrong message because their livelihood and their identity were tied to the wrong message. Those are the ones he rebuked. Those are the ones he called "blind guides" and vipers and serpents and demons and devils.

As a result he was despised, rejected and acquainted with grief. Because of the power brokers who controlled the masses, those who wanted to know more hid (as it were) their faces from him. Nicodemus comes to him at night. He hears a piece of truth. He knows it is truth, but he is in the company of people who want the one who is communicating the truth to be condemned as a liar. When he tries to stick up for him, the wrath of those who were putting their wrath upon Yeshua turned their wrath toward him and he backed down.

(Isaiah 53:3b-5) "He was despised, and we esteemed him not. Surely he hath borne our griefs, and carried our sorrows: yet we did esteem him stricken, smitten of God, and afflicted. But he was wounded for our transgressions, he was bruised for our iniquities: the chastisement of our peace was upon him; and with his stripes we are healed."

The question now that anybody would have to ask who knows *Isaiah* is this (and typically it is those who are in the Jewish community): "Is he talking about something that has happened already or something that shall happen?" When a scholar begins to look at *Isaiah*, he tries to identify whether *Isaiah* is speaking in the past tense or if he is speaking in the present tense. They would have to identify and conclude that he is speaking in the present tense. That is because this person is not in the history of the past. The only person who comes close to this is Moshe/Moses.

(Isaiah 53:6) "All we like sheep have gone astray; we have turned everyone to his own way; and the LORD hath laid on him the iniquity of us all."

No man bore the burden of a nation.

(Isaiah 53:7-12) "He was oppressed, and he was afflicted, yet he opened not his mouth: he is brought as a lamb to the slaughter, and as a sheep before her shearers is dumb, so he openeth not his mouth. He was taken from prison and from judgment: and who shall declare his generation? for he was cut off out of the land of the living: for the transgression of my people was he stricken. And he made his grave with the wicked, and with the rich in his death; because he had done no violence, neither was any deceit in his mouth. Yet it pleased the LORD to bruise him; he hath put him to grief: when thou shalt make his soul an offering for sin, he shall see his seed, he shall prolong his days, and the pleasure of the LORD shall prosper in his hand. He shall see of the travail of his soul, and shall be satisfied: by his knowledge shall my righteous servant justify many; for he shall bear their iniquities. Therefore will I divide him a portion with the great, and he shall divide the spoil with the strong; because he hath poured out his soul unto death: and he was numbered with the transgressors; and he bare the sin of many, and made intercession for the transgressors."

Paul comes along in *Romans 8* and identifies Yeshua at the right hand of the Almighty interceding on our behalf even to this day. The entire chapter of *Isaiah 53* is pertaining to the Messiah.

We can go through the other prophets and begin to identify verses and passages that refer to the Messiah. But I believe that with all that we have looked at as far as Messiah in the prophets, as in *Micah*, as in *Jeremiah*, as in *Isaiah* and as in *Revelation;* we know that is a book of prophecy. Daniel and all of these prophets speak concerning the Messiah. All of the other prophets speak concerning the Messiah.

Messiah in the *Psalms*

The *Psalms* speak concerning the Messiah. Let's take a look at *Psalm 2*.

🔍 *Psalm 2:1-3*

It is very difficult to read any of the gospel accounts without being mindful of the *Psalms*. In the second *Psalm* it says these words (and Peter quotes some of this).

"Why do the heathen rage, and the people imagine a vain thing? The kings of the earth set themselves, and the rulers take counsel together, against the LORD, and against his anointed, saying, 'Let us break their bands asunder, and cast away their cords from us.'"

Now think about this. No person in their right mind — I mean, I am not trying to justify Pharaoh, but I have to think when it comes down to trying to understand what I read. And part of understanding what I read requires the use of my imagination. With all of the information, the knowledge and the pieces that I have, I am trying to put myself in Pharaoh's skin, in Pharaoh's head. I am looking at a time when you are the most powerful person on the planet, when people bow and people worship you, when people look to you for their sustenance, for their well-being, for their provision and their protection. There is none greater than you. No one around you or anywhere close acknowledges that there is anyone greater than you. And here comes this Moses shepherd guy telling Pharaoh what he does. I can imagine.

The Pharaoh of Egypt:
The most important being on earth

Where I am about to go is only because of my imagination. I invite you to take this brief journey with me just for moment. What Moses did in confronting Pharaoh was huge. There is no scale dealing with anything in the earth other than — imagine a pauper Jew going to Hitler and telling Hitler, "You need to let the Jewish people go."

Now, Hitler of course was (by some stretch of the imagination) Christian. He believed in the God of Luther, if you would. He was an Anti-Semite, even though he was of Semitic origin. Imagine a Jewish man going to Hitler and telling Hitler to let the Jewish people go free. You can imagine how that would turn out.

Imagine if you would in the 1820's in Alabama, Mississippi or Georgia. Some Northern Black comes to the most powerful slave landowner in the South and tells him that he needs to let all of the slaves go free. What do you think would have happened to him?

It is amazing to me that Moses was able to go into the presence of Pharaoh as many times as he did and come out of Pharaoh's presence after making all of those decrees and for Pharaoh to see all of the things that Moses spoke about occurring.

Moses' life — every time he set foot in Pharaoh's presence, his life was on the line because Pharaoh was a powerful person.

When it comes down to Moses confronting this individual, we know that Moses' life was in jeopardy. Ultimately Pharaoh lost his mind, because after he let them go, what did he do? He pursued them and it cost him big time.

Who in their right mind then, would stand up against the Almighty?

Do you know that people do it every day? Some of most wicked people on the planet are individuals whose identity is so perverted to the point where they will enter into relationships with the same sex. That is wicked. That is perverted.

Even when a person says that they believe in the Almighty and they know how the Almighty feels about sex before marriage; they do it anyway. We have example after example in the scriptures of what YeHoVaH requires of us. Even though people today see the examples of what happened to them of old and the New Testament warns that these things were done for our example; people today defy the Almighty by decreeing that they don't have to do what he says in his commands.

These are Messianics, Hebrew Roots, Christians, Jews and so-called believers. I am not standing here as judge, because the word *is* the judge. When you see people violate his commands openly and then justify it or make excuses for it, where is your fear of the Almighty? There is none. There is very little of it.

It seems like the only time a person has a glimpse of fear is when their life is on the line, when they are this close to death, when the bottom of their life has fallen out and when they can't see how they are going to make it. Unfortunately it takes moments like that for a person to come face to face with the fear of the Almighty. Those moments are fleeting. After those moments pass and things begin to get back to the way a person likes them or wants them, the fear of the Almighty also flees.

This is how Israel continued to go in and out, in and out. And when the prophets were raised up, some of them decided that if we shut them up, we will shut the mouth of God. And if we shut his mouth, then we can live our lives any way we want to. We can do our own thing; every man going in their own way doing whatever pleases them.

 *Psalm 2:3-12*

This is the whole goal of taking the gospel to the ends of the earth so that people will put their trust in Messiah. It is not so you can believe. Believe what? "Oh, I believe he died for me and therefore I am saved." No, it is about putting your trust in him like you put your trust in your bank, like you put your trust in your retirement account, like you put your trust in that safe deposit box or in your investments. (I can't really say, "like you put your trust in government," because we see it will shut down on you.)

We are to put our trust in him. Those who put their trust in the Almighty through Yeshua will never be put to shame. When we put our trust in the people of the earth, it is like if you have ever signed a contract. You trust that the contract is written for your benefit. You trust when that person says, "This says this." You don't read it. You just sign it. You have just trusted that that person gave you viable information that you can believe in so you signed it.

It is like when you are signing that mortgage or whatever or that insurance policy and somebody is saying, "This document says this. Just sign it. Put your initials." You sign it. You are putting your trust in that what you are told is what is in those documents. When we put our trust in someone, what we are doing is committing our belief to them that they are communicating to us what is actually written.

When you put your trust in the Almighty, what you are saying is, "Okay. I believe that this is to my benefit. Therefore I am going to trust you and do it."

It is not, "Okay, I believe, but I don't have to do anything. I don't have to sign anything. I don't have to enter into any agreements; no covenants. I just believe." Let me tell you something. You take that into that mortgage company. "Okay, I believe that the document says what it says." They say, "Well, if you believe that, you need to sign here." "Well, I don't need to sign it. I believe it is what it is." "No Sir, you need to sign it." "No Ma'am, you need to sign it. It is not a valid agreement without your signature." Your signature says that I have read these documents and I agree with them.

That is how people enter into agreements and that is exactly how people enter into agreements with him. That is exactly how the children of Israel in the wilderness said, "Whatever you say, whatever is in the ketubah, whatever is in the agreement, whatever is in the covenant, we haven't seen it. We don't know what it says, but we will do it."

Then you have somebody who will preach a 15-minute "come to Jesus" meeting. Folks flood down the aisle giving their heart to Jesus and they don't have a clue what that means. They are entering into an agreement believing in something and they don't have a clue as to the bottom line.

As we continue on, we will pick up where we left off in the next lesson. We are stopping here in *Psalm 2*. We will pick up in the next lesson in Messiah in the *Psalms*.

Class 92 Study Summary

Key Points

1. The Messiah-Centric principle is that principle by which scripture is interpreted in relation to its center, the Messiah.

2. Yeshua taught people all things that were written about him in the law, in the prophets and in the *Psalms.* For the first one hundred years after the Messiah, there was no written New Testament, so the disciples were quite able to communicate the Messiah just from the "Old Testament."

3. Yeshua was referred to as the "son of David" because he was of the household of Judah.

4. True prophets speak on behalf of YeHoVaH, so the words they speak are of the Almighty.

5. Some of the names that the Messiah will be called when he returns will be "Wonderful, Counselor, Mighty One, Mighty God, Everlasting Father" and "Prince of Peace."

6. If someone is bankrolling your decision-making, then you are not free. You are going to come under *the* Master or you are going to come under another master. Either way it is your choice.

7. Just because healing has not yet manifested does not mean that it hasn't occurred. The word tells us that by Yeshua's stripes we *are* healed.

8. Although not mentioned by name, the Messiah can be found throughout the Old Testament (for example in *Psalm 2*).

9. Who in their right mind would stand up against the Almighty? People who do not fear YeHoVaH are those who openly violate his commands and then justify their behavior.

10. The word is the judge.

11. We are to put our trust in the Almighty. When we do that, we not only believe in him, we believe him.

Review Exercise

1. Everyone has various roles and therefore sometimes names. What are some of your names? Who calls you that and what role is it significant of? You might also think about nicknames that have been assigned to you by people you know.

I am called	By	Because

2. Do any of the above names you have completely refer to you?

_____

_____

Why or why not?

_____

_____

_____

3. Have you ever thought about what you believe about healing?

_____

_____

_____

_____

4. Does prophetic scripture back up your beliefs?

_____

_____

_____

_____

**Rate the following statements
by filling in the most appropriate number.**

(1 = I do not agree 10 = I agree completely)

Objectives:

1. I can define prophetic information about Yeshua's names and titles.

   1.◯   2. ◯   3. ◯   4. ◯   5. ◯   6. ◯   7. ◯   8. ◯   9. ◯   10. ◯

2. I can name the prophetic words in the *Psalms* relating to Yeshua.

   1.◯   2. ◯   3. ◯   4. ◯   5. ◯   6. ◯   7. ◯   8. ◯   9. ◯   10. ◯

My Journal

What I learned from this class:

_____

_____

_____

_____

_____

_____

_____

_____

_____

_____

_____

_____

_____

_____

_____

_____

_____

_____

_____

_____

Discipleship Training Class 93

Messiah-Centered Principle Recap (part 13)

It is very difficult today to turn on the news, to look at *Facebook*, the government and all of the things that are coming down and the merchants of fear out there. The bottom line is that Father has called us to occupy. He has called us to take dominion. He has called us to go and take the gospel of the Kingdom to the whole world and not to fear man. We are going forward in the power and in the authority and in his name; as he declared that all power in heaven and in earth has been given to him. He gave us this power and authority we are walking in. When you walk in the authority and the power that the Almighty has given you, the enemy recognizes you and doesn't mess with you.

Now, he tries to distract and that is the thing we have to be aware of today. There are a lot of distractions. There are a lot of things and people pulling us in different directions. But we are to keep our eyes on the author and the finisher of our faith and not deviate to the left or to the right but to stay on that straight and narrow path.

That is the beauty of this whole Messiah-Centric principle. The whole of scripture literally centers around Messiah. When our lives center around him, I am going to tell you. You are going to see the power and the authority.

You know, Yeshua was not murdered. The Jews didn't kill Jesus, as many in the church would say. He came knowing full well what he came to do and he came to lay down his life. That was his plan. That was his purpose, but somebody had to participate in that. So in order to get certain people to do what Father ordained would happen, he had to blind some folks. He had to blind some folks so they could not see his plan. That is because the Bible tells us that had the rulers of this world known who they were crucifying, they never would have crucified him.

It was not because they would have said, "Oh, he's the king." No. They would have known that the Father's plan would be to transform the world that they had control over. By not participating in his plan, Satan would still be the ruler of this world in full authority. But Yeshua has all authority now. Those who submit themselves to his authority have all power over the devil.

The Messiah-Centric principle is that principle in scripture where scripture is interpreted in relation to its center — Messiah. As we have noted, the basis for this principle is the fact that **Messiah is the central person of the Bible.**

When we started this Messiah-Centered principle, it was based upon the back of some words that Yeshua spoke in *Luke 24*.

As you recall, the crucifixion had taken place. The resurrection had occurred. There were two disciples of Yeshua on the road to Emmaus. They were troubled in heart. Yeshua joined them. They had no clue who he was. They had dialogue. In the process of this dialogue, Yeshua said these words:

(Luke 24:25-26) "Then he said unto them, 'O fools, and slow of heart to believe all that the prophets have spoken: Ought not Messiah to have suffered these things, and to enter into his glory?'"

The prophets have prophesied some things. They have spoken some things. And throughout the history of the earth as Father raised up these prophets, these prophets spoke concerning he who was to come. Yet when he came, the people who supposedly were looking for him did not recognize him.

Let me tell you something. There are people today who supposedly are looking for him, but they are not looking for him because they are too busy having church. They are too busy celebrating these pagan feasts and festivals that they have created. They are too busy following their denominations instead of being in tune with eyes to see and ears to hear what the Father is saying and doing. A lot of what he is saying and doing is tied up in his moedim; those feasts, those festivals that he established so that we would stay in tune with him. They are not practiced religiously, but with our heart and with our soul and with our mind and with our strength.

So here it is that you had these individuals who knew that the Messiah was coming. They believed that Yeshua was "the Messiah" as long as he was with them, but as soon as he was dead or crucified, their hearts turned. They began to look in a different direction. In this particular case we find two individuals who were on their way somewhere. They were on the road to Emmaus. We don't know if Emmaus was their destination. Maybe it was, maybe it wasn't. I don't know if it was. And yet once they realized who they were talking to, they changed their minds. They changed their direction. They went back to Jerusalem as we will see here.

He rebukes them. "You fools!" The prophets have spoken some things and yet they didn't believe it.

(Luke 24:27) "And beginning at Moses and all the prophets, he expounded unto them in all the scriptures the things concerning himself."

We see how Yeshua is about to tell them starting with the Torah, the law. Then working his way through the prophets, he expounded unto them in all the scriptures — in all the scriptures.

(Luke 24:28) "And they drew nigh unto the village, whither they went: and he made as though he would have gone further."

We see here that they were going to stay there and he was going to continue on.

(Luke 24:29-31) *"But they constrained him, saying, 'Abide with us: for it is toward evening, and the day is far spent.' And he went in to tarry with them. And it came to pass, as he sat at meat with them, he took bread, and blessed it, and brake, and gave to them. And their eyes were opened, and they knew him; and he vanished out of their sight."*

Their eyes were opened at the moment when he gave thanks and when he blessed. Now some would say that he took the bread and blessed it. Notice the "it" is in italics in your Bible. You always have to be aware because this scripture would indicate that he blessed the bread. No, he took bread and said a blessing. He blessed the Almighty as he did every time he would take of bread and wine. He gave thanks and he blessed the Almighty.

(Luke 24:32-33) *"And they said one to another, 'Did not our heart burn within us, while he talked with us by the way, and while he opened to us the scriptures?' And they rose up the same hour, and returned to Jerusalem, and found the eleven gathered together, and them that were with them,"*

They were trying to get him to stay with them. Notice what they said. They said, "Abide with us for it was toward evening and the day is far spent." We find out now that even though the day is far spent, that this same hour they got up and returned to Jerusalem. They went. They were on a mission. They found the eleven gathered together and those who were with them.

🔍 Luke 24:34-41

They did not believe because they were overjoyed and they wondered. Hmm. What he is trying to do is convince them that this is not a figment of their imagination that they are seeing. "Look at my hands, guys. Look at my feet, guys. It is me!" And yet they did not believe. So now he has to do something really, really natural. He asks them for meat.

🔍 Luke 24:42-43

They were expecting to see him swallow the food so they could see the food going down. He is trying to convince these individuals that he has resurrected and yet they are having a problem. He had already rebuked the two by calling them fools.

🔍 Luke 24:44

All things must be fulfilled, which were written where? In the Law of Moses and in the prophets and in the *Psalms*. We have three distinct areas of the Bible that Yeshua refers to and that speak of him.

This is important to know as we are looking at this Messiah-Centric principle and even more so today. I have been noticing recently that there are some furious attacks being hurled at the believers in Messiah who keep the Torah. Some people refer to Messianics as "messy." Some refer to Messianics as "occult."

YouTube is full of videos. Someone sent me one video that leads to hundreds more videos where churches are now starting to warn their people that this is "wicked." This is "evil." I have seen preachers preach messages from the largest congregations out there to the small rural communities. They are warning their people to stay away from you Messianics, from us.

So I say that is good news because what it says is that the word is getting out. Now unfortunately there are those out there who are into Messianic Judaism and they are mixing the truth with some traditions. This creates a problem for some people, but nevertheless the word is getting out that people need to turn back to the commands of YeHoVaH.

We need to know how to convince people who don't believe the New Testament, that this Yeshua is the one whom Moses prophesied about. He is the one whom the prophets prophesied about and the *Psalms* prophesied about. This is exactly what the disciples were able to do without a New Testament. They were able to convince hardcore Pharisees and Sadducees and scribes (mind you) that Yeshua was the Messiah.

We should be able to do that. We should be able to do this without the New Testament (mind you); without *Matthew, Mark, Luke* and *John*. We should be able to convince any Jewish believer out there from the scriptures that they adhere to that Yeshua is the Messiah just like Peter, James, John and all of the disciples of Yeshua. There were more than twelve (minus Judas).

There were hundreds of them. As a matter of fact, remember that when Yeshua rose from the grave, the Bible says that he showed himself to over 500 of his disciples.

We know that in the upper room, in the temple court or the House of YeHoVaH on the day of Shavuot there were 120 at least. But during his resurrection, during the forty days, he showed himself to the eleven. He showed himself to over 500. By the time that Yeshua resurrected from the dead, there was only one disciple (John). I should say there was only one male disciple. I have to qualify that because Yeshua's Mother was a disciple and Mary Magdalene was a disciple and the other Mary was a disciple. There were several women. They were all disciples of Yeshua.

When it came down to the disciples in the book of *Acts*, they did not have *Matthew*. All they had was the testimony of Yeshua. The testimony of Yeshua came from the prophets, from the law and from the *Psalms*. Here he says,

> *"These are the words which I spake unto you, while I was yet with you, that all things must be fulfilled, which were written in the law of Moses, and in the prophets, and in the Psalms, concerning me."*

Matthew, Mark, Luke and *John* are literally the physical life lived and the testimony that the disciples of Yeshua saw, but these were not written until years later — years later.

When Peter would stand up in the midst of them, he didn't do like we do today. "Okay, take your Bibles. Turn to the book of *Matthew*. Our text for today is…" No. He didn't do that. Peter stood up and taught. I would dare say that chances are that they did not have the scrolls with them, which is why they probably went to the temple to hear the scrolls read. Yeshua was the word. Yeshua is the word. The word dwelt in the midst of them. His word was the word and his word came from the Law of Moses. It came from the prophets. It came from the *Psalms*.

This is what he is saying, *"All these things written in the law of Moses and in the prophets and in the Psalms concerning me."*

🔍 *Luke 24:45*

They had the knowledge. They had the information. They had his words, but he opened their understanding that now they might understand. You see, if you don't understand; there are people out there who are doing Torah portions. They are reading. They are reading. They are studying, reading, reading, reading, reading and reading. The Bible says get wisdom, get knowledge, but with all your getting, get an understanding.

Do you know how you get an understanding? The best way to get an understanding of something is literally to practice it, to do it.

I was talking to my wife. We have lots of discussions. That is my best friend, so we talk all of the time. We use real-life situations. Like for instance, we have this lawn mower and this lawn mower is a riding mower. My son Alpha and my son Apostle and even my son Aaron — Aaron is old enough to know that okay, I need some training. I need to do some training before I can operate certain things. But do you know that the average child out there sees a parent do something or they see an adult do something and they think they can do it?

Your child probably thinks, your 4, 5, 6, 7, 8, 9, 10 your 12-year old probably thinks right now that they have watched you getting into the car and driving enough. What they don't see is that foot action. They don't see that steering action, but they watch you and they are convinced that they can drive a car. They think they have the knowledge because they have watched you do it. You put them into that driver's seat and the next thing you know, they are jerkin' and stoppin' and can't turn. Why? Because they haven't practiced. The more you practice driving. That is most people. There are some folks who, no matter how much they practice, they don't get it. But the more you practice driving, guess what? The better you become at it.

The more you walk in this word, the better. You can listen to this word. You can be in church all of your life. You can listen to these teachings that I am presenting to you for the next year or for the next two years, but if you don't put what I'm teaching into practice – (as James says, don't be a hearer but a doer). If you put this stuff into practice, that is where understanding comes. It comes by applying what you are learning. Now the Father is beginning to give you an understanding.

Notice. Please notice. Here it is after the resurrection and he opens their minds so that they might understand the scriptures.

Think about that. They walked with Yeshua. They watched him do the things that he did. He sent them out. They did some stuff and marveled at the fact that they had this authority in his name. And yet they were bewildered by the fact that they could not cast a spirit out of a boy. Yeshua said it is your unbelief.

The thing that happened was that they saw it and heard it, but now he is opening their mind so they might understand it. He has commissioned them or he is about to commission them to go and teach. When you practice, when you teach — this is the thing that you are going to find. As you are out there and you are communicating this truth to other people, as you are applying it — there are people out there who are talking it, but they are not doing it. I tell people all of the time. A fellow called me the other day. I tell people, "You have to keep the Sabbath."

"You ought to listen to Pastor Bailey. He's got some great teachings on the Sabbath." Then in the same voice it is like I am looking forward to the day when I can take the Sabbath off. I mean, you are working on the Sabbath, but you are telling other people that they should keep the Sabbath. What kind of testimony is that? Think about it. Are you believable?

You can tell people to do stuff, but if you are not doing it, you are not convincing. When you do it, now there is a level of convincing. You are able to convince others because it is not just something you are saying, but it is something that you are doing. It is a part of who you are.

Yeshua opens their minds so that they might understand the scriptures.

We stopped in the last lesson in *Psalm 2.* But I want to show you in *Psalm 110* as we look at Messiah in the *Psalms*, where he is referred to as "Lord."

🔍 *Psalm 110, Matthew 22:41-46*

Notice what the *Psalm* says. It says here that "The LORD said unto my Lord." Now, here in the King James in the Old Testament, the only way you know the distinction between the LORD and the Lord is that in the King James, the first LORD is "L-O-R-D." The second Lord is "L-o-r-d." That is in indication. But when you begin to look at that in the Hebrew, you can see the distinction. You can tell based on the spelling and the upper and lower cases of the same word, that there is a distinction that is being made in the English King James version from the Hebrew Scriptures.

The Greek makes no distinction. Here in **Matthew 22:41** Yeshua has been tested by the Sadducees. He silenced the Sadducees. The Pharisees come to test him and the Pharisees gather together. Yeshua asks:

(Matthew 22:42) "...What think ye of Christ? whose son is he? They say unto him, 'The son of David.'"

They didn't even think about it. The son of David, they said. Why? Wait a minute. They know that the Messiah is the son of David. Guess what?

Understand something. Here they know that this King-Priest is going to come through the line of Judah, not from the Levites. The Pharisees know this. They said, "He's the son of David." Whose son is he? The son of David.

This is interesting because there are scriptures that tell us concerning the son — *Psalm 2* that we looked at in the last lesson. It deals with the Son. We looked at that and yet there are people today who will say emphatically that God does not have a Son. They are monotheistic. Both the Jewish and the Islamic communities would make this argument.

Here they say that he is the son of David, so they are looking for a King. They are not looking for YeHoVaH. They are looking for a King to come, but they know that this is Mashiach and he is going to be a king coming through the line of David. That is important to note.

(Matthew 22:43-45) "He saith unto them, 'How then doth David in spirit call him Lord, saying, The LORD said unto my Lord, Sit thou on my right hand, till I make thine enemies thy footstool? If David then call him Lord, how is he his son?'"

He tricks them, but he does not trick them. What he does is expose their ignorance. Here they are trying to trap him, but in essence he had already said, "You people err because you don't know the scriptures or the power of YeHoVaH." So you have people who don't know the scriptures and they don't know the power.

How does the power come? The power comes from the indwelling of the Spirit. What did Yeshua say? "When the Holy Spirit comes upon you, you shall receive power." Authority is what he is saying. You shall receive *dunamis*, dynamic power, the ability to do things in the supernatural realm, the ability to see things, the ability to know the mind of Messiah.

He says, "How is it that David calls him Lord? How is he his son?"

It is a good question. No man was able to answer him (verse 46).

(Matthew 22:44) "The LORD G2962 said unto my Lord, G2962 'Sit thou on my right hand, till I make thine enemies thy footstool'"

Let's look at this particular word in the Greek. You will notice that both the word "LORD" and "Lord" is the same Greek word. This is the Strong's numbering system. Strong's system of numbering in both the Hebrew and in the Greek directs us to the actual Greek word (the Hebrew word if you are in the Tanakh or the Greek word if you are in the Brit Chadasha/New Testament).

You will see here that the word "LORD" is the same word in the Greek. That word is G2962 — *kyrios*, koo'ree-os; supreme in authority, i.e. (as noun) controller; by implication Mr. (as a respectful title): -- God, Lord, Master, Sir.

These are the words. These are the terms that this word *kyrios* could mean. One of the things that happens when I am talking to people that we are supporting in countries outside of the United States is that they refer to me as "Sir."

One of the things about Pakistan is this. I would write a letter or communicate and a gentleman I deal with says to people, "Well, I'm waiting for my Sir." This is what he says.

"I'm waiting for my Sir to get back with me." He is speaking of me when communicating to other people because I will have said that I am going to do something. It is like when we were supporting and paying the rent for the facility that was being used. In one particular case, the landlord there wanted the funds earlier and he communicated with me. Then I got the communications. And there he had communicated to the landlord that he was waiting on his "Sir" to get back with him.

I thought it was strange that every time he talked to me, he called me "Sir." But then when he responded to other people as "his Sir" he was in some sense saying I'm his lord or I'm his master (from this perspective). It was not that I am his God or that I am his Lord, but that I am his Master. You have "landlord" and this would certainly fit in there, but it felt weird for him to refer to me as his "Sir."

Notice here in the Greek that there is no distinction between *kyrios* as it relates to the Father, and *kyrios* as it relates to the Son (as it relates to Yeshua). But in the Hebrew (and this is really interesting), here the Strong's word from *Psalm 110*, the LORD in all capitals is:

H3068*YeHoVaH*, yeh-ho-vaw'; from H1961; (the) Self-Existent or Eternal; Jehovah, Jewish national name of God:--Jehovah, the Lord.

It is interesting that Strong's has the term "YeHoVaH" as the L-O-R-D (as the name).

Now, the word for "my Lord" is:

H113 *adon*, adown, awdone'; or (shortened) adon, awdone'; from an unused root (meaning to rule); sovereign, i.e. controller (human or divine): -- lord, master, owner. Compare also names beginning with "Adoni-".

So it is saying "YeHoVaH said unto my Adoni…" Now interestingly enough, when the Jews refer to YeHoVaH, they say "Adonai." You hear it in the priestly blessings as it refers to YeHoVaH, Adonai.

It is amazing if we think about it. We see that there are two words, "YeHoVaH" and "Adonai" translate as "The LORD said to my Lord." You have the two words in the Hebrew that are very distinct. But in the Jewish community and in many of the Messianic Jewish communities, instead of using YeHoVaH (the name that you cannot pronounce as they say, or the name that is too sacred to say), the term "Adonai" is replaced as the word "LORD." When in fact it is "YeHoVaH said to my Lord," and David is writing this indicating that David is now calling his son "Lord." Yeshua says, "How can David, who is the Father, call his son his Lord?"

We see that this refers to the Messiah in the *Psalms* (where David is referring to him as the Lord, the Lord of hosts). "YeHoVaH, Adonai," as he would say.

As we move forward as Messiah the Redeemer, we go to:

🔍 *Psalm 130:8; Matthew 1:21*

These things that I am trying to say to you here are really referring to how you communicate to a community of Jews the same way Yeshua did when he asked the Pharisees, "Who was David talking to?" That is an excellent scripture when you are talking to someone who says that it is impossible for Jesus to be the Messiah. You say, "Okay well, I understand where you are coming from. It is not that I agree where you are coming from, but explain this passage. Who is he talking to? Who is the Messiah? Whose son is he?" He is the son of David. Well, if he is the son of David, how is it that David calls him "Lord?"

Yeshua's wisdom stumped these religious leaders and guess what? His wisdom is being communicated to us from the Old Testament and from the *Psalms*.

In **Psalm 130:8** we see him being revealed as the Redeemer. Look at it in the context of the entire psalm.

🔍 *Psalm 130*

Who is going to redeem? It is the Messiah. This is a Messianic *Psalm*, so who is going to redeem Israel?

Looking at **Matthew 1:21**, one of the things that happen every year during Tabernacles and during Passover and the Last Great Day, is the Great Hosanna where people are saying, "YeHoVaH saves! Adonai saves!" People today are still crying out, "Adonai saves! YeHoVaH saves!"

We know that during the Passover as they laid out the palms, people would cry out, "Blessed is he who comes in the name of YeHoVaH. Hosanna! Hosanna!" We can see that this Messiah in verse 21 — this is directly in conjunction with the prophets where the virgin shall conceive. She shall call his name "Immanuel," for he shall save his people from their sins.

(Matthew 1:23) "Behold a virgin shall be with child and she shall bring forth a son and ye shall call His name 'Immanuel,' which being interpreted as 'El with us.'"

YeHoVaH is with us. God is with us, so he is going to save his people. He is the Redeemer.

We know from both the book of *Isaiah* and from the *Psalms* that he is King and Ruler (the Messiah).

🔍 *Psalm 72; Matthew 2:1-11*

Psalm 72 is a short psalm. It has twenty verses. That is not much. You can take the time to read this in different versions to get different perspectives. At first glance you would say that this is a psalm that David wrote for Solomon. But in actuality it is a Messianic psalm and we are going to see that.

We can see that by referring to verse 5. Solomon certainly did not live throughout all of the generations, yet we note that this is a Messianic psalm.

Now I want you to look at *Matthew 2* and compare. We believe that verse 10 was fulfilled when the Magi from the East came and offered their gifts of gold, frankincense and myrrh.

You are probably very familiar with this, along with the passage in *Luke* which is always pulled out around Christmas time. That is because *Matthew 2* and *Luke 2* are being used to support the birth of Jesus being on December 25. We know that this is just not true.

I am always amazed at organizations which boast on preaching the truth, on having the truth and preaching things they know are not true. They know this is not true. Ask any preacher out there, "Was Jesus Christ born on December 25?" They will tell you no. The question is, "Well, why do you celebrate December 25 as Jesus' birthday and you know he wasn't born then?" "Oh, well, you know, well, you know, well, you know."

So you claim to preach the truth, yet you knowingly support a lie. Then you teach this to the children and you tell the Christmas story. You are now adding scripture to that which you know is a lie and yet you claim to be people who preach the truth.

You also see here as David was writing *Psalm 72* for his son Solomon that it is also a prophetic psalm. We see that he is actually writing it for a king who is going to rule over all nations. Solomon did not rule over all nations. But Yeshua is the King of Kings. He will rule over all of the kings of the earth.

We keep looking at *Matthew 2* because it is a fulfillment of both the *Psalms* passage and the *Isaiah* passage. It is amazing how *Isaiah* and *Psalms* seem to focus on some of the same prophetic scripture that is being fulfilled here in the books of *Matthew*, *Luke* and of course in *Mark* and *John*.

Some would ask, "Was all of Jerusalem disturbed?" I think that the people who were in the know — because if the king is disturbed, the people who know that the king is disturbed are going to be disturbed. This lets us know something. You have to understand. If the Magi came to Herod and revealed these things to Herod, how is it that those who are not in Herod's house become disturbed?

How is it that people who don't know that the Magi — the three wise men, as part of the Christmas story. The fact of it is this. How does everybody know that Herod is disturbed so they are disturbed? This lets us know that this is not just that the Magi showed up one night. It takes a while for rumors to spread or for words to get around, even if they are not rumors. It takes a moment for that word to get around. This means that this happens over a period of time.

Now Herod wants to know, so he calls all of the high priests. We know that when a high priest is in office, there is only one high priest in the office at a time. That was not the case during Yeshua's time. There were two (Annas and Caiaphas).

One was recognized by Rome, but the other was the actual high priest. Here it says that Herod calls all of the high priests. How many high priests are there? Who is Herod calling?

That would make me do some research to try to find the answer, because it just does not sit right. It says "chief priests," so that might make some sense. But I haven't done a word study on this and I haven't looked in other versions to see what is actually going on.[1]

We note that the prophet here is Micah. The prophet *Micah* tells us in chapter *5:2* concerning this particular verse.

Because these individuals were actually astrologers, some would use this to sanction astrology. They would sanction looking to the stars to determine one's future or to plan one's life or to determine certain aspects of life; such as who you can be a mate to and who you can't, all of these kinds of things. This does not sanction astrology or horoscopes, which comes from it.

Some versions note that Herod called on them "privily." Others say "secretly." This is why it is important to have a King James Version of the Bible and a Strong's Concordance. Because when you look at these terms and you look at these words, okay, secretly, privately — is that the same? For me to call you into a private meeting is different than me having a secret meeting. That is because if I am calling a private meeting, there is a good possibility that other people know that I am having a meeting but it is just private. They are not invited to the meeting. But if I am having a secret meeting, then no one else knows.

It is important to have a King James Bible and a Strong's Concordance. This helps to be able to break down and get an understanding of what is actually being said; because now it lets you also inside the mind of these individuals.

Another thing that seems suspicious is that the king is going to worship a man. He is going to worship a king? This is saying that these Magi, these astrologers, are saying something broader than just a king. This is the Son of God. This is God manifested. Under no other circumstances has anybody been connected to, or been identified with a star. This is prophecy. This individual, this Mashiach, is literally going to speak as the Almighty, for the Almighty, on behalf of the Almighty — the word becoming flesh; God who is the word. These individuals are saying that this is not just a son of a king. This is not just another king. This is one who will be worshipped.

You had these individuals who come from hundreds of miles to worship.

And Herod is saying, "When you find him, let me know." Trickster.

There is something here, too. We see that this is Messiah, King and Sovereign. He is Sovereign. He is Ruler. There is no one over him. Herod had Rome over him. Yeshua — there is

---

[1] If something just seems a little odd, then I need to stop for a moment and pause to kind of look at it a little more closely. As I said, there is only one high priest in the office, except during the time of Yeshua. There was one in office, but there were actually two high priests living — one actual high priest and one acting high priest. So a priest stays in the office typically until he is no longer able, which generally means that he is dead. We now wonder how many high priests Herod had at this time.

no one over him but the All-Sufficient One, YeHoVaH. Here what we see is that they worshipped him. But notice what the Bible says here.

> (**Matthew 2:11**) *"And when they were come into the house, they saw the young child with Mary his mother, and fell down…"*

This is bowing, possibly a prostration of their physical beings.

There is a posture in worship. Worship has been reduced to singing songs, songs of worship and praise and worship. But with worship really comes a posture, a lifting of the hands, a bowing of the head, a falling upon one's face, a prostration.

We see that the *Psalms* reveal Messiah as Son. The *Psalms* reveal Messiah as King and Ruler. The *Psalms* reveal Messiah as Redeemer. We see that in the *Psalms*, Yeshua began to share with them all things about him from the Law of Moses (which is actually the law given to Moses), from the prophets and from the *Psalms*. Of course the most recited psalm of all is *Psalm 23*. "YeHoVaH is my shepherd." That psalm is certainly referring to YeHoVaH, Yeshua the Messiah, our Shepherd, the Good Shepherd, the true Shepherd. As Yeshua said himself, "I am the true Shepherd. I am the only Shepherd that has authority. I am not a hireling. I am not a thief. I am not a robber. I am the Good Shepherd."

This Good Shepherd is (again) *Psalm 23*. It is the most recited and probably the most memorized in its entirety of all of the *Psalms*. I don't think we need to go to *Psalm 23*. Almost everyone knows *Psalm 23* and that is Messiah in the *Psalms*.

In the next lesson we are going to get into the parable principle. You will notice that most of Yeshua's ministry and teaching dealt with parables. We are going to look at the parable principle and understand one. A parable is not something that you can preach as doctrine. Many people try to preach the parable as doctrine when in actuality, it is a story. We will find out a little more about that.

Class 93 Study Summary

Key Points

1. Father has called us to occupy. He has called us to take dominion. He is calling us to go and take the gospel of the Kingdom to the whole world and not to fear man.

2. The entire scripture literally centers around the Messiah. That is the Messiah-Centric principle.

3. Yeshua the Messiah was not murdered. The Jews didn't kill Jesus, as many in the church would say. He laid down his life for all of mankind.

4. There are people today who are supposedly looking for the Messiah, but they aren't really looking for him. They are too busy celebrating pagan feasts and festivals they have created.

5. There are three distinct areas of the Bible that Yeshua refers to as speaking of him. That is the law, the prophets and the psalms.

6. There are people today who are teaching that the Messianic faith is "evil" or "of the devil." It is good news in a way because the word is getting out.

7. We should be able to communicate the Messiah using just the books of the Old Testament.

8. For the first one hundred years when the disciples preached the Messiah, they didn't have the New Testament. They didn't have *Matthew, Mark, Luke* or *John*.

9. The more you walk in the word, the more aligned with it you become. We are to become one with the word.

10. The Pharisees knew that the King-Priest (Messiah) would come from the line of Judah, not from the Levites. They called him the son of David, so they were looking for a King to come. They weren't looking for YeHoVaH. Father tricked them because he concealed the full truth from them.

11. When the Holy Spirit comes upon us, we will receive *dunamis* or dynamic power.

12. In the King James Bible, the only distinction between the LORD and the Lord is in the way the word is spelled (in all capital letters or in upper and lower case letters).

13. YeHoVaH is with us. God is with us. He is going to save his people. He is the Redeemer.

14. Many people claim to preach the "truth" yet they knowingly support lies in the form of religious traditions and doctrines that are not biblical.

15. It is important to have a King James Bible and a Strong's Concordance as part of your studies because they will help you get an understanding of the words used.

16. The psalms reveal the Messiah as the Son.

17. A parable is not something that you can preach as a doctrine. A parable is a story. Despite this, people attempt to do just that.

This is the reading list of the **Messiah-Centered principle scriptures**. If you notice, some of these are entire chapters, while others are individual scriptures. Be sure to study each one carefully and to glean all that the Holy Spirit may be telling you while studying them.

Entire Chapters:

Acts 2, 6, 7, 28	Deuteronomy 18	Exodus 19
Genesis 12	Hebrews 7-9	Isaiah 53
Leviticus 16	Mark 11	Matthew 1-2
Numbers 19	2 Kings 18	

Chapter/Verse(s):

Acts	1:8	3:11-26	4:1-4	6:7-15	7:58	10:38-43
	17:2	17:11	18:24-28	28:25-28		
Colossians	1:16					
Daniel	7:13-14	9:25-26				
Deuteronomy	18:15-20					
Ephesians	3:10-11					
Exodus	17:6	19:4	25:1-9	26:31	29:8-9	29:20
	32:1-7					
Galatians	5:16-26					
Genesis	1:1	1:26	3:14-15	8:20		
Hebrews	2:17	3:1-6	7:11-8:1	8:7-8	8:11-13	9:1-6
	9:8-9	9:11-28	10:7	13:8-16		
Isaiah	7:14	9:6-7	53:1-12	56:1-8		
Jeremiah	23:4-6	31:31-33	33:14-18			
John	1:1-17	1:19-21	1:41	1:45-46	3:3	3:11-21
	4:25	5:39	6:31-51	7:37-44	8:55-58	
Leviticus	16:1-34	24:5				
Luke	7:11-19	11:47-51	24:1	24:10-53		
Mark	11:17					
Matthew	1:1-25	2:1-11	13:14-18	13:53-58	21:1-11	21:42
	22:29	22:41-46	26:53-57			
	27:62-66	28:1-15				
Micah	5:1-2					
Numbers	17:10	19:7	20:1-13	21:4-9		
Psalms	2:1-12	40:6-7	72	110	130:8	
Revelation	1:3	1:13-16				
Romans	1:1-2	8:26-34	11:5-8	11:19-20	11:26	15:4
1 Corinthians	5:7	10:1-12	15:3-4			
1 John	1:19-21	3:1-11				
1 Kings	8:6					
2 Kings	18:1-4					
2 Peter	2:5					
2 Timothy	3:15-16					

Discipleship Training Class 94

Parable-Centered Principle (part 1)

Objectives:

As a Discipleship student, at the end of this class you will be able to:

- Describe how Yeshua used parables
- Define the five steps of interpreting a parable
- Explain how parables were utilized in the Old Testament writings

---

We are going to be looking at the parable principle; or as some would term it, the Parabolic principle. We are going to call it the parable principle. We are going to be looking at the parables in the Bible and get an understanding as to why Yeshua decided that he would speak to the multitudes in parables.

The parable principle is known as the principle by which any parable is interpreted by discerning its moral and elements. When we look at this principle, we have to know the definition.

A parable is a short, simple story from which a moral lesson may be drawn. It is an earthly story with a heavenly meaning.

We are going to find that Yeshua spoke to the multitude in parables. However, when he was alone with his disciples, he spoke to them. He shared in one place that the prophets longed to hear the things that they were hearing and yet they were privileged and we are privileged.

Unfortunately today many are looking at the teachings of Yeshua (especially the parables) and they are teaching the parables as if they were literal. Again, we are going to find that **a parable is a short, simple story from which a moral lesson may be drawn.** We are also going to see that a parable is somewhat fictitious. When you begin to teach fiction in a sense where it is scripture (when in fact it is a story that is used to bring or to teach a moral lesson), it is easy to make mistakes when teaching from the parables.

When you begin to do research about parables and the parable principle, you are ultimately going to stumble into this guy named Mark Bailey.[2] He is the most recent individual who has been really teaching on the parable principles, but he actually cites this guy, Adolph Julicher.

---

[2] Not a relative of mine.

What we see is that Mark Bailey is Vice-President for Academic Affairs. He is the Academic Dean and Professor of Bible Exposition at Dallas Theological Seminary in Dallas, Texas. Many of the teachers that I know of, all seem to quote him.

Mark writes:

> "A turning point in the study of Jesus' parables came with the work of Adolph Julicher who sought to expose the inadequacies of the allegorical method of interpretation and asserted that each parable taught a single moral truth. In answer to Julicher, C.H. Dodd (another scholar who is quoted a lot) and Jehoakim Jeremias sought to discern more specific lessons from Jesus' parables by focusing on their major referent — the Kingdom of God.
>
> Dodd and Jeremias attempted to interpret the parables in their historical context in the life of Jesus and in the gospel record. More recent trends have tended to see the parables as literary art at the expense of historical interpretation. Consequently, some writers have returned the approach that sees multiple meanings based on the subjective philosophical self-understanding of the interpreters, rather than the historical objectivity of Jesus and his message.
>
> The past fifteen years or so have been dominated by sophisticated literary criticism and structuralism which seems to be more concerned with the style of augmentation than the historical interpretation. From the pendulum-like extremes of Julicher and the multiple meanings allowed by the extremes of the philosophical, linguistic movement, a more cautious balance is being sought by recent conservative writers. Though authors such as Robert Stein, David Wynham, Craig Bloomberg, and John Sider have sought to interpret Jesus' parables more conservatively, it remains to be seen how many will join their efforts.
>
> Parables are distinguished from other literary figures in that they are narrative in form but figurative in meaning. Parables use both simile and metaphor to make their analogies and the rhetorical purposes of parables are to inform, convince, or persuade their audience.
>
> Pedagogically, Jesus utilized parables to motivate hearers to make proper decisions. To his original audience, the parables both revealed and concealed new truths regarding God's kingdom program. Those who rightly responded were called disciples and to them it was granted to understand the mysteries of the Kingdom. The same truth was concealed from those who, because of hardened hearts, were unreceptive to the message of Jesus.
>
> A parable may be briefly defined as a figurative narrative that is true-to-life and is designed to convey, through analogies, some specific spiritual truth usually relative to God's kingdom program. A proper interpretation of Jesus' parables should be given attention to and looking at the following five steps."

I am trying to make a point here and I will let you in on it in just a moment.

The five steps that he talks about are:

1. Understand the setting of the parable.
2. Uncover the need that prompted the parable.
3. Analyze the structure and details of the parable.
4. State the central truth of the parable and its relationship to the Kingdom.
5. Respond to the intended appeal of the parable.

Now, did you get that? This is a lot of theological mumbo-jumbo. These guys tend to blow smoke up each other's skirts and basically quote one another and create this smoke-screen. The fact of the matter is that parables in the Bible are either interpreted by the one who spoke it or gave it, or else the audience has no clue as to what is being conveyed.

Yeshua specifically spoke to his audience for a specific reason in parables which he himself unveils in his teachings. In *Matthew 13:10*, after one of these teachings when he was speaking a parable, the disciples came to him.

(Matthew 13:10) *"And the disciples came, and said unto him, 'Why speakest thou unto them in parables?'"*

They know that he is speaking, but he is speaking in a parable, so they asked the question, "Why are you doing this Yeshua?"

(Matthew 13:11) *"He answered and said unto them, 'Because it is given unto you to know the mysteries of the kingdom of heaven, but to them it is not given.'"*

There is something that is being said here that Yeshua is conveying to those who are listening to the truth. You have to understand something. Yeshua was the word made flesh. Yeshua was the one and seemingly the only one who had a perfect understanding of YeHoVaH's word. He not only taught it, but he lived it and demonstrated it to his disciples so they would know how to live it and how to communicate these truths.

Up until Yeshua's day, what had been done is that the religious leaders had given the people (or were giving the people) manmade rules and regulations based upon their interpretation of the word. That same thing is going on today.

Yeshua said:

(Matthew 13:11) *"He answered and said unto them, 'Because it is given unto you to know the mysteries of the kingdom of heaven, but to them it is not given.'"*

Notice the question. Why are you speaking unto them in parables? He said, "It's for you to know. I am speaking in parables to them because it is for you my disciples, to know the mysteries of the Kingdom. But to them it is not given."

They are going to be a people that Paul refers to as forever learning, but never coming to the knowledge of truth. They will always be getting more and more and more information and more and more and more knowledge, so their heads are being puffed up.

We are surrounded by people like this. They always want to tell you what the word says. But when it comes to living an authentic life as a disciple of Yeshua, it is highly suspect and seriously questioned.

We look at people around us and we know. You don't have to talk to people to know whether or not they are living a Torah-centered, Spirit-filled life. Listen to their words. Listen to their conversation. Look at who they communicate with. Who are their best friends?

Someone said this to me a long time ago. It bears repeating because there is a lot of truth to it. If you want to know what kind of person you really are, look at the people you hang around with. Look at the people you spend your time with. Look at the people you prefer to be with. Look at them and they will tell you who you are. You don't even have to ask them. Just look at what it is. There is an adage which says that birds of a feather flock together. There is a reason why you are drawn to people that you are drawn to and why people who are drawn to you are drawn to you. It is because there are things that you have in common.

Therefore you can tell what kind of person you are by the people you hang around.

Yeshua said:

(Matthew 13:12) "For whosoever hath, to him shall be given, and he shall have more abundance: but whosoever hath not, from him shall be taken away even that he hath."

In other words, the more you attain in the Kingdom that is of truth, the more the Father is going to reveal his truth to you. This is why I say to people that it is so important that you begin with the basics and the things that you know to do, to do them. The thing that you have affirmed to be truth, walk in it. **One of the most critical truths that we come into is the Sabbath day.**

There are certain things that are not going to be revealed to the world until they embrace YeHoVaH's Sabbath. But embracing the Sabbath and walking in the Sabbath and living the Sabbath is the beginning. There are people who keep the Sabbath, but who reject the other commands. They reject the feasts. They reject the holy days of YeHoVaH. Keeping the Sabbath is actually the beginning.

We can see from the latter portion of verse 12. You will find that the church around us and the people around us who are in these churches seem to be getting further and further and further away from the Almighty. They are compromising more and more and more as it pertains to the word of YeHoVaH.

(Matthew 13:13) *"Therefore speak I to them in parables: because they seeing see not; and hearing they hear not, neither do they understand."*

It is an interesting statement that Yeshua makes; that they see but don't see. They hear but they don't hear. Why? It is because they aren't listening. They are not listening. They hear the words, but they are not hearing with their spirit. They are not allowing these words to take residence in their being. You see, **you have to become one with the word.** But if you are simply looking for information, if you are looking for revelation, if you want to find deep things, if you are simply searching the scriptures so that you will have more knowledge; wisdom and knowledge are wonderful. But without understanding, it's hard to apply them.

What is most important is that you get an understanding.

(Matthew 13:14) *"And in them is fulfilled the prophecy of Esaias, which saith, 'By hearing ye shall hear, and shall not understand; and seeing ye shall see, and shall not perceive:'"*

He uses this phrase and when we hear it, we need to take notice and pay attention. In this particular case Yeshua makes our work a little easier. That is because he tells us what prophet he is speaking of. Unfortunately the King James uses the word "Esaias." The same King James in the book of Esaias in the Old Testament used the word "*Isaiah.*" This (for modern readers) can be a little bit confusing because the person now starts looking in their Old Testament for "Esaias." They are looking for the prophet Esaias but they won't find it. For some reason or another the King James translates Esaias instead of *Isaiah.* This is one of the challenges that the King James presents to us and why it is important that we do word studies. A simple word study will let us know that he is talking about the prophet Isaiah.

Yeshua is quoting the prophet in a prophecy.

(Matthew 13:15) *"For this people's heart is waxed gross, and their ears are dull of hearing, and their eyes they have closed; lest at any time they should see with their eyes and hear with their ears, and should understand with their heart, and should be converted, and I should heal them."*

This is a terrible statement. Understand something. If you see what you are seeing here in light of the word, what you will see is that you have people who have eyes but they can't see. It is a reference to a blind person. This is the worst kind of blindness.

You see, having no eyes and not being able to see is one form of blindness. But having eyes and still not being able to see, that is the worst type of blindness. They have eyes, but they have closed them. They are saying, "I don't want to see that. I don't want to know that. I know that but I am not going to do that."

They have ears they hear with, but they don't hear. What does he say? Look at verse 15 again. It seems as if the healing comes from being converted or from having an understanding that the one who is able to heal them is the one that they are supposedly looking for. But they don't see him because they have this idea of how he is going to come.

You see, when we define this type of ideology in modern day terms, the Baptists think they are the only ones who have the truth. The Methodists think they are the only ones.

Whatever denomination you are a part of, they think they are the ones who have the truth and they only see their truth.

I had a precious brother write to me. One of the people who used to watch our program on the Internet said that they don't watch us anymore. That is because one day they were in on the broadcast and they heard me say that I speak in tongues. At that point they shut us down. Up until this point they were being blessed by the teachings. The ministry was encouraging and inspiring them. But they heard me say that I speak in tongues and at that moment they determined that I had a devil.

It's like how did you come to that determination from that statement? Forget the fact that up until that statement they had been tremendously blessed by the ministry. That is a preconceived idea. Somebody taught them that if you speak in tongues, you must be of the devil or that it is a demonic spirit. When they heard me say that, that thought kicked in. Never mind the fact that I am preaching truth and transforming lives and that their lives have been transformed and blessed by the teachings. All of that goes out the window because of a statement that stirs up preconceived ideas. It is all because of a notion that they had been taught in one of those whorehouses called churches, or Messianic synagogues (seat(s) of Satan).

You will find that people make some dumb statements, but they supposedly have the truth.

(Isaiah 6:9) *"And he said, 'Go, and tell this people, Hear ye indeed, but understand not; and see ye indeed, but perceive not.'"*

This is somewhat challenging to me. If you look at the context of what is being said in the King James, Isaiah is prophesying on behalf of the Almighty. It is as if the Almighty is saying, "Go tell these people that you will hear but you won't understand. You will see but you won't perceive." That doesn't seem right.

(Isaiah 6:10) *"Make the heart of this people fat, and make their ears heavy, and shut their eyes; lest they see with their eyes, and hear with their ears, and understand with their heart, and convert, and be healed."*

Obviously we have some issues here with the translation. In the Septuagint (which is the Greek translation of the Hebrew Scriptures), here is how this verse reads:

(Isaiah 6:9-10, Septuagint) *"Say to these people, 'You will be ever hearing but never understanding; you will be ever seeing, but never perceiving. This people's heart has become calloused; they hardly hear with their ears, and they have closed their eyes.'"*

This is what is going on. When we look at a particular passage of scripture, I am telling you. Yeshua is speaking to a people. Understand that he knows who they are. He was sent to them.

Later in that same chapter of *Matthew* we read:

(Matthew 13:34) *"All these things spake Jesus unto the multitude in parables; and without a parable spake he not unto them:"*

Now what we see is that he is speaking to the multitude in parables.

(Matthew 13:35) *"That it might be fulfilled which was spoken by the prophet, saying, 'I will open my mouth in parables; I will utter things which have been kept secret from the foundation of the world.'"*

There is that phrase again. In this particular case one can make the assumption (since he mentioned Isaiah before) that he must be speaking about Isaiah again. That is because he does not mention which prophet. This statement makes our work a little bit more challenging, but then he gives us a serious clue as to what the prophet spoke.

We see here that the prophet (this is Old Testament or a prophet from the Tanakh saying this) is using the term "parable," which tells us that parables were spoken in the Old Testament. Most people think that parables are a New Testament principle, but parables were conceived in the Old Testament. We will be looking at that a little bit later.

The question is, which prophet? Well, we get a clue in *Psalm 78.*

Psalm 78

I was reading this particular psalm. It is really amazing when you do your due diligence to understand the words of Yeshua. I understand. Hear me. I can understand why the church world, the Christian Church, focuses upon the words of Jesus. That is because (in essence) Yeshua is "the Prophet" that was prophesied. As we look at the Messiah-Centric principle, we understand that all scripture focuses on Yeshua. Yeshua is the one. As the woman at the well, the Samaritan woman said, "When he comes, he is going to tell us all things."

Yeshua is the one whom Moses said that YeHoVaH was going to raise up a Prophet like him and when he comes, he is going to speak for YeHoVaH. And everything that this Prophet says, we must do. Those who do not listen to this Prophet, their souls would be required of them. It will be required of them. Basically what he is saying is that **you need to listen to what Yeshua said.**

I understand why the church focuses on the words of Yeshua. But if you don't understand Yeshua's context and what Yeshua was saying — most of what Yeshua spoke came straight from the Old Testament, from the Tanakh. To have an understanding of what Yeshua said, you can't look at everything Yeshua said. As a matter of fact, very little can you look at as far as what Yeshua said from a Greek or from a Western perspective. You have to look at what he said in the context of what the prophets spoke and of what the Torah taught.

If you take Yeshua out of that context, you will not understand what he is preaching or what he is teaching. You can't throw away the Old Testament. You can't throw away the law. The law is important. It is vital for interpreting the words of the Prophet that we must listen to.

He says things that without that understanding there is no way we will understand. This is why the majority of the church doesn't have a clue. They don't understand and cannot live according to the word because it is out of its context.

Psalm 78 is a prophecy. Remember it was spoken by the prophets saying, "I will open my mouth in parables."

(Psalm 78:2) *"I will open my mouth in a parable: I will utter dark sayings of old:"*

Compare this:

(Matthew 13:35) *"That it might be fulfilled which was spoken by the prophet, saying, 'I will open my mouth in parables; I will utter things which have been kept secret from the foundation of the world.'"*

Yeshua is quoting from the *Psalms,* but wait a minute! He said it was spoken by the prophet. What prophet spoke this in the *Psalms*?

Psalm 78 is a maschil of Asaph. *"Oh my people, hear my teaching. Listen to the words of my mouth."* A maschil of Asaph? Wait a minute. Weren't the *Psalms* written by David? A great majority of *Psalms* were written by David, but David did not write all of the *Psalms*. This particular *Psalm* is a *Psalm* — a maschil of Asaph. This is interpreted as or believed to be some form of literary art song. But it is also a song of instruction that is supposedly spoken by one of authority, one who is a leader, one who is in charge.

David wrote quite a few *Psalms* for Asaph, but Asaph wrote *Psalms* himself. And in this particular *Psalm* it is referred to as a prophetic *Psalm*. Well, who is this Asaph? Asaph was a Levite. Asaph was a Psalmist. Asaph was a prophet.

(2 Chronicles 5:12) *"Also the Levites which were the singers, all of them of Asaph, of Heman, of Jeduthun, with their sons and their brethren, being arrayed in white linen, having cymbals and psalteries and harps, stood at the east end of the altar, and with them an hundred and twenty priests sounding with trumpets:"*

Asaph was a Levite of the Gershunite family. He was appointed over the service of praise in the time of David and Solomon. He led the singing and sounded cymbals before the Ark, so he was a song leader. He would be what you would today call a praise leader; the one who leads the praise. He would be the one who in the church is called a praise leader.

(2 Chronicles 29:30) *"Moreover Hezekiah the king and the princes commanded the Levites to sing praise unto the LORD with the words of David, and of **Asaph the seer**. And they sang praises with gladness, and they bowed their heads and worshipped."*

Asaph was a seer or a prophet. He was a Levite, but he was also a prophet.

Although we find the word "parable" in the New Testament in reference to Yeshua's ministry, the use of parables was conceived in the Tanakh (in the Old Testament).

Let's return to *Psalm 78*. It is not one of those *Psalms* that you would memorize. It's one of those *Psalms* that you would probably start reading and say, "Man, this is boring. This has nothing to do with me, so I will just pass this up and find one of those *Psalms* that I like." There are people who have favorite *Psalms*. "I love that *Psalm*. That's my favorite." But this *Psalm* is a prophecy. Remember what Yeshua said.

(Matthew 13:35) *"That it might be fulfilled which was spoken **by the prophet**, saying, 'I will open my mouth in parables; I will utter things which have been kept secret from the foundation of the world.'"*

We see *Psalm 78* verses 1 and 2 stating:

(Psalm 78:1-2) *"Give ear, O my people, to my law: incline your ears to the words of my mouth. I will open my mouth in a parable: I will utter dark sayings of old:"*

What an opening.

Psalm 78:3-7

Oh, it gets interesting. It is worthy of reading in its entirety. This prophecy that Yeshua quotes a couple of verses of — understand that to the people that he is speaking to (in this case he is talking to his disciples), when he opens his mouth and utters parables, those who were knowledgeable in the word would know that this parable, this *Psalm* is one of rebuke. It is one of correction and one that does not invoke fond memories like some of the *Psalms*.

Psalm 78:8-17

It starts to take a turn here. It is about to get ugly. Can you see that as Yeshua is invoking this particular *Psalm*? He says, "I know the people that I am speaking to. They have closed their eyes. They are blind. They are intentionally blinding themselves. They have the word, but they are just like their Fathers. I gave my word to them that the Fathers would teach their children and the children would teach their children and those children would teach it to their children. That way they won't be like their Fathers who were a rebellious and stubborn and stiff-necked people. And yet here it is, generation after generation after generation." Yeshua is dealing with a stubborn, stiff-necked and rebellious people of whom he declares that their Father is the devil.

He says, "I am going to speak to this people in parables. I am going to give them the word, but they are not going to hear it. I am going to show them the fulfillment of scripture, their scripture, but they are not going to see it. That is because they are dull of hearing and blind. They are following blind guides. They have adopted traditions and commandments that were made of men. They have created a religion that has absolutely nothing to do with me, but they claim that it is based in my word. I am going to speak to them knowing that they are not going to listen. I am going to show them things knowing they are not going to see. They think they know, but the more they hear what I have to say, the less they are going to understand. The knowledge that they have is going to be removed from them. Their hearts are going to be hardened."

This is exactly some of the things that we are dealing with as we are trying to relate to our religious brothers and sisters and parents and uncles and aunts and co-workers and former church members, but that didn't stop Yeshua from communicating. "I am going to tell these people the truth, but they are not going to hear it. I am going to show them the word, but they are not going to see it. They are tired. They don't want to hear. They are dull of hearing. They have heard but they have not put what they have learned to practice. Therefore they are hearers and not doers. They always want to know more, but they are not applying what they know."

He says, "What I am doing is simply the fulfillment of the prophet Asaph and the prophecy is the 78th *Psalm*." When we look at the *Psalm*, people sometimes think about the Messiah and a Messianic *Psalm*. But this is a *Psalm* that is basically an indictment. It is saying that you people are just like your Father and your ancestors; not like the patriarchs (Abraham, Isaac and Jacob), but stubborn, stiff-necked and rebellious people.

Basically you are going to prove (as he goes on to say in another place), "I am going to prove that you are just like your Fathers because your Fathers killed all of the prophets — all of them." Then the Father who sent the prophet decided that okay, he is going to send his only Son. Yeshua spoke that in a parable. He is going to send his only Son and you are going to kill him. "We are done with him. We don't have to listen to this individual anymore because we have killed all of his servants and we have killed his only begotten Son. Now we are a righteousness unto ourselves. We will establish our own righteousness." (This is basically what they did).

After seeing all of that in verses 17-20, we can see that they were never satisfied.

🔍 *Psalm 78:21-32*

Some individuals came to Yeshua and he spoke to them about the parable concerning the rich man and Lazarus. As he was speaking to them, somebody cried out, "Let Lazarus dip his finger into some water." Or send someone to tell my brothers so they don't come to a place like this. Yeshua said, "What difference is it going to make?" They have Moses. They have the prophets. They have the word. They hear it, but they don't do what is says. They see it, but they don't see it. They are not interested in doing it. They are interested in satisfying the requirements of their religion. Their religion gives the false sense of comfort that they are alright, even though they read the word that is right there before them. They discount the word that is right there before them for their religion. They teach for commands the commandments of men and they make the Law of YeHoVaH of no effect.

"We don't have to keep that law. Jesus gave us a new law — love, the law of love. All we have to do today is to love God with all of our heart, all of our mind and with all of our strength and love our neighbor as ourselves and we have kept the whole law. That's all we have to do."

And then the alternate question, "Well, what does that look like and how do you know you are doing it?"

"Well, I don't know, but one thing I do know is that is what the word says. It says that all I have to do is to love God with all of my heart, with all of my soul and with all of my strength and love my neighbor as myself and I have kept the whole law."

"Well, have you done that?"

"Well, no."

"Are you trying to do that?"

"Well, yeah."

"Well, how do you know, if you don't know what that looks like?"

You see, this is the blindness that Yeshua is trying to expose. You have a person who says, "That makes sense." Then they run to their Rabbi. "Well, that's not what that literally means." Or they run to their priest or they run to their pastor or their apostle or their elders. "That's not what that literally means. All you gotta do is this, this and this and you are in good standing with us. And if you are in good standing with us and this is the true church of God, then you are in good standing with God. That is because to be in good standing with God, you have to be in good standing with us. We are the ONLY representation, the TRUE representation of God in the earth."

This is serious business.

Read the rest of *Psalm 78*.

Although we find the word "parable" in the New Testament in reference to Yeshua's ministry, the use of parables was conceived in the Tanakh/Old Testament. The word "parable" in the Old Testament Hebrew is the word *mashal*, meaning "properly a pithy maxim, usually of a metaphorical nature: hence a simile; a proverbial saying, parable, similitude, resemblance."

You look this up and it's a "pithy maxim." That is obviously two words. You think okay, what does the word "parable" or *mashal* mean in the Hebrew? Oh. It's a pithy maxim. What is a pithy maxim?

"Pithy" is the use of a few words in a clever and effective way, according to Webster's online dictionary. A "maxim" is a succinct formulation of a principle, rule or basic truth about life. So it is a clever and effective use of words to formulate a principle, rule or basic truth about life.

The word *mashal* is translated "parable" in the following passages:

Numbers 23:7, 18; 24:3, 15, 20, 21, 23

Job 27:1; 28:1

Psalms 48:4, 78:2

Ezekiel 17:2; 20:49; 24:3

Micah 2:4

Habakkuk 2:6

These are the places where you will find the word "parable" in the King James. I want us to take a moment and look at a couple of these, because in order to understand some of these things, you have to look at the context.

When you get the understanding and meaning of a parable and how parables are used, you have to be convinced that you cannot teach a parable as a literal message. It is a story that comes alongside a truth to try to give an understanding of the truth that the parable is coming alongside to highlight. It is not the parable, but the truth that is trying to be highlighted by the parable. It is a clever saying and an effective use of words to formulate a principle.

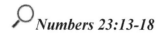 **Numbers 23**

When you look at this chapter, you recognize it as a story of a prophet. There was a prophet by the name of Balaam. There was a king by the name of Balak who wanted the prophet Balaam to curse Israel. Now, Balaam was one of these prophets, kind of like a prophet for hire except today prophets for hire have become "prophe-liars." Balaam had enough connection (if you would) to know some things. And that was to truly inquire of YeHoVaH even though in his heart he had a desire for material possessions.

In verse 7 we see *"...and he took up his parable."* Remember that a parable is a clever and effective use of words to formulate a principle. He picks up this parable. Pay attention to this.

(Numbers 23:7-9) "And he took up his parable, and said, 'Balak the king of Moab hath brought me from Aram, out of the mountains of the east, saying, Come, curse me Jacob, and come, defy Israel. How shall I curse, whom God hath not cursed? or how shall I defy, whom the LORD hath not defied? For from the top of the rocks I see him, and from the hills I behold him: lo, the people shall dwell alone, and shall not be reckoned among the nations.'"

He is speaking in a parable.

(Numbers 23:10-11) "Who can count the dust of Jacob, and the number of the fourth part of Israel? Let me die the death of the righteous, and let my last end be like his! ¹¹And Balak said unto Balaam, 'What hast thou done unto me? I took thee to curse mine enemies, and, behold, thou hast blessed them altogether.'"

How does he bless them? Because he didn't curse them. He didn't curse them. Based upon what Balaam said, he declared that he had blessed them, but Balak didn't give up.

Numbers 23:13-18

In both of these places, he speaks. He takes up this parable. Notice how preceding his taking up of the parable, YeHoVaH puts a word into Balaam's mouth. YeHoVaH says in verse 16, *"And YeHoVaH met Balaam, and put a word in his mouth, and said, Go again to Balak and say thus."* So he put a word in Balaam's mouth.

Numbers 23:18-23

Now we see that he picks up a parable. YeHoVaH puts a word in his mouth and basically comes to the conclusion that **you can't curse what YeHoVaH has blessed**. Now, in the midst of this story of an almost backslidden prophet, there is some good news and it is great news for us. It is the fact that what YeHoVaH has blessed, you can't curse. What YeHoVaH has blessed, you can't curse.

For me, this is of the utmost importance because I know that the blessings and the curses come from one thing. The blessings come from obedience and the curses come from disobedience to one thing.

The blessings come from obedience to the law. The curses come from disobedience to the law.

Deuteronomy 28 makes it very clear that if we diligently hearken to do all of these commands that YeHoVaH has given us today, all of these blessings will come upon us in abundance. ***Deuteronomy 28:15*** says that if we diligently hearken NOT to do all of these commandments, then all of these curses will come upon us. And it lists the curses that he is speaking of.

The blessings come from walking with YeHoVaH in his commands. The curses come from not walking with YeHoVaH in his commands. There are people who claim to be walking with YeHoVaH, but who are not keeping his commands. There are people who are claiming to be walking with YeHoVaH who are Spirit-filled and they believe that they don't have to keep his commands. There are people who claim to be walking with YeHoVaH, but they are keeping the commandments of men, based upon the commandments of YeHoVaH.

You have to decide what camp you are in.

You have to decide. Are you keeping traditions or are you standing on his truth? Are you building your spiritual life off of principles based upon the word or are you building your life in the word? There are churches and synagogues and Messianic communities that are standing on the principles that are based upon the word.

There is religion and then there is true religion. True religion is based in, found in, standing upon and keeping the commands of YeHoVaH.

I want to deviate just a moment to build on that statement.

James 1:21-22

It is not that truth that sets you free. It is the word that you do. It is what you put into practice. Knowing the truth and not doing the truth is like not having the truth. It is better not to know the truth than to know it and not to do it. Having the truth and not doing the truth is a great deception. This is what James says.

🔍 *James 1:23-25*

It's interesting. "The perfect law of liberty." What James is saying is that the law is freedom. The world and the church want to say that the law is bondage. **There is nowhere in the Bible where it says that the law is bondage**. As a matter of fact, the Bible tells us that the law is not bondage. It is not burdensome. It is not too hard for us to do. James says that if you want freedom and liberty, it is in the law; the perfect law of liberty.

You have to understand something. When James wrote this and when James said this, there was no New Testament Bible. James was not talking about *Matthew, Mark, Luke* and *John*. James was talking about the perfect law of liberty. He was talking about this law that YeHoVaH had given that had been misinterpreted, mistranslated and miscommunicated by all who came before Yeshua. Yeshua not only did not come to destroy it, but to show us how to live it the way it was intended to be lived. James now refers to this law as the law that is able to save your souls. It is the engrafted word, the perfect law of liberty. Being a doer of this perfect law of liberty shall make a man blessed in his deeds.

🔍 *James 1:26-27*

This is not getting entangled in the world; not taking advantage of the orphans and the widows. This is not misusing the word or misrepresenting it. It is not being a false witness or a bad ambassador, but one who looks into the law of liberty and continues therein. It is one who knows. **YeHoVaH in his law shows us how we are to live.**

Yeshua comes along and says, "You know, these people are so full of their religion. They are so full of themselves. They are so full of their own righteousness." YeHoVaH has sent prophet after prophet, after prophet, after prophet. Their Fathers have killed the prophets. They are just like their Fathers.

The people today — many are just like their Fathers or their religious ancestors. If this old-time religion was good enough for my Daddy and my Momma and my Grandmamma and my Granddaddy, it's good enough for me. I was born this and I will die this. I was born and bred a certain religious belief system and this is what I am going to continue therein.

Then they are going to places where you have individuals preaching parables. I did a teaching and it is called *Maximizing Your Talents.* In this particular teaching I took one of those parables and literally revealed it as it was. Many people have taken that particular parable and turned the "talent" into spiritual gifts. They have turned the talent into abilities. They have turned the talent into something that is not even in the context of the scripture or the verses. This particular teaching, *Maximizing Your Talents* actually deals with what Yeshua was dealing with.

What was important was that what they did with their talent determined whether they were a wicked servant or a good or a righteous servant — all from the talent.

It has nothing to do with spiritual gifts and abilities, as the church and many in the Messianic community want to teach. Learn what it is.

The Renewed Covenant — There are all of these teachings and I am really surprised. I know people are taking advantage of them on the Internet, but you all need to get some of these teachings. We have put a lot of energy and time into getting the true gospel of the Kingdom on disks that you can have, just in case it is true that the Internet disappears; just in case it is true that they shut down the Internet or Wi-Fi or whatever the case may be. If you have your own hard copy, they can't shut that down. All you need is a good DVD player and an old tube and you are good to go with some great teaching whether you can access it on television or not.

Class 94 Study Summary

Key Points

1. The parable principle is that principle by which any parable is interpreted by discerning its moral and elements.

2. A parable is a short, simple story from which a moral lesson may be drawn. It is an earthly story with a heavenly message. A parable is somewhat fictitious.

3. Yeshua is the word made flesh. He is the only "man" who has a perfect understanding of YeHoVaH's word (because he is the word).

4. Up until Yeshua's day, instead of giving people the word, religious leaders gave them their interpretations along with their manmade rules, regulations and traditions.

5. One of the most critical truths we come into is the Sabbath day.

6. You have to become one with the word. Otherwise it is simply information and knowledge. Without wisdom you won't have understanding and without the Holy Spirit, you won't have revelation.

7. We need to listen to what Yeshua said. We are to listen to the Prophet that YeHoVaH sent. Everything that this Prophet said for us to do, we must do. It is said in the word of those who do not listen to him, that their souls will be required of them.

8. You have to look at what Yeshua said in the context in which it was spoken. If you take it out of context, you won't understand what he is preaching or teaching.

9. A "maschil" in the Bible is a song of wisdom.

10. Although we find the word "parable" in the New Testament in reference to Yeshua's ministry, it was first conceived in the Tanakh (Old Testament).

11. Yeshua knew the people he was talking to (religious leaders). He said they were blind. He said they intentionally blinded themselves with their religion. That is why he spoke to them in parables.

12. You can't curse what YeHoVaH has blessed and you can't bless what he has cursed.

13. The blessings come from obedience to the Law. The curses come from disobedience to the Law.

14. There is religion and then there is true religion. True religion is based on, founded in and is standing upon and keeping the commandments of YeHoVaH.

15. Nowhere in the Bible does it say that the Law of YeHoVaH is bondage.

16. In his Law, YeHoVaH shows us how we are to live.

Review Exercise

1. Were you surprised to find out that parables are in the Old Testament?

_____

_____

_____

Why or why not?

_____

_____

_____

2. A parable has been defined as a "pithy maxim." How would you reword that definition into your own words? Keep your definition true to the lesson information.

_____

_____

_____

_____

3. Have you ever picked up a parable or used a fictitious story in your own life to communicate some idea to someone? What were the circumstances and why did you use a story? How did you do that? Did it have the desired effect?

_____

_____

_____

_____

_____

_____

_____

_____

4. Select a parable and do an in-depth study. Which parable will you dive deeply into? What things of significance did you learn; especially anything you found out that you really didn't know or hadn't thought of before?

_____

_____

_____

_____

_____

_____

_____

_____

_____

_____

5. What are some similarities and what are some differences between Yeshua's parables and say, Aesop's Fables?

_____

_____

_____

_____

_____

_____

_____

_____

_____

_____

Rate the following statements
by filling in the most appropriate number.

(1 = I do not agree 10 = I agree completely)

Objectives:

1. I can describe how Yeshua used parables.

    1.◯   2. ◯   3. ◯   4. ◯   5. ◯   6. ◯   7. ◯   8. ◯   9. ◯   10. ◯

2. I can define the five steps of interpreting a parable.

    1.◯   2. ◯   3. ◯   4. ◯   5. ◯   6. ◯   7. ◯   8. ◯   9. ◯   10. ◯

3. I can explain how parables were utilized in the Old Testament writings.

    1.◯   2. ◯   3. ◯   4. ◯   5. ◯   6. ◯   7. ◯   8. ◯   9. ◯   10. ◯

My Journal

What I learned from this class:

_____

_____

_____

_____

_____

_____

_____

_____

_____

_____

_____

_____

_____

_____

_____

_____

_____

_____

_____

Discipleship Training Class 95

Parable-Centered Principle (part 2)

Objectives:

As a Discipleship student, at the end of this class you will be able to:

- Explain your understanding of parables through the Greek word *parabole*

We are going to be looking at the parable principle itself, but also a passage of scripture that surrounds this lesson's teaching. It is actually also going to help us into a better understanding of one of these doctrines that are prevalent in some communities that is dealing with the whole deliverance movement.

As we are looking at the parable principle, we saw in the last lesson that the word for parable in the Old Testament is from the Hebrew word *mashal*; meaning "properly a pithy maxim, usually of a metaphorical nature: hence a simile: a proverbial saying, parable, similitude, resemblance."

Pithy is the use of a few words in a clever and effective way. A "maxim" is a succinct formulation of a principle, rule or basic truth about life. So putting those together we have a clever and effective use of words to formulate a principle, rule or basic truth about life.

We saw how the word *mashal* is translated in a number of passages in the Old Testament; and we looked at *Numbers 23*. We looked at the issue with Balaam and Balak and how Balaam picked up a parable as he was instructed by the Almighty and began to speak it.

The word pops up in **Psalm 78:2**. This *Psalm* is powerful. It is unfortunate that as he revealed himself in days of old in all the things that he did in the midst of them; they still would not repent. Today we are living in a time when we can see not just on a national and international level, but many of us can see on a personal level. I have made it a point in my life where when things are happening in my life or around my life, I need to examine myself. That is because I know that number one, all things work together for good for those who love Messiah and who are called according to his purpose (those who walk after the Spirit and not after the flesh). We know that the Father will work things out for us.

The deal is that when things are not going right in my life; if something is not going the way I think it should be going (especially if the Father is instructing me to do something and things are just not falling into place), then the first thing that I do is examine. Am I doing something I am not supposed to be doing? Am I not doing something that I am supposed to be doing? I am doing a thorough examination of myself.

I am my worst critic and you should be your worst critic as well. But at the same time we shouldn't be so hard on ourselves when we find or see things or places where we have fallen short that we beat ourselves up. We repent. We confess. We know that he is faithful and just to forgive us and to cleanse us.

The thing is though that the Father was revealing certain things to his people in days of old. The more he did, it is as if they refused to see. Okay, Father is resisting us. Father gives grace to the humble, but he resists the proud. When we look at this issue of parables, I want us to look at *Ezekiel*.

Ezekiel 17 and 18

Ezekiel 17 is where we see the Father speaking. We are going to find this word "parable." As we have noted in the verses here is the word *mashal*. This translates in the English to the word "parable," but it is not just parable that it translates into (we will look at that in just a moment).

The Father is instructing his prophet to speak a riddle and to put forth a parable to the House of Israel. You have to understand something. A parable is a clever use of words. It is a story that comes alongside. The problem is that people try to interpret a parable. Most parables (all parables really) that are given in scripture are generally interpreted by the person who gave it.

If I want to know the interpretation of a parable, I don't need to try to do a word study on the parable itself. I need to look for the interpretation of the parable from the one who gave the parable. We are going to find out that here YeHoVaH gives a parable, but he also gives the interpretation of the parable, so there is no need for me or anybody else to try to interpret this parable.

This brings into place another basic rule of scripture reading and interpretation. Whenever you are looking at a passage of scripture, don't stop at a verse. If you don't understand a word, look it up. Scripture interprets scripture.

Oftentimes I have people who want me to interpret a verse of scripture, and it is like, if you read a little further on, you will get the interpretation. Don't get stuck.

The riddle or the parable begins in verse 3. We can take some time and get into what is going on here. But what I want to show you was the parable that Ezekiel is speaking that was given to him by YeHoVaH to speak to the people. Not only did Ezekiel speak this parable, but now the Father gives him the interpretation. In other words, the reason why he gave the parable was to give a story to come alongside a story.

Now he is saying, "Here is what the parable means. Here is the parable, but here is what the parable means." In the eighteenth chapter, again the parable here is interpreted by the one who gave the parable. It is unfortunate that too many individuals have tried to reinterpret scripture. In other words, they read a portion of scripture and then try to give a meaning. Now they are putting their own private interpretation to a word in the scripture.

A good example is if we look at the book of *Acts*, concerning Peter. The vision that he had was about the sheet that came down full of abominable things. He heard a voice saying to "rise and eat." Peter gives the interpretation of his vision. The Father gives Peter the interpretation of this vision and yet even though Peter has given the interpretation that it had absolutely nothing to do with eating things that are unclean but to call no man unclean, a majority of people insist that this vision instructs Peter to eat unclean things. They swear that through this vision Father is now saying that it is okay to eat swine and shellfish and things without scales. It is now "okay" to eat unclean things based upon Peter's vision, when Peter himself gave the interpretation.

Isn't that amazing?

Ezekiel 18

This particular passage of scripture is also rooted in a parable according to verses 2 and 3. The word "proverb" here is the Hebrew word *mashal*. In the book of *Proverbs* verse 1, the word there is *mashal*. We will look at that, but the word "proverb" in some places is the Hebrew word *mashal*. It is the same word for "parable."

What are you saying when you say this? Do you know what you are saying? One of the translations of this is that because the Father ate sour grapes, the children's teeth are going to be bad. That is the idea. In other words, the children are going to suffer because of what the Father ate. The Father did something and it is going to be transferred and visited upon the children.

Here in the book of *Ezekiel*, Father is about to address something. He says in verse 3,

"'As I live,' saith YeHoVaH Elohim, 'you shall not have occasion any more to use this proverb in Israel.'"

Don't use it anymore. Stop it.

What is he saying? He is saying that the Father is not responsible for the child's behavior. But he is also saying that the son, the child, is not responsible for the Father's behavior. How many of us use (as an excuse) the behavior of our parents to justify our behavior? How often have we heard, "Well, *you* did it." How often have you rebuked your spouse saying, "Well, the boy is just like you" or "the girl is just like you. Have you forgotten? You used to be that same way."

How many times have our children used the guilt trip on us to blame us for their behavior? How many times have you used it to blame your parents?

This is what YeHoVaH says to his people in verse 4,

"Behold, all souls are mine; as the soul of the father, so also the soul of the son is mine: the soul that sinneth, it shall die."

In other words, you are responsible for your own behavior. You can't blame someone else for your behavior.

A husband and wife could have two children. Let's say one is named Cain. The other one is named Abel. One murders the other one. They both come from the same parents. Is Adam or Eve responsible or are the parents responsible for Cain's actions? It happened even after YeHoVaH instructs Cain about his behavior before he murders his brother. YeHoVaH himself instructed Cain and yet Cain did what Cain did even though YeHoVaH himself instructed him.

Was Adam or was Eve responsible for Cain's behavior? No. Cain is the one who had to pay for what Cain did. This is what is in verses 6-9. Then in verses 10-13 you have a righteous Father and a son who is unrighteous. Did the son get that from his Father?

When a Father is not the best Father, can the son (this unrighteous son) say, "Because of you I am the way I am?" Why is it that children and grownups who blame their behavior on their parents always look for the negative behavior of the parent as if the only thing a parent has ever done is negative? What about all of the righteous right things that the parents did? Oh, that doesn't count. That is irrelevant.

Some of you out there have allowed your children to hold you hostage to something you did long ago. They keep throwing it up in your face. You cower down and give in to their demands because they are using that against you even though you have repented and even though you have asked Father to forgive you. Father has forgiven you. He has cast it as far as the East is from the West. But those children, that spouse or that sibling remembers. They want to hold you hostage even though the Father has freed you.

I say today to be free. Walk in the freedom. You are not responsible for someone's behavior. You are responsible for your behavior. You have contributed to the behavior of someone. Your job is to repent and to confess it, even to the person that you have wronged. Then move on. This is what the Father says.

Every person, this son's blood shall be upon him (verse 14).

Now you have a Father who is righteous and who now has a wicked son. But this wicked son has a son that sees all of his Father's sins which he has done and considers it and doesn't do such things.

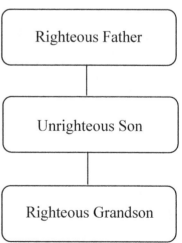

This son's son has seen all of the abominations, all of the wickedness of his Dad and all of the bad things that this Dad did. This child grew up in that house. This child was probably abused by this Father, neglected by this Father, ignored by this Father and mistreated by this Father.

And yet this son is nothing like his Father. He doesn't eat on the mountains where his Father ate. He doesn't lift up his eyes to the idols of the House of Israel like his Father did. He hasn't defiled his neighbor's wife like his Dad.

(Ezekiel 18:17-18) *"That hath taken off his hand from the poor, that hath not received usury nor increase, hath executed my judgments, hath walked in my statutes; he shall not die for the iniquity of his father, he shall surely live. As for his father, because he cruelly oppressed, spoiled his brother by violence, and did that which is not good among his people, lo, even he shall die in his iniquity."*

Now some people would say, "Well, wait a minute." What we are looking at here is all of the attributes that these deliverance ministries use to justify or to create this whole "generational curse" issue that tells people they need to be delivered from demons.

Let me tell you something. If someone has convinced you that you have a demon, then you have allowed that spirit, that convincing to get into your mind. Now you are convinced that you have a demon and the only thing that can help you is if this demon that you have been convinced that you have is cast out.

In order to justify a prophetic ministry, there has to be prophecy. In other words, to justify a healing ministry, there has to be healing. In order to justify a deliverance ministry, there has to be people with demons. So now we have to teach that the reason your behavior is the way your behavior is, is because you have been opened up to generational curses. This is where these spirits have traveled down your Father, your Father and your Father. Now you have to go back into your past. You have to search your soul. You have to look at the impact that your father had on you.

You were abandoned. You were molested. You were this and you were that, and all of these kinds of things. Now, does that have an effect on people? Absolutely. But psychologists, sociologists and deliverance ministries are trying to get people to point the blame at someone else because you are "fine." It "isn't" your fault.

Listen. If you are out there sleeping around and you are promiscuous, it's your fault. Now, if you are being raped and forced upon, then that is a whole other issue. We aren't talking about that. But if you are out there and you are putting that crack pipe to your mouth and you are pouring that alcohol down your throat, that is not a demon. That is you.

Here is the thing about deliverance ministry. You can't cast you out.

You can go to deliverance ministry and have people pray over you, but you cannot be cast out of you. The only thing you can do is repent. "Well brother, you are talking about the parable. Why are you preaching so hard?" Well, let me tell you something. I have been in one of the premier deliverance ministries on the planet. And the moment you get rid of one demon, you have two more that you have to get rid of.

In other words, you will always need deliverance. You will always be getting deliverance from this and deliverance from that and deliverance from this. That is because the deliverance ministry has to justify its existence.

Everything is a demon now. Everything is a devil.

(Ezekiel 18:19) *"Yet say ye, Why? doth not the son bear the iniquity of the father? When the son hath done that which is lawful and right, and hath kept all my statutes, and hath done them, he shall surely live."*

That is the whole idea. The iniquities of the Fathers are being visited to the third and fourth generation of them that hate me; but showing mercy, showing love to the thousands of generations of them that love me and keep my commands.

Notice what the Father did. The Father kept the commands of the Almighty. Notice what his son did. His son did not keep the commands of the Almighty. But then he had a son who kept the commands of the Almighty. See? It is all about the commandments. It is not about demons. It is about obedience.

When you walk in obedience to the word of YeHoVaH, you have the covering and protection of the Almighty. When you don't walk in obedience to the Almighty, I don't care how much deliverance you get. You have no protection. You have no covering because these ministries are teaching that you need to be delivered. You need to be delivered. You need to be delivered but you don't have to keep the commands.

How are you going to get delivered from you?

You see, it is all about what you allow, the teachings that you receive and the things that you believe. If you believe you have a demon, you surely have one. All things are possible to them that believe. If you believe you are seeing things, you surely are.

I am not trying to get you to deny that you don't have issues. That is not the issue. The issue is keeping his commands. The one who has the power to deliver you is saying that you need to keep his commands. But the one who is ministering deliverance is saying that you don't have to keep the commands. Jesus delivered you from that.

Jesus delivered you from the commands, but now you need deliverance from the demons that come because you have been delivered from the commands.

These are the words of YeHoVaH. They are not Ezekiel's words. They are not Arthur Bailey's words. But the people who are doing all this deliverance ministry don't read this portion of the word and this is not a vision. I know they would much rather be prophesying and trying to interpret the valley of dry bones and the wheel within the wheel, but this is the direct word from YeHoVaH.

(Matthew 4:4) *"Man shall not live by bread alone, but by every word that proceeds from the mouth of YeHoVaH."*

There are people out there who want to blame their parents and they want to blame these people and those people. Every time you shift the blame onto someone else, you have shifted the responsibility away from yourself.

Now someone else is responsible for your actions. YeHoVaH says, "No, you are going to be responsible for your own actions."

Yes, my Dad was an alcoholic and I picked up his alcoholism, but I had other family members who didn't. They told me through some of the training and courses that I went through that some of this skips generations. One child could be susceptible to it and another child not, and yet it is in the DNA, so now they want your medical history.

How is it that you both come from the same parents, you both have the same DNA structure and yet one child is susceptible and another child is not? One child is a rebel and the other child is a saint and yet it is the parents' fault?

Now you have rebellious attitudes with rebellious actions and it is "your" fault, not the person who is acting in rebellion.

They are going through. "It's your fault." "I'm sorry. What do you want me to do?" "Well, I need counseling. You have to pay for counseling. I'm not responsible for my behavior. I'm not responsible for my actions. If you hadn't abandoned me, if you hadn't left me, if you had let me have that, if you would have done this for me. But you didn't do it because you didn't care."

So now I am going to prove to you that your actions or lack thereof are responsible for my behavior. It's your fault. Father says, "You can blame who you want, but when it comes down to it, the one who sins is the one who is going to pay for their behavior."

Parents, you might be able to go to jail for your children. You may be able to give them all the help that they need, but when it comes down to standing before YeHoVaH, you can't stand before YeHoVaH for your child. They are on their own. Your role at this point is to give them truth and not back up — to stand and not give in.

(Ezekiel 18:26-31) *"When a righteous man turneth away from his righteousness, and committeth iniquity, and dieth in them; for his iniquity that he hath done shall he die. Again, when the wicked man turneth away from his wickedness that he hath committed, and doeth that which is lawful and right, he shall save his soul alive. Because he considereth, and turneth away from all his transgressions that he hath committed, he shall surely live, he shall not die. Yet saith the house of Israel, 'The way of the LORD is not equal.' O house of Israel, are not my ways equal? are not your ways unequal? Therefore I will judge you, O house of Israel, every one according to his ways, saith the Lord GOD. Repent, and turn yourselves from all your transgressions; so iniquity shall not be your ruin. Cast away from you all your transgressions, whereby ye have transgressed; and make you a new heart and a new spirit: for why will ye die, O house of Israel?"*

It is amazing. Here the Father says, "Make for you a new heart and a new spirit." How are you going to do that? How are you going to do it? He says, "I will put a new heart in you. I will give you a new heart and put my Spirit in you."

You see? Here is the deal. The person has to be willing to turn to YeHoVaH. They have to be willing to say, "Okay. I'm wrong. I take responsibility for my actions. I'm no longer going to blame someone else for my behavior. Father, I come to you and I need you now to give me a new heart. I need your Spirit within me."

And Father says, "I have been waiting for this moment." He has been waiting for this very moment. Father can't force a new heart into a rebellious person. He can't give a new Spirit to a person who is operating in their own evil, wicked, foul, rebellious spirit. **They have to come to a place of repentance.**

One of the quickest ways of getting them to that place (sometimes it seems like a lifetime) is when you turn them over. It's like "I'm not going to bow down to appease your rebellion any longer. You have used that for the last time. You have blamed me for your behavior and I've done everything that I know to do. I've done everything that I know to do and all I can do is say to you that I'm sorry. I apologize. That is all I can do. Now it's on you.

You can continue to blame me for your behavior, but you have to understand. I didn't put one joint to your mouth. I didn't go and buy one pack of cigarettes for you. I didn't go and buy that alcohol and force it down your throat. I didn't lie down with the dogs you lie down with. You went against my counsel. You went against my standards.

These things that you are dealing with are your own actions. You can't blame me for having a child out of wedlock. You can't blame me for becoming an alcoholic or a drug addict. You can't blame me for the life you have right now because I didn't do this or I didn't do that. The only person you can blame is yourself. And I at this moment will no longer receive the blame from you. Those days are over. I'm not going to jail for you. I'm not going to hell for you.

(Ezekiel 18:32) *"'For I have no pleasure in the death of him that dieth,' saith YeHoVaH Elohim: 'wherefore turn yourselves, and live ye.'"*

As we can see, YeHoVaH says to Israel, "Don't say that anymore. No longer can you say that the Father has eaten sour grapes and the children's teeth are set on edge. No longer can you say that the Father is responsible for the wickedness of the son. Every person is responsible for their own actions."

Stop taking the blame. Stop taking the guilt. Stop allowing people to manipulate you and control you.

The word *mashal* is translated in these further passages in the Old Testament:

Deuteronomy 28:37

1 Samuel 24:13

1 Kings 4:32

2 Chronicles 7:20

Psalm 69:11

Proverbs 1:1, 6; 25:1

Ecclesiastes 12:9

Isaiah 14:4

Jeremiah 24:9

Ezekiel 18:2-3

 *Proverbs 1:1*

Here is a good place to get people reading the *Proverbs* of Solomon. That word "proverb" there is the word *mashal*. Here is where we get the word "parable." We will find that the book of *Proverbs* is literally a book of parables. It has many parables. Here is what it says about them:

(Proverbs 1:2-4) *"To know wisdom and instruction; to perceive the words of understanding; To receive the instruction of wisdom, justice, and judgment, and equity; To give subtlety to the simple, to the young man knowledge and discretion."*

We look at the book of *Proverbs* and find that the book of *Proverbs* — the word here in verse 1 and the word in verse 6 is the Hebrew word *mashal,* which is the word from which we get "parable."

When we look at the Greek, the word "parable" is **parabole** (para-boley).

I want to look at something from the last lesson. It is important for us to understand what Yeshua did and said because we find:

(Matthew 13:13-14) *"Therefore speak I to them in parables: because they seeing see not; and hearing they hear not, neither do they understand. And in them is fulfilled the prophecy of Esaias, which saith, 'By hearing ye shall hear, and shall not understand; and seeing ye shall see, and shall not perceive.'"*

The main reason why Yeshua spoke in parables was to fulfill the prophecy of *Isaiah.* We looked into this a little deeper in the last lesson, so I encourage you to review that material.

People are ever learning but never coming to the knowledge of truth. There are people in our environments and in our circles and in some of our homes and synagogues and churches and temples who go from one deep thing to another. For them it is all about the information and the conversation in getting deep. For them it's all about the four levels of Torah. It's all about the midrashing. They just want to talk.

They want to have very deep conversations to try to impress you with their information and with their knowledge. They want you to know that they are not dumb. They are not stupid. They are not ignorant to the scriptures.

They have read many books and they are knowledgeable on many levels and they have great conversation, but their lives are a wreck.

Their homes are falling apart. Their children don't respect them. Their wives don't respect them. At their jobs and with their co-workers, it's like talk-talk-talk-talk-talk. You know you have a lot of knowledge, but you are not doing anything. What are you doing with it?

We know these people. They are heady. They are high-minded. They can get into any conversation. They know a whole lot about a whole lot, but that is it. It's knowledge. They are always hearing but never understanding. They are always seeing but never perceiving. Their hearts are calloused. They hardly hear with their ears and they have closed their eyes.

We know people like this because I deal with them. I don't deal with them much because you get into conversations with them and you know it's like we will talk for hours and walk away. The next week we have the same old conversation on a different subject.

I have chosen personally not to engage in a lot of those conversations. For me, it is not about what you say as much as it is about what you are doing. I want to know if you believe what you are saying. That is because if you believe what you are saying, you are going to be doing what you are saying.

This is the thing about Yeshua. Yeshua did and taught. He did not just teach. There are people who just teach. They are always teaching. Teach, teach, teach. Are you doing what you are teaching? Do you believe what you are saying?

If I believe what I am saying, I am going to do what I am saying. And when I teach what I am doing, then there is a passion with what I am saying. I am not just giving you stuff off of the top of my head. I believe this. I know this to be true. It works!

The word works.

You have people who are saying one thing and doing something else. The Bible has a word for that. What is it? It's a hypocrite. There are a whole lot of hypocrites. They are Torah terrorists. They know and they always want to tell you.

Look at your family. Look at your home. Look at your life. You have a lot of good information. Why don't you apply it? Why don't you live it?

Now come the excuses. It's a whole bunch of excuses.

No excuses. Do it. You will see that it works. It works!

From the Greek, a parable is:

*"A similitude, a **fictitious narrative** (of common life conveying a moral): a placing of one thing by the side of another; a comparison of one thing with another; a narrative, fictitious but agreeable to the laws and usages of human life by which either the duties of men or the things of God, particularly the nature and history of God's kingdom, are figuratively portrayed; a short discourse that makes a comparison; it expresses a single complete thought."*

It is critical in the New Testament to understand the parable principle, because when Yeshua spoke to the multitude, he spoke in parables. He spoke in parables because he was fulfilling scripture. When he got alone with his disciples, he gave the interpretations of what he was trying to say to the multitude. He is saying that these people just want to hear, hear, hear. It's like okay, what new thing? We are on the cutting edge. We are looking for a new thing. God has to do a new thing. It's a new thing, a new thing, everything is a new thing.

What are you doing with the old things? These things you ought to have done. Folks are letting go of the things that they ought to have done and are looking for the Father to do a new thing.

Of course he did a new thing in Jesus. He said we don't have to do all of that old stuff (or so they say).

The word *parabole* is translated "parables" and it is also translated as "comparison."

(Mark 4:30) *"And he said, 'Whereunto shall we liken the kingdom of God? Or with what comparison shall we compare it?'"*

You will find that there are some things that people don't like to be compared to and yet there are certain things where they say, "Okay, I can accept that. You can compare me with that."

The new girlfriend doesn't like to be compared to the old one. That is a problem. I am trying to make a point. Well, you can find a better way to make that point.

The word *parabole* translated "parable" is also translated as "figure." (*Hebrews 9:9, 11:19*)

(Hebrews 9:8-9) *"The Holy Ghost this signifying, that the way into the holiest of all was not yet made manifest, while as the first tabernacle was yet standing: Which was a figure for the time then present, in which were offered both gifts and sacrifices, that could not make him that did the service perfect, as pertaining to the conscience;"*

The word *parabole* translated "parable" is also translated as "proverb." (*Luke 4:23*)

(Luke 4:23) *"And he said unto them, 'Ye will surely say unto me this proverb, Physician, heal thyself: whatsoever we have heard done in Capernaum, do also here in thy country.'"*

Notice that there are people who look at Yeshua as the master physician. What are they comparing him to? The term "physician" is a word that we relate to as "doctor." Now the idea that Yeshua uses this as a parable is speaking not of himself, but of what the people are saying.

I remember that the old folks used to say, "Oh, he's a doctor who's never lost a patient." We are not patients, but that kind of language brings to mind physicians and pharmakeia and medicine and doctor/patient relationship. "He's the master physician." Yeshua isn't a doctor. Doctors can't heal. Doctors prescribe medicine. They "practice."

Yeshua is a healer, not a physician. He uses this parable. He says, "You are going to say to me, 'Physician, heal yourself.'"

The word *parabole* is translated "parable" in:

Matthew 13; 15:15; 21:33, 45; 22:1; 24:32

Mark 4:13; 7:17

Luke 5:36; 6:39; 12:6, 41; 18:1, 9; 19:11; 20:9, 19; 21:29

Parable — throughout the Bible.

From a theological point of view, a parable is:

*"...a **fictitious, but true to human life** story that is designed to illustrate by way of comparison, some spiritual truth."*

In the parables that Yeshua spoke, he would say a parable. At times his disciples would get to him privately. In one case as we looked in *Matthew 13* he asked, "Why do you speak to the people in parables? Why? Why do you do that?"

"So that it will be fulfilled as the prophet said. These people are always hearing."

Here is the thing about religious people. Religious people are simply fulfilling a duty. Religious people go to church. When I was a person in church, people would ask me what church I go to and I would facetiously say, "You are looking at him." I did not understand church as I understand it today.

But here is what I did understand. I understood that the church was not a building but the people. That is the understanding that I had. But it's a congregation. It's an assembly. The church, the assembly is not the building that they are assembled in, but the ones who assemble.

My mind had to move away from it because I grew up thinking that we went to church. I have been part of churches that if you did not go to church, you were "breaking God's commandments." What?

If you didn't go to church, you were "sinning," so to keep from sinning, what do we do? We go to church. Why? I'm not a sinner. I'm not a sinner! I go to church because I don't want to sin. But when I get to church I'm taught, "You're a sinner saved by grace."

Okay, I'm doing all of this stuff to *not* be a sinner, but when I come here you are telling me that I *am* a sinner, so what is the point in doing all of this stuff? There is a lot of confusion.

I do this because I don't want to be a sinner. I don't want to sin.

Religious people do things. They do things to appease their religious belief systems. They are not necessarily doing things to please the Almighty as much as they are doing things to please their system of belief and the things they are taught as to how to be a good member of this "church," this assembly.

Now, when it comes down to the Almighty, he says that we are to remember his Sabbath day and to keep it holy. Remember his Sabbath day and keep it holy. Remember his Sabbath day and keep it holy.

Then he gave us additional convocations that are part of his feast days. The things that we do, we don't do out of religion. We are not trying to fulfill some obligation to a system. We are obeying the commands of the Almighty. That is what we do.

Religious people are part of a system. We are not religious people. We are people of the Almighty. We are obeying his commands because we are in his Kingdom where he rules. He is the one who calls the shots, not us.

Religious people are simply fulfilling obligations to a system. We are not. We are walking with our Messiah in obedience to his commands. We are looking to the day that we hear, "Well done, good and faithful."

I pray that those are the words you will hear; words that you desire to hear and that you are doing what you need to do. It is not about works. It is about obedience. People can call it whatever. "You are trying to work your way." No, I am not trying to work my way.

Don't you all teach that you have to work out salvation? What does that mean? It sounds like work to me. Now, if you are just saved by grace you shouldn't have to do any work. Nothing.

We will pick up with parables in the next lesson.

Class 95 Study Summary

Key Points

1. All things work together for the good of those who love Messiah and who are called according to his purpose. This means those who walk after the Spirit and not after the flesh. We know that the Father will work things out for us.

2. When things are not going well in life, we are to examine ourselves to see if there is anything that we need to repent of and correct. We need to be our own worst critic.

3. A parable is a clever use of words. It is a story that is partly fictitious.

4. Sometimes people want a verse of scripture interpreted when if they would simply read a little further on, they would find the interpretation for themselves.

5. The Father is not responsible for the child's behavior and the child is not responsible for the Father's behavior. In other words, you are responsible for your own behavior. You can't blame someone else for your behavior.

6. Cain still murdered his brother, even after YeHoVaH himself instructed Cain in what his behavior should be and before he committed murder.

7. Some people allow their children or loved ones to hold them hostage to some past action when they should repent, forgive and move on. We should walk in freedom and not allow others to do this to us. Father casts our sins as far as the East is from the West.

8. You can go to as many deliverance ministries or services as you like. The only thing that is going to keep any demons away is if you keep the commandments and walk in the word with Yeshua and have his testimony.

9. The word "parable" is also translated as "comparison."

10. Some people look at Yeshua as the "master physician," but Yeshua is not a doctor. He healed us. He is a healer. Doctors only practice medicine.

11. The church is not a building. It is a congregation, an assembly or a group of people. It is the persons who assemble.

12. Religious people do things to appease their religious belief systems. They aren't necessarily doing things to please the Almighty as much as they are doing what they were taught in order to be a good member of their church organization or denomination.

13. Religious people are part of a system. We are not religious people. We are people of the Almighty. We are obeying his commands because we are in his Kingdom and he rules. He calls the shots, not us.

Review Exercise

1. Who is the most well qualified to interpret a parable?

_____

_____

2. Does the tenet of "let scripture interpret scripture" hold well for parables?

_____

_____

3. How does the concept of a comparison fit with the idea behind parables?

_____

_____

_____

_____

4. Why do you think that John did not include any parables in his gospel?

_____

_____

_____

_____

5. Have you read all of the parables Yeshua taught? If not, commit to doing that soon. Remember. Don't read only the passage of the parable, but also the interpretation given.

Parables of Yeshua

1. The parable of the sower
- *Mark 4:1-20*
- *Matthew 13:3-23*
- *Luke 8:5-15*

2. The parable of the seed growing secretly
- *Mark 4:26-29*

3. The parable of the mustard seed
- *Mark 4:30-32*
- *Matthew 13:31-32*
- *Luke 13:18-19*

4. The parable of the tenants
- *Mark 12:1-11*
- *Matthew 21:33-46*
- *Luke 20:9-18*

5. The parable of the budding fig tree
- *Mark 13:28-32*
- *Matthew 24:32-36*
- *Luke 21:29-33*

6. The parable of the faithful servant
- *Mark 13:33-37*
- *Matthew 24:42*
- *Luke 12:35-48*

Parables of *Matthew* not found in *Mark*

7. The parable of the wheat and tares
- *Matthew 13:24-30*

8. The parable of the leaven
- *Matthew 13:33*
- *Luke 13:20-21*

9. The parable of the hidden treasure
- *Matthew 13:44*

10. The parable of the pearl
- *Matthew 13:45-46*

11. The parable of the net
- *Matthew 13:47-50*

12. The parable of the lost sheep
- *Matthew 18:12-14*
- *Luke 15:3-7*

13. The parable of the unmerciful servant
- *Matthew 18:23-35*

14. The parable of the laborers in the vineyard
- *Matthew 20:1-16*

15. The parable of the two sons
- *Matthew 21:28-31*

16. The parable of the wedding feast/banquet
- *Matthew 22:1-14*
- *Luke 14:15-24*

17. The parable of the ten virgins
- *Matthew 25:1-12*

17b. The parable of the talents
- *Matthew 25:14-25:30*

18. The parable of the two debtors
- *Luke 10:30-37*

19. The parable of the Good Samaritan
- *Luke 10:30-37*

20. The parable of the rich fool
- *Luke 12:16-21*

21. The parable of the lost coin
- *Luke 15:8-10*

22. The parable of the prodigal son
- *Luke 15:11-32*

23. The parable of the unjust steward
- *Luke 16:1-8*

24. The parable of the rich man and the beggar Lazarus
- *Luke 16:19-31*

Rate the following statements
by filling in the most appropriate number.

(1 = I do not agree 10 = I agree completely)

Objectives:

1. I can explain my understanding of parables though the Greek word *parabole*.

1. ○ 2. ○ 3. ○ 4. ○ 5. ○ 6. ○ 7. ○ 8. ○ 9. ○ 10. ○

My Journal

What I learned from this class:

_____

_____

_____

_____

_____

_____

_____

_____

_____

_____

_____

_____

_____

_____

Discipleship Training Class 96

Parable-Centered Principle (part 3)

Objectives:

As a Discipleship student, at the end of this class you will be able to:

- Define how comparing instances of the same parable as chronicled in two or three of the gospels reveals more about the parabolic lesson
- Explain why parables, while they are teaching vehicles, can't be used to establish doctrine

---

We are looking at the parable principle, part 3. I am always thrilled by the fact that we can learn together. This is the day that the Father has called us to come together and to be disciples. Yeshua said that we are to go and teach. And we know that in the process of going and teaching and equipping the saints as we are commanded to do, that that is what draws us closer. We learn more about him. We take on his yoke. We pick up his burden and learn of him.

I am excited that you will allow me to pour into your life and I am excited that your life has been one that has chosen to be poured into.

We are headed somewhere. I believe that we are in the end times. I am not one who says that flippantly. We know that based upon what Yeshua said, that the true gospel of the Kingdom has to be taken to the ends of the earth. Up until this point we know that the true gospel of the Kingdom has not been taken to the world.

There is another gospel and this gospel is the gospel about Jesus. That is the gospel that has been preached in this country and sent from this country around the world.

Yeshua didn't come to preach a gospel about himself. He came to preach the gospel of the Kingdom. That is the gospel that Yeshua preached.

Our goal is to get the gospel of the Kingdom, the gospel that Yeshua preached to the ends of the world. Then (he said) the end will come. There is a reason for this gospel of the Kingdom going forth and that is to be a witness. You see, the Father wants to make sure that everybody has an opportunity to hear the true gospel so that when they stand before him, there are no excuses — no excuses, whatsoever.

Because he has ordained us in this hour to take the gospel of the Kingdom to the ends of the earth, it lets me know that we are actually in the end times. And you are chosen. I have been chosen. We have been chosen to be part of YeHoVaH's plan to take the gospel of the Kingdom to the ends of the earth.

We know that the parable principle is that principle by which any parable is interpreted by discerning its moral and its elements. We are going to look and see today that it is not wise to try to build doctrine upon a parable. Unfortunately that is exactly what is occurring. And because of that, there have been many errors associated with the interpretation of scripture based upon individuals building doctrines upon parables.

The definition of a parable is "a short, simple story from which a moral lesson may be drawn." It is an earthly story with a heavenly meaning. Nevertheless a parable is a story. It is a story from which we can draw lessons.

The word "parable" in the Old Testament as the word *mashal* means "properly a pithy maxim, usually of a metaphorical nature: hence a simile: a proverbial saying, parable, similitude, resemblance." When we begin to look at parables, it is one of the words that is not necessarily mentioned here, but it is alluded to as an allegory.

Many of you who are familiar with John Bunyan's *Pilgrim's Progress* know that it is an allegory. It is full of stories that have meanings that you can associate with them, but it is an allegory nonetheless.

A parable is similar. The word "parable" in the New Testament is *parabole*. We looked at that in the last lesson. The word parable is "a similitude, a **fictitious narrative** (of common life conveying a moral); a placing of one thing by the side of another; a comparison of one thing with another; a narrative, fictitious, but agreeable to the laws and usages of human life."

Notice that the words "fictitious narrative" are in bold. **A *parabole* is a fictitious narrative.** When we look at a *parabole*, it by definition is a fictitious narrative. Then we see "…by which either the duties of men or the things of God, particularly the nature and history of God's Kingdom are figuratively portrayed; a short discourse that makes a comparison; it expresses a single complete thought."

These are a lot of nice words saying that it is a fictitious narrative. It is critical in the New Testament to understand the parable principle. That is because when Yeshua spoke to the multitude, he spoke in parables.

From the last lesson and from a theological point of view, **a parable is a fictitious but true to human life story that is designed to illustrate by way of comparison, some spiritual truth.** When you look at a parable, each person can interpret it differently.

In the New Testament, *parabole* is referred to as:

(1) a proverb (**Mark 7:17; Luke 4:23**), (2) a typical emblem (**Hebrews 9:9; Hebrews 11:19**), (3) a similitude or allegory (**Matthew 15:15; Matthew 24:32; Mark 3:23; Luke 5:36; Luke 14:7**); (4) ordinarily 8, in a more restricted sense, a comparison of earthly with heavenly things, "an earthly story with a heavenly meaning" (*Easton's Illustrated Dictionary*).

Now as we noted in the last lesson, the use of parables originated in the Old Testament. It is not a New Testament concept, nor did it originate in the New Testament. It originated from the Old Testament and we looked at several examples in the last lesson.

The Hebrew word *mashal* is a similitude in the Old Testament and is used to denote (1) a **proverb** (according to *1 Samuel 10:12; 1 Samuel 24:13; 2 Chronicles 7:20*) and (2) a **prophetic utterance** (*Numbers 23:7; Ezekiel 20:49*). We noted Balaam as he talked about picking up a parable or sharing a parable with Balak. We also noted in *Ezekiel* where he picked up a parable to prophesy to the children of Israel. It is also used to denote (3) **an enigmatic saying** (*Psalm 78:2; Proverbs 1:6*).

One of the things that I want us to look at really quickly is in the *Proverbs*. The book of *Proverbs* opens up with the Hebrew word *mashal*. As we noted, one of the definitions of this Hebrew word is defined as a proverb.

(Proverbs 1:1-4) *"The proverbs of Solomon the son of David, king of Israel; To know wisdom and instruction; to perceive the words of understanding; To receive the instruction of wisdom, justice, and judgment, and equity; To give subtlety to the simple, to the young man knowledge and discretion."*

When we look at the *Proverbs*, we see an enigmatic saying in verse 6: *"To understand a proverb, and the interpretation; the words of the wise, and their dark sayings."*

Nathan used a parable when confronting David with a harmless story of a rich man and a poor man living in the same city.

Read *2 Samuel 12:1-14*

My wife and two of my sons and I took another college tour. This time we went over to Columbia to the University of South Carolina. Interestingly enough, while we were on the college campus there was a setup where individuals were handing out Bibles. They had people on the campus and they were handing out these little cards. They were saying that if you go to that station over there you can get a free Bible. This is what they were saying — a free Bible.

Well, we get over to the station and my son Alpha decides that he wants a Bible. It was false advertising. He went over there and sure enough, they gave him a book, but the book was the New Testament only. It was the New Testament. They said that this was "the Bible." Now, do you see the problem here? You have the Bible, but it is only a New Testament. A person who is not familiar with the Bible would assume that this is the whole Bible. If you have never had a Bible in your hand and somebody is giving you a Bible, you assume that this is the Bible. It may not be for years because you know, one thing you don't note is that people who aren't in a religious setting may never come in contact with the Bible.

It used to be that if you went to someone's home, they would have the family Bible sitting on the table. Those are not common anymore. You can go to people's homes and you can be there for days and hours. You can go to dormitories. You can go to apartments. You can go to condominiums. You can go into all kinds of places. Many hotels used to have the Gideon Bible. Many don't have them anymore.

My point is that a person can go through their entire life and never come into contact with a Bible. To think that we live in a society and in a generation where you can literally go through your whole life without ever coming into contact with a Bible if you don't actually go to church. It used to be that if a person went to a church, they would have the pew Bible (for those churches that had pews).

Today you can go to many of these seeker-friendly congregations or to many of these ministries or these mega ministries. You can't find a Bible in the place other than the one the preacher is preaching from *if* he is preaching from the Bible. Many preachers preach from their notes.

They handed my son this book. Actually he got one for me, for my wife and for his brother as well as for himself. He had four Bibles. I told my son, "This Bible isn't a Bible. This is the New Testament. The New Testament doesn't constitute a Bible."

We walked a little further and there was a fellow who had the "Yeshua" shirt on. He was handing out tracks. He was from a Messianic congregation there in Columbia. I introduced myself and handed him one of my cards. He gave me one of his cards and we talked for a moment as we continued on to the tour.

The point that I am trying to make here is how a person in our generation who comes into contact with a supposed "Bible" (that is only consisting of the New Testament) could be fooled into thinking that it is the whole Bible and be shocked to find out that there is another portion of the Bible that is not included with the Bible that he or she has.

Unfortunately this is where the Christian Church is. It is operating on what they call the Bible, but which is actually the New Testament. The assumption is that everything in the New Testament is all they need to know. It would be easily assumed that because Yeshua used the parable, that the parable initiated or the parable originated with the teachings of Yeshua. The fact of the matter is that parables are throughout the Old Testament. Yeshua was using a principle that had been used hundreds of years prior to his birth.

In *2 Samuel 12,* Nathan is using a parable.

(2 Samuel 12:1) "And the LORD sent Nathan unto David. And he came unto him, and said unto him, 'There were two men in one city; the one rich, and the other poor.'"

The back story here (and you should read it) is that David has decided that he is going to have a marital relationship with the wife of an individual who serves in his Army. To hide his sin, he has the husband killed. David did not murder him with his own hands, but YeHoVaH accused David of murder since it was by David's order that Uriah was killed.

What you want to do here is to identify that there are certain ways that you approach people with power. There are certain ways that you approach people with power and you have to exercise wisdom. We know. I have been a part of congregations. I am sure that you have seen people. I know many people right now who supposedly are knowledgeable of the word, but who are in dire straits because they don't know how to deal with people.

They don't know how to relate with people. They think they can talk to people any kind of way. They think that because they have the truth, that they don't need protocol or tact or wisdom. You can approach individuals in a way that would bring backlash that if one operated in wisdom, that wouldn't happen.

Nathan is approaching the king. Now yes, he is the spokesperson for YeHoVaH, but you need to understand that a lot of YeHoVaH's spokespersons were killed. They were murdered, assassinated by the very people YeHoVaH sent them to speak to. Nathan could have easily been ordered to death. It was just like how Uriah was killed by the hand of David through an order. Nathan too could have been killed. So Nathan approaches the king and he uses wisdom. He used a parable.

(2 Samuel 12:1b-3) "There were two men in one city; the one rich, and the other poor. The rich man had exceeding many flocks and herds: But the poor man had nothing, save one little ewe lamb, which he had bought and nourished up: and it grew up together with him, and with his children; it did eat of his own meat, and drank of his own cup, and lay in his bosom, and was unto him as a daughter."

People today have pets, but they don't call them pets. They call them a member of their family. That dog, that cat, that pig or that parrot (whatever it is) is part of their family and they care for it as such. Nathan is saying that this man had this ewe lamb that was just like his own daughter.

(2 Samuel 12:4-9) "And there came a traveler unto the rich man, and he spared to take of his own flock and of his own herd, to dress for the wayfaring man that was come unto him; but took the poor man's lamb, and dressed it for the man that was come to him. And David's anger was greatly kindled against the man; and he said to Nathan, 'As the LORD liveth, the man that hath done this thing shall surely die: And he shall restore the lamb fourfold, because he did this thing, and because he had no pity.' And Nathan said to David, 'Thou art the man.' Thus saith the LORD God of Israel, 'I anointed thee king over Israel, and I delivered thee out of the hand of Saul; And I gave thee thy master's house, and thy master's wives into thy bosom, and gave thee the house of Israel and of Judah; and if that had been too little, I would moreover have given unto thee such and such things. Wherefore hast thou despised the commandment of the LORD, to do evil in his sight? thou hast killed Uriah the Hittite with the sword, and hast taken his wife to be thy wife, and hast slain him with the sword of the children of Ammon.'"

In other words, you used a foreign army to do your dirty work.

(2 Samuel 12:10) "Now therefore the sword shall never depart from thine house; because thou hast despised me, and hast taken the wife of Uriah the Hittite to be thy wife."

Now here is a question. With David being a man after YeHoVaH's own heart, do you think that David said, "Today I am going to despise the Almighty. I am going to violate his commands?"

No, he did not. Those were not his words, but his actions exactly communicated that. You see, there is nobody out there in their right mind (unless they are truly satanic) that will say, "Today I am going to despise God." And yet there are people out there who are committing adultery. There are people out there who are fornicating. There are people out there who are doing all manner of immoral commandment-breaking, lawless deeds.

They are not saying it. They are not saying, "I am going to do this to despise you." They are doing it to please themselves.

When we put our own needs above his commands, that is exactly what we are saying with our actions. That is not with our mouth because we would probably never say that with our mouths. I don't think any believer in their right mind would leave on purpose to intentionally violate his commands. But if one is not conscious of his commands, at that moment they decide they want to do something that satisfies themselves. They are not thinking about the commandments of the Almighty. They are only thinking about themselves.

Now, interestingly enough, YeHoVaH knows that, so he says, "Here is a reminder." If I have these tzitzits on and here it is and I'm about to go out there and commit adultery, it would be almost impossible for me to take down my pants without seeing these strings. Now, I know that is a little graphic, but the fact of the matter is that in the process of me about to do something that would be a violation of his commandments, my eyes more than likely will glance at these strings and remind me of his commandments.

It should bring conviction to me. You and I both know that when a person has purposed in their own heart to do that which pleases them, then trying to reason with them is almost impossible. I know, I know, I know, but, yeah, but, yeah.

There is a chance that when I look at these...

You have to also know that typically for a person to wear these strings, they have already determined that they are going to take YeHoVaH's laws seriously. There are people out there who purpose in their heart that they are serious about the things of YeHoVaH, but they have not taken that step to wear these strings as a reminder.

When a person comes to a point where they say, "I am going to wear these strings as a reminder," they are serious. I deal with people on a regular basis. Do you know what they say to me? "I don't need strings to remind me of the commandments. I don't need to wear strings to remind me of my love for God. My love for God is in my heart. My love for God — I think about it all the time."

YeHoVaH says, "Yeah, I know you say you love me, but if you love me, you will keep my commandments. And my commandment is that you wear your tzitzits as a reminder to keep my commandments. So here. Keep my commandments. But I know that when you get caught up in the things of your own heart and your own desires, then you are going to forget my commandments. These serve as a reminder so that you don't forget."

Chances are, if a person gets to the point where they purpose in their heart that they are going to wear these things every day, then there is a good chance that in the process of them violating the commands that they may glance at these at some point and say, "Do you know what? I shouldn't be doing that."

Why would that need to happen? You say, "Oh, man, I shouldn't be doing this." You should (in your own heart) not be doing it in the first place, but we are people and we forget.

So he says,

(2 Samuel 12:9-14) *"'Wherefore hast thou despised the commandment of the LORD, to do evil in his sight? thou hast killed Uriah the Hittite with the sword, and hast taken his wife to be thy wife, and hast slain him with the sword of the children of Ammon. Now therefore the sword shall never depart from thine house; because thou hast despised me, and hast taken the wife of Uriah the Hittite to be thy wife.' Thus saith the LORD, 'Behold, I will raise up evil against thee out of thine own house, and I will take thy wives before thine eyes, and give them unto thy neighbour, and he shall lie with thy wives in the sight of this sun.' For thou didst it secretly: but I will do this thing before all Israel, and before the sun. And David said unto Nathan, 'I have sinned against the LORD.' And Nathan said unto David, 'The LORD also hath put away thy sin; thou shalt not die. Howbeit, because by this deed thou hast given great occasion to the enemies of the LORD to blaspheme, the child also that is born unto thee shall surely die.'"*

We see here that again, **the wages of sin is death**. Something is going to die. The wages of sin is death. The way of a sinner is hard.

Classification of Parables

There are major differences of opinions among Bible scholars over the definition and classifications of the parables in the Bible. A few scholars accept only those parables designated by scripture as such. In other words a parable says, "This is a parable. He picked up a parable. This is a parable."

The passage that we just read did not indicate that this was a parable. It did not say, "And Nathan gave a parable to David." No. YeHoVaH put a parable in Nathan's mouth, just like Ezekiel picked up a parable. He gave Nathan a parable. Nathan used this parable to get David to a point where he identified that what this fictitious individual had done was deserving of death; only to be communicated that this fictitious individual was a type of David and what David had actually done. So this fictitious individual was used to bring David face to face with himself.

And David recognized it.

The majority of scholars who have written on the subject of parables allow for a broader definition. Although many agree that a parable is an extended simile, there is much disagreement over where the boundary line should be placed between simile and parable.

You might say, "That is a lot of mumbo-jumbo." Well, I am going to tell you that it gets serious.

When attempting to interpret a parable, the interpreter must always allow scripture to interpret scripture.

Have you ever had a person who said, "I'm going to tell you a riddle"? The person who is giving the riddle already knows the answer, but now you have 25-30 people trying to figure out the riddle. "Is it this?" "Is it this?" The person who gave the riddle knows the answer, so who is best qualified to give the answer to the riddle other than the person who gave the riddle?

It is the same thing with scripture, the same thing with parables, the same thing with visions, with dreams and with prophecy. If the Father speaks to a prophet to speak certain things, he may withhold the meaning from the prophet. But if he gives him a dream or a vision, then he more than likely will reveal the dream or vision.

We find in scripture that there are individuals who had dreams and visions that they could not interpret. Someone who had the relation with the Almighty was able to interpret the dream or the vision.

But if the person who has the dream or vision gives you the interpretation of the dream or vision, why would you argue with the person who gave the interpretation or who had the dream or the vision? Why would you argue with them when they had it revealed to them by the one who gave them the vision? Why would you then reinterpret the vision? Some people want to reinterpret Peter's vision. They indicate that through Peter's vision in *Acts,* now YeHoVaH is saying that people can eat all kinds of abominable things. That's ridiculous!

Since parables are draw from the cultural background of those speaking the parable, the interpreter should research the manners, customs and material culture involved in the parable he or she is interpreting. That is only logical.

Doctrine should NEVER be founded solely upon parabolic teaching. Although parables primarily illustrate doctrine, any doctrine they do teach must be viewed in its harmony with the clearly defined teachings of the scripture.

Parables are used in only three of the gospel narratives: *Matthew, Mark,* and *Luke. John* doesn't use parables, but *Matthew, Mark,* and *Luke* extensively use parables. Major translation errors have been perpetuated through history due to the improper interpretation of parables. We are going to see one of the major ones. A major translation error that exists today is the improper interpretation of the "parable of the tenant" that is found in all three gospels:

Matthew 21:33-46; Mark 12:1-12; Luke 20:9-19

When we look at this parable and compare each passage, we find that combined, it is the sole reasoning behind the replacement theology doctrine. "The church" has replaced Israel and America has even become God's new Holy Land or the new Israel.

People don't say that, but when you talk about "God bless America" and that the Constitution has been founded upon the Bible, and "In God We Trust," people will boldly say today that America is a "Christian nation." In essence, America was at one point considered to be the only "Christian nation" whereas the gospel came out of Jerusalem, out of Zion. Now the gospel is coming out of America.

Let's look at this particular parable because I think it is important for us to look at it. When we look at it we are going to find some troubling things, I think. I don't necessarily have to convince you that they are troubling. I think that you will be convinced yourself.

In Matthew's account we see that it is called a parable, so we don't have to guess. We see a householder who has a field and a winepress and he has "let it out." In other words, he rented it. You are probably familiar with the legal term "sublet." You don't see the term "let," but you will see subletting in languages that are associated with rental contracts. If you are one who is renting the apartment, it means you either can or cannot sublet it or rent it out to other entities. Here he let it out or rented it to husbandmen and went into a far country.

Modern day theologians have said that this is the interpretation of the parable. The husbandmen were the Jews, the land was Israel and the servants were the prophets. YeHoVaH sent the prophets and YeHoVaH was the householder. So you have YeHoVaH who has his land. He sublet it out to the Pharisees and the Sadducees and now he sent the prophets. The people were the fruit. He sent the prophets. They killed the prophets. He sent his son. They killed the son. Now the Father killed them and took the land and gave it to another group of people, "the church."

That is the interpretation.

One of the principles that I didn't get into and I don't see the need to get into is the principle of numerology or the numerical principle. That is because this same principle says okay, with three supposedly being the number of completion; because this parable is written in three of the gospels. There is some crazy stuff circulating that people are buying into and the preachers are preaching this. They are preaching that the church has replaced Israel based upon these teachings, these parables and their interpretation.

Here we have a parable that is mentioned in three of the gospel narratives. Therefore it is interpreted that this is the exact parable by interpretation. Interestingly enough, Yeshua does not give an interpretation of the parable. It is clear that it is a parable, but he doesn't explain the parable. The religious leaders perceived that it was a parable against them. They saw that it was based upon the scripture reference that was used about the stone that the builders rejected having become the chief cornerstone. But the parable isn't explained.

"The Parable of the Tenant" Side-by-Side

Matthew 21:33-46	*Mark 12:1-12*	*Luke 20:9-19*
[33] Hear another parable: There was a certain householder, which planted a vineyard, and hedged it round about, and digged a winepress in it, and built a tower, and let it out to husbandmen, and went into a far country: [34] And when the time of the fruit drew near, he sent his servants to the husbandmen, that they might receive the fruits of it. [35] And the husbandmen took his servants, and beat one, and killed another, and stoned another. [36] Again, he sent other servants more than the first: and they did unto them likewise. [37] But last of all he sent unto them his son, saying, They will reverence my son. [38] But when the husbandmen saw the son, they said among themselves, This is the heir; come, let us kill him, and let us seize on his inheritance. [39] And they caught him, and cast him out of the vineyard, and slew him. [40] When the lord therefore of the vineyard cometh, what will he do unto those husbandmen? [41] They say unto him, He will miserably destroy those wicked men, and will let out his vineyard unto other husbandmen, which shall render him the fruits in their seasons.	[1] And he began to speak unto them by parables. A certain man planted a vineyard, and set an hedge about it, and digged a place for the winefat, and built a tower, and let it out to husbandmen, and went into a far country. [2] And at the season he sent to the husbandmen a servant, that he might receive from the husbandmen of the fruit of the vineyard. [3] And they caught him, and beat him, and sent him away empty. [4] And again he sent unto them another servant; and at him they cast stones, and wounded him in the head, and sent him away shamefully handled. [5] And again he sent another; and him they killed, and many others; beating some, and killing some. [6] Having yet therefore one son, his well-beloved, he sent him also last unto them, saying, They will reverence my son. [7] But those husbandmen said among themselves, This is the heir; come, let us kill him, and the inheritance shall be ours.' [8] And they took him, and killed him, and cast him out of the vineyard. [9] What shall therefore the lord of the vineyard do? He will come and destroy the husbandmen, and will give the vineyard unto others.	[9] Then began he to speak to the people this parable; A certain man planted a vineyard, and let it forth to husbandmen, and went into a far country for a long time. [10] And at the season he sent a servant to the husbandmen, that they should give him of the fruit of the vineyard: but the husbandmen beat him, and sent him away empty. [11] And again he sent another servant: and they beat him also, and entreated him shamefully, and sent him away empty. [12] And again he sent a third: and they wounded him also, and cast him out. [13] Then said the lord of the vineyard, What shall I do? I will send my beloved son: it may be they will reverence him when they see him. [14] But when the husbandmen saw him, they reasoned among themselves, saying, This is the heir: come, let us kill him, that the inheritance may be ours. [15] So they cast him out of the vineyard, and killed him. What therefore shall the lord of the vineyard do unto them? [16] He shall come and destroy these husbandmen, and shall give the vineyard to others. And when they heard it, they said, God forbid.

⁴²Jesus saith unto them, Did ye never read in the scriptures, The stone which the builders rejected, the same is become the head of the corner: this is the Lord's doing, and it is marvelous in our eyes? ⁴³Therefore say I unto you, The Kingdom of God shall be taken from you, and given to a nation bringing forth the fruits thereof. ⁴⁴And whosoever shall fall on this stone shall be broken: but on whomsoever it shall fall, it will grind him to powder. ⁴⁵And when the chief priests and Pharisees had heard his parables, they perceived that he spake of them. ⁴⁶But when they sought to lay hands on him, they feared the multitude, because they took him for a prophet.	¹⁰And have ye not read this scripture; The stone which the builders rejected is become the head of the corner: ¹¹This was the Lord's doing, and it is marvelous in our eyes? ¹²And they sought to lay hold on him, but feared the people: for they knew that he had spoken the parable against them: and they left him, and went their way.	¹⁷And he beheld them, and said, What is this then that is written, The stone which the builders rejected, the same is become the head of the corner? ¹⁸Whosoever shall fall upon that stone shall be broken; but on whomsoever it shall fall, it will grind him to powder. ¹⁹And the chief priests and the scribes the same hour sought to lay hands on him; and they feared the people: for they perceived that he had spoken this parable against them.

Some theologians decided that they would devise their interpretation and surely it is the Father, the prophets, Israel and Yeshua. Therefore they killed the Son. They crucified him. So God now took the promises and nullified the Old Testament. He came up with a New Testament with a different people that he is now going to save. Then once he saves all of these people, he is going to turn back toward those individuals that he had taken.

Come on. You see the replacement theology, the rapture and all of that. It is wound up in the interpretation of a parable that gives no interpretation. We have replacement theology, America and the new Holy Land. God shed his grace on thee, America the Beautiful. People are outraged that based on the recent past administration in the White House, people are declaring that this is "no longer" a Christian nation. Think about it. When has it ever really been that?

We know there was a time when people did adhere to biblical principles, but at what point in America's history were the commandments of YeHoVaH ever adhered to? **The only laws that were instituted in this "holy nation" were Sunday blue laws to protect sun god worship. The Sabbath was always desecrated. The commandments and the feasts and festivals were never acknowledged.**

So yeah, it may have been a Christian nation. It's a Christian nation that preaches a Jesus that is anti-Torah. He is one who abolished the Sabbath day and decided any day could be a Sabbath.

He is one who said that we "no longer" have to keep those "Jewish feasts," so let's create some feasts of our own.

So now we have a new Holy Land, a new Savior, a new set of laws and a New Testament that nullifies the Old Testament. Now you have organizations around the country distributing "the Bible" which is only a partial scripture. Instead of the law coming from Zion/Israel, the gospel is sent from America.

I know that one of my former disciples in the Christian Church was trying to bait me. He posted something on *Facebook*. It said, "Why is it that people are offended by the gospel and not the law?" I was tempted to bite, but I chose not to. I wanted to say, "Well, what law are you talking about? What gospel are you referring to? What is 'the gospel?'"

People are offended by the gospel because people who hear the gospel say that something is wrong with that gospel. I mean, something <u>is</u> wrong with it. So you are saying — let me get this straight. God came down in the form of his Son and said:

- You no longer have to keep my rules.
- I'm going to pay the price for you because I gave you a bunch of rules you couldn't keep.
- I'm sorry I gave you that cursed law.
- I repent. I apologize. I'll pay the price for your sins.
- Now all you have to do is believe.
- You don't have to do anything I say. We're good now, right?

They are saying, "Huh?" Man makes all of these laws, these ridiculous laws and you are saying that we don't have to do anything? "You don't have to do anything. Just believe. You don't have to keep any laws, no commands. Just love me."

So folks are saying, "You know, there has to be more to it than that. I know there is more to it than that." Isn't that what most Christians are saying? "There has to be more to it than this. We're missing something."

I hear this all of the time. This was me. It is like, "So, let me get this straight. All I have to do is to go to church on Sunday. I don't have to keep a Sabbath, but I can act like any day is the Sabbath and any five minutes of any day or any hour of any day can be my Sabbath." The ridiculousness of it is that I know that even though I am saying that any day can be a Sabbath day, I don't keep a Sabbath day any day.

Do you understand this? How many people who call themselves Christians that you know say, "Any day can be a Sabbath day" and they actually keep any day as a Sabbath day? You can probably count them on one hand, because they don't. I was really thinking and now I understand even more so. James said that **a person who knows the law but who doesn't keep the law; a person who hears the word but who doesn't do the word deceives themself.**

Imagine I am saying, "Any day is a Sabbath day." Now clearly I read in the Bible, "Remember the Sabbath day and keep it holy." I can't get around that, but by declaring that every day is a Sabbath, what am I declaring? Every day is a Sabbath now. Okay, every day is a Sabbath, so which day am I keeping as a Sabbath? I am keeping every day as a Sabbath.

Well, what do you mean? I am entering into his rest. What rest are you entering into? Because what I see is strife, hypertension, anger, malice, wrath, carnality and worldliness.

What rest are you entering into?

People are saying that all we have to do is love him. Well, how do you do that? Every day is a Sabbath. How do you keep every day as the Sabbath? Well, any day is a Sabbath. What day do you keep a Sabbath? I don't even have to talk to you. Why are you getting upset at me? I am just simply trying to understand your doctrine. That is all. You are getting upset at me because you can't explain it? Because you are just talking? Talk, talk, talk. You are blowing smoke, but you are blowing smoke up the wrong chimney. I just so happen to know that what you are saying may sound good, but you don't even believe what you are saying. There is no way you can practice what you are preaching.

I wanted to ask this guy, thinking that people are not offended by the law. You are. The moment you mention law to one of these guys, they are all upset. "We don't have to keep the law! The law was done away with!" Wait a minute. Calm down. People aren't offended by the law because they are not hearing it. The only ones that are offended by the law are the ones that have that other gospel. The world is not offended by the law.

Most religious people want a set of principles to live by. They want something to govern their lives. This is why people get into Buddhism or Taoism. It is for discipline. This is why people get into martial arts; for discipline. This is why people get into Islam; for the discipline. This is why people get into Jewish tradition or some form of discipline; something to do on a regular and consistent basis as an outpouring or as an outward showing of my faith. For the "Christian," the only thing they do is go to church.

I was watching a program and one of the gospel singers was "twerking[3] for Jesus." How do you "twerk" for Jesus? Come on, close your legs. But the praise leader is "twerking for Jesus." It is like when I first came out of the world, they used to say, "I still dance. I just got a different partner now. My partner is named Jesus. Instead of me bumping out there with the world, I bump with Jesus. We do the double bump." Yeah, right. So now instead of the law coming from Zion, the gospel is sent from America.

There is a popular book out there that a lot of folks are jumping on board with; something about harbingers. I know it is a number one seller. What the author is alluding to is that all of the signs that Israel faced, America is now facing. It is like, okay. Wow. America is now the New Israel. That is what the book is saying. All these things that happened to Israel are now happening in America. America is on the same course that Israel was on.

---

[3] Those of you who know what twerking is, I don't have to explain it. If you don't, you don't want to know.

When you have a holy nation like America, a Godly nation like America, a Christian nation like America (the new Holy Land) of course it feeds into that whole replacement theology. America has become the new Israel. God has turned his eyes off of Israel and put his focus on America. America is a holy nation and America is responsible for getting the gospel of Jesus Christ to the whole world.

So now the author writes that all of the things that took place in Israel; they can see the pattern now taking place in America. That is because after all, America is the "new Israel."

Then when you look at politics, politicians want to say that the biggest heart cry of Jerusalem being divided is coming from Israel. What they are doing is coming from America. Americans are talking about how if you divide Israel, it is "God's judgment." This is prophetically coming from America based upon Christian interpretation and some Messianic interpretation of some prophecies. The fact of the matter is that Jerusalem has been divided hundreds of times.

But now because it is America, America is the one who is determining that if you now divide Jerusalem, all of these things are going to happen. You have all of these politicians who people want to jump onto the bandwagon. I am not trying to wade off into any muddy water. The water is already murky when you start dealing with the Tea Party and what party most closely aligns with the Bible, the Republicans or the Democrats and who stands for abortion and who doesn't stand for abortion and who stands for same-sex marriage and who doesn't stand for same-sex marriage and all of this other stuff. Of course it is Republican against Democrat. Then it is the more conservative Republicans among moderate Republicans.

It is all about the Bible. All of these people who are doing all of this fighting and arguing and standing on biblical principles are Sunday worshippers. They are people who are arguing from a Sunday worship perspective and who don't even have an understanding of YeHoVaH's commands. People who see the scripture through skewed lenses are trying to interpret the Bible based upon some misinterpretations of parables that give them the voice of YeHoVaH; when they can't even get the Sabbath right.

Yeah, they sound "spiritual." They sound religious. I am not trying to knock. I am just simply speaking fact. It is the "lesser of two evils," but the lesser of two evils is still evil. It is just less evil than the other evil. It sounds like "the lesser of two evils." You start off with two evils and you just choose the lesser evil. Why choose evil at all?

"We have to take our country back." It is not your country. It never was. The earth is YeHoVaH's, the fullness thereof and they that dwell therein. It is his! And until we serve him, **those who build this nation except he builds it, the labor is in vain.**

It is really time for us to turn back to the scriptures and believe what the scriptures teach; not people's interpretation, especially people's interpretation who are already approaching the Bible from a Sunday worship perspective. Do you think that just because millions and millions and millions of people are worshipping on Sunday that they are going to force Sunday worship on the Creator? "Well, we never liked the Sabbath. We chose Sunday so you join us on Sun-day, O God."

(Isaiah 2:3) *"And many people shall go and say, 'Come ye, and let us go up to the mountain of the LORD, to the house of the God of Jacob; and he will teach us of his ways, and we will walk in his paths: for out of Zion shall go forth the law, and the word of YeHoVaH from Jerusalem.'"*

The word came to this country already skewed. By the time the "gospel" hit the shores of America, it was a gospel about Jesus. It was a death/burial/resurrection gospel. It wasn't keeping YeHoVaH's commands. We will keep the commands we want to keep and the rest of them we won't keep. We will redefine the Bible and determine what God is accepting and what he is not accepting. And if enough of us, a majority of us, declare Sunday to be the Sabbath, then God himself has to adjust.

Yeshua asked his disciples a question. We will get into this next lesson too, because this is so vital. I want you to have a chance to think about it.

(Mark 4:13) *"Then Yeshua said to them, 'Don't you understand this parable? How then will you understand any parable?'"*

At face value, it would seem as if he is saying, "If you get the understanding of this parable, then you will understand all of the parables," but that isn't what he is saying. He is saying that basically if he is speaking in parables so they don't get it, how in the world are they going to get it unless he interprets it?

This is where it is important for us to put our faith in the Almighty to show us what he is saying versus the interpretations that are given to us by the various organizations that we have become a part of.

We will pick up with the "Parable of the sower" in the next lesson with *Matthew 13, Mark 4* and *Luke 8*. This parable is going to give us some insight into parables. We will have a better understanding once Yeshua explains this parable, since he is saying that this is the pinnacle of parables. This is the parable of all parables and that when he gives us the explanation of this parable, we are going to have a better understanding of the Kingdom and of YeHoVaH's word.

After that we'll get into the interpretation of prophecy. Now we are going to get into where the rubber meets the road. Then this Discipleship series will conclude with the ordinances and leadership piece; understanding and looking at leadership in a congregational setting and what the Bible has to say about it. I want us to really understand eldership, deaconship, leadership and all of that as we bring our Discipleship Training into the home stretch.

Class 96 Study Summary

Key Points

1. There is another gospel being taught. It is the gospel "about" Jesus. Yeshua didn't come to preach a gospel about himself. He came to preach the gospel of the Kingdom. That is the gospel that Yeshua preached, not the one we see in churches today.

2. Because we have been ordained in this hour to take the gospel of the Kingdom to the ends of the Earth, it lets us know that we are actually in the end times.

3. A parable (*parabole*) is a fictitious narrative that is a true to human life story designed to illustrate, by way of comparison, some spiritual truth.

4. Tzitzits are reminders to us to keep the Father's commandments. Some people say they don't need to wear tzitzits, but if they are not wearing them, they have already forgotten the commandment to wear them.

5. When attempting to interpret a parable, the interpreter must always allow scripture to interpret scripture.

6. A major translation error that exists today is the improper interpretation of the "parable of the sower." Some people claim that the husbandmen were the Jews, the land was Israel and the servants were prophets. Wrong interpretations are the reasoning behind the replacement theology doctrine that is in churches today.

7. Although America is considered to be a "Christian nation," in reality the country wasn't founded upon the Torah. It wasn't really founded upon the Bible.

8. At one point the gospel was coming out of Jerusalem, out of Zion. Now it is coming out of the United States of America. (But that is another gospel.)

9. James says that someone who knows the law but who doesn't keep it and who hears the word but who doesn't do what it says, deceives themself.

10. Every day is not the Sabbath. The Sabbath is the seventh day of the week.

11. Until we serve YeHoVaH, those who build this nation are building it in vain. Unless he builds it, the labor is in vain.

12. The word came to America already skewed. By the time it reached these shores, it was the gospel "about" Jesus, not the gospel that Yeshua preached.

Review Exercise

1. Through the word *mashal*, we see that a parable can be:

(1)_____, (2)_____ or even a

(3)_____ .

2. Explain the following statement: *"Parables sometimes illustrate doctrines, but they do not establish doctrines."*

_____
_____
_____
_____
_____
_____
_____
_____
_____

3. Look up the definition of "allegory" and write that here:

_____
_____

Does a parable fit that description? Why or why not?

_____
_____
_____
_____

Rate the following statements
by filling in the most appropriate number.

(1 = I do not agree 10 = I agree completely)

Objectives:

1. I can define how comparing instances of the same parable as chronicled in two or three of the gospels reveals more about the parabolic lesson.

    1. ○   2. ○   3. ○   4. ○   5. ○   6. ○   7. ○   8. ○   9. ○   10. ○

2. I can explain why parables, while they are teaching vehicles, can't be used to establish doctrine.

    1. ○   2. ○   3. ○   4. ○   5. ○   6. ○   7. ○   8. ○   9. ○   10. ○

My Journal

What I learned from this class:

_____

_____

_____

_____

_____

_____

_____

_____

_____

_____

_____

_____

_____

_____

_____

_____

_____

_____

Discipleship Training Class 97

Parable-Centered Principle (part 4)

Objectives:

As a Discipleship student, at the end of this class you will be able to:

- Explain the parable of the sower in depth
- Define information from the parable as it relates to our mission to make disciples

The parable principle (as we have noted) is the principle by which any parable is interpreted by discerning its moral and interpreting its elements. When we begin to look at the parables, we note that a parable is "a short simple story from which a moral lesson may be drawn." It is an earthly story with a heavenly meaning.

The word "parable" in the Old Testament Hebrew is the word *mashal,* meaning "properly a pithy maxim, usually of an metaphorical nature: hence a simile: a proverbial saying, parable, similitude, resemblance."

The word "parable" in the New Testament Greek is *parabole.*

A parable is "a similitude, a fictitious narrative (of common life conveying a moral); a place of one thing by the side of another; a comparison of one thing with another; a narrative, fictitious but agreeable to the laws and usages of human life, by which either the duties of men or the things of God, particularly the nature and history of God's Kingdom are figuratively portrayed; a short discourse that makes a comparison; it expresses a single complete thought."

It is critical in the New Testament to understand the parable principle because when Yeshua spoke to the multitude, he spoke in parables. From a theological point of view, a parable is a fictitious, but true to human life story that is designed to illustrate by way of comparison, some spiritual truth.

(From the Easton's Illustrated Dictionary) In the New Testament a parable might be a:

Proverb	*Mark 7:17; Luke 4:23*
Typical (as in "a type") emblem	*Hebrews 9:9; Hebrews 11:19*
Similitude/allegory	*Matthew 15:15; Matthew 4:32, Mark 3:23, Luke 5:36; Luke 14:7*
Comparison of earthy with heavenly things, "an earthly story with a heavenly meaning."	

As noted, the use of parables originated in the Old Testament. The use of parables as Yeshua is using them is not something that originated with Yeshua. We looked at some verses and saw that the use of parables was something that was all the way back in the book of *Genesis*.

Picking up from lesson 96 now, Yeshua asks his disciples a question:

(Mark 4:13) *"Then Yeshua said to them, 'Don't you understand this parable? How then will you understand any parable?'"*

What Yeshua is saying to them is that the parable that he is challenging them on, he is saying that if you can understand this parable, this parable will help you to understand all the parables that we will find in the New Testament. Yeshua is really about to let them know that when it comes down to the Kingdom of YeHoVaH, this parable is the one that they needed to get.

The parable of the sower is a critical parable. We are going to be looking at these particular passages:

Matthew 13:1-23; Mark 4:1-20; Luke 8:4-24

The key to a parable (as we have noted) is that it is important. If a person shares a parable, if a person shares a proverb, if a person shares a riddle, they generally know what it is they are saying. The riddle is for you to figure out. They already have it figured out and they are seeing if you are going to get it.

The parable is like a riddle. In some places it is referred to as a proverb. So when we look at this parable, it is important to properly interpret a parable, especially when the one who shares the parable is giving you the understanding. Why would someone choose a different understanding than the understanding that the one who is presenting the parable is giving?

People use interpretative measures in places where there is no need to use it, if the one who gives the parable or who gives the riddle gives you the interpretation.

Matthew 13:1-23

Remember that at one point his disciples said, "Why do you speak to the multitude in parables?" Yeshua said to them, "There are prophets and there are those of old who would have loved to hear the things that you are hearing, but they couldn't. They didn't. And yet those things that you are hearing are so valuable." He was saying to them that he spoke to them in parables because they were really dull of hearing.

It is unfortunate today that people go in and out of church. They go in and out of Messianic synagogues and Messianic communities, shuls or whatever you want to call them. They go in and out of congregations all around the country, but they are dull of hearing.

When it comes down to the Kingdom, I look at it as something quite simple. The Almighty created it. The Almighty created us. The Almighty says, "This is my Kingdom. This is my world. I made it." The Almighty created rules that we are to live by in his Kingdom. He says, "If you live by these rules, you will do well. You will live long. You will prosper. And if you don't, you are going to have some problems." Therefore it is so simple to me that in the Kingdom of YeHoVaH, we live by YeHoVaH's rules, or we get out of his Kingdom.

The bottom line is when the Almighty begins to reveal to us what it is that he requires of us, oftentimes because we have heard so many teachings, we have read so many books. When it comes down to the actual doing of what the word requires us to do, most people (many people) are dull of hearing.

When it comes down to living out the commands that are the simple truth of the gospel, hear, obey, hear, listen and do, don't be a hearer only, but be a doer of what the word says.

It boils down to living out the word; not just knowing it, but doing it.

What is really interesting in this passage in *Matthew* is that I have heard so many different sermons and so many different spins on this particular parable. Yeshua gives us the interpretation at the end.

Notice that the disciples knew in this message that he was sharing with the people. They didn't get it. Think about it. Why would the disciples come to Yeshua and ask this question? They didn't get what he was saying. The people didn't get what he was saying and yet only the disciples asked the question. Did the people ask the question? Obviously not. They went on about their business. But the disciples came and asked why.

"Why do you talk to the people like that? Why do you speak to the people in parables?" We see his answer in verse 11.

Now imagine. These people have heard a message. They have heard a word. They have just heard a word from the Master. They were probably excited that they got to sit in the audience and listen to the Master teach. And yet they went away thinking that they had an understanding, but they had no clue as to what was going on.

This is one of the challenges that I have with people who are all over the place. When you are over here listening and over there listening and over there getting a word, you are getting all of this information. You are getting all of this knowledge, but where is the application? Where is the basic simple application as to how you live all of these teachings and all of these messages out in your daily life?

What happens is that people collect information. They collect sermons. They collect leaders. They collect teachers. They go from this place to that place to that place to this other place. And the bottom line is how are you applying it or are you just accumulating knowledge?

What Yeshua is saying is that to them that have —you are going to see what he means a little bit later. **To have information and not apply that information is like not having information at all.**

As a matter of fact, the more diverse the information you get, the less you will apply the information you are gathering. Now you have a lot of information that you are not doing anything with. It is better not to even have the information. That is because now it is like, "How do I apply it? What do you do with it?"

Yeshua is saying that people who are gathering information and going from place to place are really sick. They are not whole. I am not saying that. Yeshua is saying that. I am saying what Yeshua is saying. I see it. I see it on a regular basis. I see it in people who struggle and in people who are having issues with relationships. I see it in people who are not knowing how to walk out their faith. I see it on so many different levels.

The moment that I say something to people — you shouldn't have too many teachers. You shouldn't have a lot of teachers. You shouldn't be listening to all of these different preachers. "Oh, you just want everybody to listen to you." No, you don't have to listen to me, but here is what I do know. If you are over here and they are preaching against prosperity and you are over here and they are preaching prosperity, which one are you going to believe? You are over there and they are preaching against healing and you are over here and they are preaching healing; or you are over here and they are preaching prophetically and prophesying and over there they are speaking in tongues. Over here they are saying they shouldn't be prophesying. Prophesy is "dead." Then over there they are against speaking in tongues. So now you are hearing this message and that message and that message and this message.

Do you see how these messages can contradict one another? Because messages that we hear contradict one another, we don't do anything since we don't know what to do. How can you do anything with that?

What I think doesn't matter. What I teach is what I believe. You can tell what I think from what I teach. When I teach, I have had people say to me, "Well, you shouldn't be speaking in tongues. Tongues is of the devil." Then I say, "Well, do you see me manifesting the works of the devil?" I mean, when you listen and you hear and you watch and you see and you have the privilege of being around me, do you see me manifesting the works of the devil? Then how do you surmise that speaking in tongues is the work of the devil from someone in whom all you have seen are the works of the Spirit manifesting in their life?

You see, that is a mindset that was given at some point in your journey and that has stuck in your spirit. The moment you hear something that goes against what has been stuck in your spirit, you reject it.

The bottom line is that speaking in tongues is a work of the Spirit. So is the interpretation. "Well, we don't need all of that stuff." Then the Father and you have a disagreement. As much as I read the word, not one time do I see the Father (who loves his people) give his people something they didn't need. If we didn't need it, he wouldn't give it to us.

Back to the sower.

(Matthew 13:17) *"But blessed are your eyes, for they see: and your ears, for they hear."*

How is that? Why would he say that to them? The difference between the disciples and the people is that the disciples pressed in to get an understanding by simply asking the question, "Why are you speaking to the people in parables?"

The people did not press in. That is the difference between the multitude and the true disciples. The true disciple is not going to go the way of the multitude. Yeshua said it very clearly in that the way of the multitude is broad. Broad is the way that leads to destruction. Narrow is the way that leads to life, but few people find it. Many people get on the broad way. They are simply satisfied with hearing the message. They are not going to do anything with it. They don't even have enough understanding to do anything with it.

The disciples pressed in. Yeshua says, "You are blessed."

(Matthew 13:17-18) *"For verily I say unto you, 'That many prophets and righteous men have desired to see those things which ye see, and have not seen them; and to hear those things which ye hear, and have not heard them. Hear ye therefore the parable of the sower.'"*

Now, those are beautiful words. What he is saying is this: "Right now I am about to give you the interpretation of this parable." I can imagine that in the multitude there were individuals who, if they had recording devices, recorded the message. They probably got the DVD.[4] They would have had the message, and they can go into it and peruse the message. They can pull out their word study tools and just dissect the message. Then they come up with the interpretation. This person comes up with their interpretation and now preaches a sermon series on the interpretation of the parable of the sower.

This person has a different interpretation and preaches a sermon series on the interpretation of the parable of the sower. Now you have all of these DVD packages and televangelists and these TV preachers and *YouTube* videos with their interpretation of the parable of the sower. None of these people stuck around to hear the interpretation. Only the disciples pressed in and

---

[4] Well, they didn't have DVDs, but I'm sure if they had had DVDs and MP3s and *YouTube* back in that day, they probably had the message.

asked the question. Yeshua probably wouldn't have given them the parable of the sower's interpretation had they not pressed in and asked the question.

Now *YouTube* and all of the web sites are filled with video teachings on the interpretation of the parable of the sower. None of those individuals heard the interpretation from Yeshua, but they pulled out their tools to interpret this particular parable and came up with their own interpretation. They are so convinced that this is the proper interpretation. Why? Because "God" showed them it was.

Oh, boy. God showed you. Oh, wow. Can't argue with that. They are so strong and bold to proclaim, "I am confident. I will stake my life on this interpretation."

And yet had they stuck around like the disciples and pressed in, they would have received the interpretation. And here it is:

(Matthew 13:19) *"When any one heareth the word of the kingdom, and understandeth it not, then cometh the wicked one, and catcheth away that which was sown in his heart. This is he which received seed by the way side."*

That was the multitude. When anyone hears the word of the Kingdom and doesn't understand it, you see this. They heard the word. They went away. Do you think they understood it? Absolutely not. The enemy now comes and takes that word. How does he take that word?

This is why I tell people that when you come to House Of Israel, this is a place where spiritual warfare is constantly raging. Those of you who join us on *Livestream* for our live broadcasts, those of you who see our videos on *YouTube*, those of you who get the DVD teachings know that when you hear these teachings; it seems like after you have received these teachings, the warfare begins to rage. Why? Because the enemy is coming to try to keep you from putting that word into practice.

He knows that if you take truth and you walk in truth, then his control in your life is diminished. The more truth you take and apply, the less he can work with you. The less he can manipulate you and control you and tap into your emotions. He doesn't have a problem with people running all over the place; no problem at all. Oh, you want to hear some messages? There are a ton of messages. Try this teacher and try this teacher and try this teacher. And he will give you teaching after teaching after teaching because he knows you get all of this information. You get all of this teaching. You get all of this contradictory teaching in your spirit. You are not going to do anything but get obese in the word and constipated in the spirit.

He has no problem with that.

When it comes down to hearing the message and then putting the message into practice, the enemy has to stop this process, so the warfare comes. The distractions come. It could be a simple child issue. It could be a spouse issue, a family issue or a job issue. It could be a number of things.

You just hear a word and you are excited about it and you get ready to go out and go home and your car has a flat. You are driving along the street singing the melodies of the Spirit and somebody jumps in front of you. Your child goes ballistic. You get a phone call during service. It is a number of ways. You have to look at it and see how the enemy distracts you. How does he keep you from taking that word and applying that word?

He is coming immediately so that word doesn't get put into practice.

(Matthew 13:20) "But he that received the seed into stony places, the same is he that heareth the word, and anon with joy receiveth it;"

This is the person who receives and runs out and says, "I'm going to do something with that today." This is the person who heard a word. Now they want to go out and preach the sermon. There is no root. They haven't tested the word. They haven't stood. They haven't received the opposition and stood steadfast. The word hasn't been put through the test in their lives.

(Matthew 13:21) "Yet hath he not root in himself, but dureth for a while: for when tribulation or persecution ariseth because of the word, by and by he is offended."

The person says, "I am convinced from this message. I am going home and I am taking that Christmas tree and I am going to throw it in the trash." Then the children say, "Momma, Daddy, why are you throwing the Christmas tree in the trash? Does that mean we aren't going to celebrate Christmas this year?" "No! I have had enough. There are going to be some changes around here. We are getting rid of every idol and all pagan idolatry." Now here comes Grandma. Here comes Grandpa. "Child, have you lost your mind? Are you okay? Don't you know that Christmas is Jesus' birthday?" Then it's, "Oh my God, what have I done?"

The next thing you know, there is opposition, persecution and resistance. The word gets choked. People start hiding their tzitzits. They put them in their pocket. They don't want people to know. We have to sneak to do what we do instead of being open and bold as a lion. So opposition comes.

(Matthew 13:22) "He also that received seed among the thorns is he that heareth the word; and the care of this world, and the deceitfulness of riches, choke the word, and he becometh unfruitful."

A person who is ambitious and wants to be wealthy is going to have a real issue with the Sabbath. They are a person who is business-minded and entrepreneurial. The world has convinced us that in order for us to be prosperous, in order for us to be wealthy — especially if we are in a cash business or some form of public service like retail. There are a lot of businesses out there where you are dealing directly with the public. If you want to have a shop, a coffee shop, or retail shop or chain of shops, you have to deal with the issue of what you do on the Sabbath. What do you do on the feast days?

Those things are the deceitfulness of riches. They choke the word. People begin to compromise. Pretty soon it is hard to walk with YeHoVaH knowing that there is compromise in your heart. Most people are either all in or they are all out, except for religious people. Religious people feel that knowledge is power and that having the information is good enough.

But a person who is serious about their walk with the Almighty is either all in or they are all out.

I have talked to people who I could tell they are serious about their knowledge of the Almighty. They will use words like "I don't play with God. I'm either going to serve him with all of my heart or I'm not going to serve him at all." I have respect for that, but that is not the way. The way is to serve him with all of your heart. Why won't a person serve him with all of their heart? Because of the deceitfulness of riches, because of the cares of this world, because they know that they have ambition in their heart to pursue things and this word is going to get in the way of the things that they are pursuing.

They pursue all of their worldly things until they get to a certain point where they say, "Okay, I built my kingdom. I have all of the things that I want. Now I can serve God with all of my heart." Unfortunately that is how some people live.

And then…

(Matthew 13:23) "But he that received seed into the good ground is he that heareth the word, and understandeth it; which also beareth fruit, and bringeth forth, some an hundredfold, some sixty, some thirty."

What he is saying is that there are people who are going to hear the word and they are not going to develop any root. There are going to be people who get excited about the word, but because they have persecution and tribulation, they are going to get offended because they have to stand on something that people they want to like them are offended by. Then there are those who because they want to be wealthy, they want to be known, they want to build a name for themselves, they are not going to be as fruitful.

But then there are going to be those who are going to say, "Okay, I hear what you are saying Father and I'm willing to sacrifice the things that need to be sacrificed in order to please you. I truly believe that if I please you, all of the things that those people are seeking, the things that I used to seek, if my ways please you, you are going to give me those desires. Or at some point, the things that I used to desire are no longer going to be a desire of mine."

When we are in the world, our desires are worldly desires. When we come into the Kingdom, now we begin to reexamine the desires that we had while we were in the world. Some of those desires will go away. Some of the things (we will find) are desires that were planted in us by the Almighty himself, so they don't go away. We continue to pursue them, but we pursue him first.

This is what this parable is saying.

In *Mark 4* we see it from a similar, but different perspective.

 *Mark 4:1-20*

Notice verse 10:

*"And when he was alone, **they that were about him with the twelve** asked of him the parable."*

Mark shows us a little bit more. *Mark* shows us that it wasn't just the twelve. There were those who were "about him." There were those who pressed in, those who didn't walk off after the message, those who weren't looking at their timepiece saying, "He is preaching too long." They come to do their Sabbath thing, but they have other things that they need to do, so hurry up.

I am not judging people, but I have no choice but to judge one's behavior. There are many reasons why people have to go. If people have to go, they have to go. The fact is though, I have been in places where people ask me, "How long is the service? How long is the teaching?" Why would a person ask that question?

Chances are it is because they are on a regimen or they have other plans. They will decide to drop in when they don't have other things to do and that is up to them. Whatever you do, that is totally up to you.

But here is the thing. In *Mark* we see that there was the multitude. There were those who were beside the twelve and then there were the twelve. The twelve asked and those who were with him (besides the twelve), we find.

If you notice, over in *Matthew 13* it says, *"and the disciples came."* (verse 10). In *Mark* we read that they who were about him with the twelve, asked of him. This is why it is important, especially when there are similar stories (the same story) in different parts of the gospel narratives. It is important to bring them together and to do a comparison. When you bring them together and compare them, you get a broader picture, a broader view. That is because one may say one little something, one little thing that now, "Oh! It was not just the twelve. It was more than just the twelve."

You might say that is insignificant. Is it? No, it is not. There are those who may not necessarily have been hand-selected by the Messiah who are passionate for learning the truth. They are putting that truth into practice and wanting to know, "What did you mean?" They too were disciples.

We are going to find out later that Yeshua had more than twelve disciples. He had over 500 disciples. At one time he had a great multitude of disciples until he preached one message and most of them left.

*(**Mark 4:11-12**) "And he said unto them, 'Unto you it is given to know the mystery of the kingdom of God: but unto them that are without, all these things are done in parables: That seeing they may see, and not perceive; and hearing they may hear, and not understand; lest at any time they should be converted, and their sins should be forgiven them.'"*

In one place it says that they may be healed. Here it says that their sins may be forgiven. Interestingly enough, when we begin to look at sins and sickness, there is definitely a relationship. First of all, sickness and disease entered into the earth via sin. Sin manifests itself in a multitude of ways according to the Torah.

To the world today, people don't think of sin as eating a ham sandwich. They don't think of sin as eating a double bacon cheeseburger. They may count their calories. There are many people that are very health conscious. They are thin or at their right weight. They exercise. They get their cardiovascular work. They do all of these things and yet they put abominable things into their bodies. They eat things like shrimp, lobster, crab and bacon and ham and Canadian bacon and all of these things. They would never consider those things as sin.

They would consider overeating and obesity possibly as sin. There are many people in the Christian community who don't see that eating shellfish and pork and things that the Bible forbids is sin because they pray over it. They ask Jesus to bless it and they don't consider it to be sin.

And yet they go to the doctor and they have hypertension, migraines and cancers of all kinds. Their body is shutting down and locking up on them. They can't figure it out. They find out that they have all of these toxins in their body that can't find a way out. Now all of a sudden they are doing EKGs and MRIs. But they say, "I'm not a sinner. I'm not a person who is out there committing adultery, lying and stealing." They don't consider the things that YeHoVaH says are sin.

Sin is defined according to *1 John 3:4* as a violation of the commandments. When we violate YeHoVaH's commands, we are entering into sin. And the wages of sin is death. Sickness is one way to bring about death.

We should die of old age. Believers should die of old age, not because of some cancer, not because of some heart attack, not because of some heart disease or some sickness that sucks the life right out of us. We should die of old age. Why? Because we are honoring YeHoVaH's commands. His commands say that if we do his commands and live, that our days will be long.

I want to be like Moses. Okay, not in the sense that Moses disobeyed the commands, but in the sense that Moses didn't die. YeHoVaH put him to sleep. We should just go to sleep one day and enter into the hereafter. That is the plan of the Almighty.

But the wages of sin is death. Sin is defined as the violation of Torah. Torah says that we should not put these things into our bodies.

We see again in verse 13:

"And he said unto them, 'Know ye not this parable? and how then will ye know all parables?'"

He is saying that if you understand this parable, you are going to understand all of the parables.

Mark 4:14-20

How does Satan take the word? Satan is a spirit. How does Satan come and take the word? How does he do that?

I am constantly having to be on guard to protect the word in my heart. That means that I have to — if I have been given a good word, I know that for me it is important for me. If I hear the word of the Father, I write it down. Notes are good. Notes are always good; especially if you go back and revisit the notes. Having a bunch of notes that you don't do anything with is just having a bunch of notes that you don't do anything with.

But notes are good if you go back and revisit them, so I know that one of the things that the enemy uses to distract us is busyness — busy, busy, busy. You always have things to do. People are on the phone calling. People need you over here. People need you over there. Pretty soon you are so distracted to the point where you say, "Okay, what did the Father say to me back there?" It is gone.

I know it was a good word. Why didn't you write it down?

The enemy immediately comes.

Those who hear the word, they receive it. The way you know that you have received the word is when you start walking in it. That is how you know you have received it. Otherwise all you have done is heard it. The Bible says be a doer, not just a hearer. When you receive the word, you are doing it. You are doing what it says. The instructions that you have been given, you are now applying them.

Finally in *Luke 8* we see the parable again. In here it says that the seed falls on a rock, instead of "stony." We see that he preaches this sermon. He preaches this message. And when you see statements like "He cried," it doesn't mean that he wept. That means typically at the top of his lungs. He shouts with everything in him. It is that important.

Now you also see even more so that the disciples are hearing and they have heard other messages. But with the emphasis that he is putting on this, it is like that teacher. Remember when he says, "Make sure you pay attention to what I am about to say, because this is going to be on the test." Yeshua is saying, "You need to hear what I just said."

The disciples ask, "What does this mean? Why are you emphasizing this?"

They press in. Some people won't press in.

In *Matthew* it doesn't say that he cried out nor does it say that in *Mark*. In *Matthew* it says it was the twelve. In *Mark* it said it was those with the twelve. Then *Luke* adds another dimension and says, "Now he cries out."

Can you see the importance of comparing all of these renditions together? When you are researching and studying, you want to find out all of the information surrounding this particular passage instead of reading a few verses and now it is like, "What does this mean?"

Now you are contemplating and meditating. I tried to get an understanding. Read the rest of the passage. If you read the rest of the passage and not stop midway through it, this is called context. We spent a great deal of time on the context principle. You have to get the right context. Once you understand where the context begins and you read to where the context ends, and there is a transition into another thought, generally you are going to find your answer. You are not going to find your answer in two or three verses.

Sometimes a context — like this one in *Matthew*, we are looking at 23 verses, not two or three verses. This is not a sermon where you read one verse and preach for an hour or you read the first part and you preach for a six-DVD series. You have to read the entire 23 verses. Then you have to go to *Mark* and read another 20 verses. Then you go to *Luke* and read another 20 verses. And guess what? You are right now at 63 verses of scripture in three different gospels, to get an understanding of a parable. That is a full understanding and not a partial understanding.

This is one of the reasons that I try to keep my messages simple, even though I take forever to answer a question. I want to be thorough so that a person now understands, instead of walking away thinking that they understand. There are many people who come into our teachings and I try to be very aware.

We might have a couple hundred people or more. Then as soon as I do the benediction, the Aaronic blessing, the numbers have a tendency to drop. That is because some people have come in. They have got a word and they are gone.

Then we spend another two hours or an hour and a half in Q and A. We are helping to bring understanding to something that was said that somebody may not have necessarily been interested in because they have done their Sabbath duty. They have come in and have heard a word. "Okay. I gotta get over here. I hope he gets done in time because my other teacher is coming on at a certain time and I have to go over there."

The Bible says to get wisdom and to get knowledge, but with all of your getting, get an understanding. You can't apply something you don't understand. When people are giving you all of this mysticism and these four-levels-of-Torah and they are talking over here and the deep things, basically what they are saying is this:

"Now I am going to teach you some things that are impossible for you to understand. That's because you're going to need a deep Torah teacher like myself to guide you. After all, you are only on the first level. But you have to be wise enough to get all the way down to the fourth level and you can't attain that because that is only for the deep Torah teachers."

And it is like, "Wow. That is deep." Yeah.

I am not trying to knock. I am just putting it out there. People are running all over the place. They are not getting an understanding. Five years later their head is spinning. They are back in a church somewhere or they are in a synagogue somewhere or they just left it altogether.

I learned something a long time ago. I was sharing it recently with a brother. You don't put your faith in men. Your faith should always be in Elohim. Men will disappoint. I try very hard to live a life that is open. I am very careful about what I let come in and what is being taught here. The last thing I need is for controversy that is unnecessary. There are some things that are controversial when you begin to go after deeply held traditions that you find are not scriptural.

I know for some people, when they found out that Santa Claus wasn't real, it is like life was no longer worth living. When they found out that the Easter Bunny was a fairy tale and there was no Tooth Fairy and Christmas is pagan, some people just lost it. They started to become a Muslim. They started practicing Buddhism and all kinds of other stuff because their foundation was shaken to the core.

Don't put your faith in men. Put your faith in the Almighty. I have had men, I'm telling you, from the very time I set foot in church. The reason why I ran so long is because I had seen so many ministers fall. There are pimping ministers, drug-dealing ministers, fornicating and adulterous ministers and drug-addicted ministers. It is sad. I didn't want anything to do with that. I ran from God for a long time.

When I returned, my first pastor died. I still don't know the circumstances surrounding his death. That is something. My next pastor was in an adulterous relationship. My next pastor was found out to be bisexual. The next pastor was supposed to be my mentor in the Missouri Synod Lutheran. I come to find out that his faith had been so shaken. The son was identified as a homosexual and his whole doctrine changed. Every denomination, every one of them, every ministry that I have been a part of that I have considered myself a member of has been disappointing.

But I wasn't there for them. **I was there to learn from him through them.** They got off track. I kept moving, which means that I can't just sit here. I'm done here. The cloud has moved. It is time for me to go. What I am seeing, I know that the glory of YeHoVaH is not on that. And I want to be where he is and he is not in this.

I have seen so many people's lives and their families turned upside down because the preacher failed. The preacher went off the deep end.

Did that preacher die for you? Did he shed his blood for you? Get a grip.

You don't put your faith in men. You put your faith in YeHoVaH. He uses men. He uses women. And if he is using someone in your life, glean from them and learn from them. Learn as much, glean as much. But if they are giving you things that are impractical, that is just heady and high-minded; do you know that the Bible says that knowledge just puffs you up? It gives you a big head.

Your question is what do I do with what you just taught? What do I do with this? Every message that you get you should ask yourself, "What do I do with this? How do I walk this out? How do I live this?"

If I am convicted in an area, that means that I may need to repent or I need to come up or I need to cut some things off or leave some things or whatever. When the word of YeHoVaH is coming, you will know that the word of YeHoVaH is coming. That is because there is going to be some spiritual warfare. The spiritual warfare is the enemy coming to steal it. He is coming to take that word to make sure that you don't get it.

He doesn't just come and take it if it never took root or if it wasn't even something worth taking. I mean, he is not going to come and take the message that he inspires the preacher to preach. They can't do anything with that. So keep giving it to them because they will never do anything with it except get a lot of information that they want to piggyback over here and run it by this person over there. They are always learning, but never coming into the knowledge of truth.

(Luke 8:15) "But that on the good ground are they, which in an honest and good heart, having heard the word, keep it, and bring forth fruit with patience."

They heard the word and keep it. They do it. They receive it. They hold onto it. When the enemy comes to get it, he gets a black eye. He gets nothing. They hold onto it. They keep that word and bring forth fruit with patience. Are you seeing this?

(Luke 8:16-18) "No man, when he hath lighted a candle, covereth it with a vessel, or putteth it under a bed; but setteth it on a candlestick, that they which enter in may see the light. For nothing is secret, that shall not be made manifest; neither anything hid, that shall not be known and come abroad. Take heed therefore how ye hear: for whosoever hath, to him shall be given; and whosoever hath not, from him shall be taken even that which he seemeth to have."

I think we have gotten to the end of that parable. As you can see, Yeshua has given us three parables. He has given us the parable of the sower in three places: *Matthew 13:1-23; Mark 4:1-20; Luke 8:4-24.* In all of those places we see that *Matthew* gives us the ground work. *Mark* gives us a little bit more. *Luke* gives us a little bit more. So when we put *Matthew, Mark* and *Luke* together, we are looking at 63 verses of scripture here.

We are doing our homework to get an understanding of the parable of the sower. We are not taking a few verses and running off somewhere. We are looking at it from every angle. We are not adding to it or taking away from it. We are not trying to interpret it through our own interpretative measures. We are listening to the author who is giving the interpretation of it so we cannot go wrong. Yeshua the word is explaining the word he just gave that others walked away from and didn't get an understanding.

This brings us to the conclusion of the parable principle. In the next lesson we are going to pick up on the interpretation of prophecy. We are going to look at the interpretation of prophecy very intensely. That is because when you think about Messiah Yeshua (the Spirit), Yeshua is the Spirit of Prophecy from *Genesis* to *Revelation*.

We know that they are looking at a book of prophecy where YeHoVaH begins by saying, "And he spoke." The Bible ends with the Spirit and the bride saying, "Come."

Class 97 Study Summary

Key Points

1. The parable principle is that principle by which any parable is interpreted by discerning its moral and interpreting its elements.

2. It is critical in the New Testament to understand the parable principle because when Yeshua spoke to the multitudes, he spoke in parables. The use of parables however, originated in the Old Testament.

3. In the New Testament a parable might be used as a proverb, a type or emblem, a similitude or allegory or as a comparison. It is an earthly story with a heavenly meaning.

4. When it comes down to the Kingdom, the Almighty made everything there is. He also created rules by which we are to live in his Kingdom. He owns all of it, even us. We must live by his rules or we cannot be part of his Kingdom. That means we have to not only know the word; we also have to do it. We must become one with it.

5. Having information and not applying it is like not having information at all. There is no point in knowing the word if you do nothing with it and if you won't walk in it.

6. We should not have too many teachers because it causes contradiction and confusion.

7. Speaking in tongues is a work of the Spirit. It is not a work of the devil, although some people teach that it is. The Father loves his people and does not give them anything that is not good for them.

8. Just because someone claims that "God showed them" or "Thus sayeth the Lord" doesn't mean that it was God who was speaking. We must try all spirits and know those among whom we labor and walk.

9. When we hear the message and try to put it into practice, the enemy will come to try to stop us. That is because when you walk in the word, he can't control you so he will try to steal the word. He will use distractions and opposition. He will use people we know and love.

10. A person who is ambitious and who wants to be wealthy in the world will have a real issue with the Sabbath. We cannot love riches and love the Almighty. We cannot serve two masters. If we are serious about this walk, we will be either all in or all out.

11. Some people will hear the word but they won't develop any root in it. That is because when persecution comes, they will compromise. They will not stand on what they have heard.

12. We have no choice but to judge one another's behavior. Those who bear fruit are those who are walking in the Kingdom. We must judge people's fruit.

13. Satan is a spirit. He tries to take the word as soon as it is given. That is why it is important to write it down or record it in some way so that we remember it and can walk it out.

14. When we are reading or preaching, it is important to compare renditions of the Bible and to do word studies to obtain the full meaning of the passages in question.

15. Don't put your faith in men. Put your faith in the Almighty. The Almighty uses men and women so we can glean from them, but look to the Father for wisdom and revelation.

16. If you feel conviction in any area, it means that you need to repent. You may need to cut some things off or leave some things. When the word of YeHoVaH is coming, you will know it because there will be some spiritual warfare. That is the enemy coming to try to steal that word to make sure that you don't receive it and walk in it.

Review Exercise

1. Have there been times during your spiritual walk that you could identify with any of the soils in the parable of the sower? What were the times and what was it like?

_____

_____

_____

_____

_____

_____

_____

_____

2. What does this parable tell us about our individual and corporate evangelism efforts?

_____

_____

_____

_____

_____

_____

_____

_____

3. Yeshua describes four responses or outcomes of the word being sown. Does that necessarily mean that only one in four people are ever going to "get it?" Why or why not?

_____

_____

_____

_____

_____

Rate the following statements
by filling in the most appropriate number.

(1 = I do not agree 10 = I agree completely)

Objectives:

1. I can explain the parable of the sower in depth.

   1. ○ 2. ○ 3. ○ 4. ○ 5. ○ 6. ○ 7. ○ 8. ○ 9. ○ 10. ○

2. I can define information from the parable as it relates to our mission to make disciples.

   1. ○ 2. ○ 3. ○ 4. ○ 5. ○ 6. ○ 7. ○ 8. ○ 9. ○ 10. ○

My Journal

What I learned from this class:

_____

_____

_____

_____

_____

_____

_____

_____

_____

_____

_____

_____

Discipleship Training Class 98

The Interpretation of Prophecy (part 1)

Objectives:

As a Discipleship student, at the end of this class you will be able to:

- Define prophecy and the interpretation of prophecy
- Define words and concepts involved with prophetic writings
- Explain the two natures of prophecy

Father has really been revealing things to me. So you are going to be (I believe) really inspired as I have been inspired in seeing things that I have never seen before. As the Father is revealing himself more and more, what we find is that the more we grow closer to the Father, the more he trusts us with insight into his word.

Because of the major significance of prophecy and the countless problems involved with misinterpretation, we are going to spend several lessons on the subject. Prophecy is far more complex than historical or poetic literature. There is historical and poetic literature in the Tanakh.

The interpretation of prophecy presents one of the greatest challenges to the interpreter in applying the science of hermeneutics. Since prophecy is also scripture, some prophecy can be interpreted by applying valid scriptural principles of interpretation. We have been dealing with this area of hermeneutics and the principles of hermeneutics. You are going to find that when dealing with prophecy, there are some major challenges that are there.

As we look at prophecy or prophetic books, there is a mixture of "Thus saith Yahweh." There is a mixture of visions and dreams. We have to be able to distinguish the difference between the visions, the dreams and the "Thus saith YeHoVaH." We will look at that as we look at the interpretation of prophecy.

Prophecy is defined by the *Free Merriam-Webster Dictionary* as follows:

1. An inspired utterance of a prophet

2. The function or vocation of a prophet; specifically: the inspired declaration of divine will and purpose

3. A predication of something to come

The *Free Dictionary* gives us a bit more specificity:

1. a. An inspired utterance of a prophet, viewed as a revelation of divine will
   b. A prediction of the future, made under divine inspiration
   c. Such an inspired message or prediction transmitted orally or in writing

2. The vocation or condition of a prophet

3. A prediction

Wikipedia says:

"Prophecy is a process in which one or more messages that have been communicated to a prophet are then communicated to others. Such messages typically involve divine inspiration, interpretation, or revelation of conditioned events to come (cf. divine knowledge)[5] as well as testimonies or repeated revelations that the world is divine."

We are looking at these external definitions. When I say "external definitions," they are those that are not necessarily biblical as far as the Bible and the word. We are going to look at the biblical word that is translated "prophecy," but the definition of prophecy is very similar to the ones that we just looked at.

There are several words in scripture that are used to refer to prophecy. We are first going to look at the Hebrew. The Hebrew is the origin or has become known as the origin of scripture. In Seminary and in theological institutions, they will teach that the Old Testament was written in Hebrew and the New Testament was written in Greek and yet we know that there are Hebrew Scriptures.

For instance is the book of *Hebrews*. The book of *Hebrews* has the actual name "Hebrews." It is ironic that the book of *Hebrews* would be a Greek Scripture. When it comes down to the Septuagint, when it comes down to the era and time, we see that there is certainly a correlation, but just the idea that the book of *Hebrews* is written in Greek is strange.

We also note that there are Hebrew versions of the book of *Matthew*. The Hebrew *Matthew* (we find) has some variation from the Greek *Matthew* that we have.

When we look at the Hebrew words (because we are restoring the Hebrew Roots), understand that the faith that is known today as "Christianity" evolved from the Hebrew Scriptures.

When we look at the Hebrew, we look at several words that are used to refer to prophecy.

1. Chazah

2. Massa

---

[5] "cf." means "compare for example."

3. Naba

4. Nebuwah

5. Nataph

We are going to look at these words.

The Old Testament Hebrew *Chazah* means "to gaze at; mentally to perceive, contemplate (with pleasure); specifically to have a vision of; to see, behold with the eye; to see as a seer in the ecstatic state." This word is translated as several words in the Hebrew Scriptures. This is why it is important that when we begin to look at the Strong's, every time you see a particular word in the Bible, it is important that you do a word study. That is because you can see "prophecy" and "behold" and not necessarily make the connection.

There are words that have different meanings even though it is the same word. You can't assume that if it means this over here, that it means the same thing over there. There are different words that are defined as *Chazah*.

Chazah

Behold	*Job 23:9; Psalms 17:2; 27:4*
Look	*Isaiah 33:20; Micah 4:11*
Prophecy	*Isaiah 30:10*
Provide	*Exodus 18:21*
See	*Isaiah 1:1; 13:1; Ezekiel 13:6-8* *Habakkuk 1:1*

I encourage you to look at some of these particular scriptures. I need to get to a certain point. It is important for you to understand that you can't look at prophecy and a vision in the same way. You can't interpret them in the same way. We will cover that a little bit later.

🔍 *Job 23:9*

Remember that one of the words associated with *chazah* as prophecy, is "to gaze at." So we can see that "it is to behold with the eye." When Job says, "I cannot see him," it is a word that is also translated from the Hebrew *Chazah*; which means "a prophecy."

Another is to "look upon" — we see to gaze on, to look on. Then there is prophecy in *Isaiah 30.*

🔍 *Isaiah 30:10*

It is an interesting verse. We are looking at the verse particularly for the word; not to try to interpret what is going on in this verse, although there are some extraordinary things that are happening here.

One of the translations is "provide" and of course "to see." We see this word *chazah* translated as all of those words in the chart.

Another word is *Massa* meaning "a burden; specifically tribute or abstractly porterage; figuratively an utterance, chiefly a doom, especially singing; mental, desire." You hear people talk about prophetic songs and prophetic singing.

Massa

Burden	*Isaiah 13:1; 15:1; 17:1; 19:1* *Jeremiah 23:33, 34, 37* *Habakkuk 1:1*
Carry away	*2 Chronicles 20:25*
Prophecy	*Proverbs 30:1; 31:1*
Song	*1 Chronicles 15:22, 27*
Tribute	*2 Chronicles 17:11*

Let's take a quick look at *Proverbs*.

🔍 *Proverbs 30:1; 31:1*

This is really interesting and we are going to see this a little bit later. We have to lay a foundation so that when we get there you already have an understanding. You are going to find that there are some prophecies and prophetic utterances that are spoken by people who do not have a book ascribed to them. There are prophets who wrote. There are prophets who were recorded. We have prophetic books.

Theology and theologians in the study of theology deal with this idea. When we begin to look at the Bible (the scriptures), there are major prophets and then there are minor prophets. These major prophets are determined by the length of the book. The minor prophets are determined by the length of their book.

I remember when I first heard "major prophets" and "minor prophets." My mind said, "Okay, there are some prophets that are more significant than others." That is the idea that my Western mind goes to. You have a senior pastor and then you have pastors or you have a first gentleman or a first family and then you have a second family; just like you have the President and you have the Vice-President. That is the way my Western mind was operating.

A major prophet is a prophet with more stature. It is a prophet more significant than the minor prophet, when it really entails basically the length of their writings. That's it.

If the Almighty is speaking to that person, you might say that one is a major and one is a minor, but it is the word of YeHoVaH that they are speaking. You can't minimize his word, because the minor prophet is speaking his word. The major prophet is speaking his word. So why are they called "major" and "minor?"

Theology answers that question with, "it is the length of their writings."

We see in *Proverbs 31* that Lemuel's Mother is teaching him a prophecy. We have come to know this prophecy as proverbs about the virtuous woman, the "*Proverbs 31* woman," when in fact there is prophecy. Now the question is, where does this prophecy come from? It says that the Mother taught him this prophecy. There is some interesting stuff that we are going to find out in the scriptures in this study.

Naba / Nebuwah

Prophesy	*1 Samuel 10:11* *Jeremiah 2:8; 26:11; Ezekiel 37:7* *Joel 2:28; Amos 3:8*
Make self a prophet	*Jeremiah 29:26, 27*

Another word that is translated "to prophesy" is *Naba* — "to prophesy; i.e. speak (or sing) by inspiration (in prediction or simple discourse); prophesy under influence of divine spirit, in the ecstatic state."

When we began to look at *Wikipedia* and the *Webster* online dictionaries, we saw these definitions. Although they gave no Hebrew word, it is the same Hebrew definition from the Hebrew word.

Jeremiah 29:26-27

What you see here going back to verse 25 is that there are people who make themselves a prophet. We are going to see this further on in this teaching. There are people (as I say), who were sent. There are people who just went. There are people who look at what ministers, apostles, prophets, evangelists, pastors and teachers do and they say, "I can do that."

It's not new. When YeHoVaH gives the children of Israel the Torah, He says that there will be those who will say, "Thus saith YeHoVaH" when YeHoVaH has not said. There will be people who will speak as if they have the authority of the Almighty, who don't have the authority of the Almighty. How do you know the difference? How do you distinguish between a true prophet and a false prophet?

The Torah gives us the answer to that. You won't know this outside of the Torah and yet we find today that people will say, "That is a false prophet." **How do you know that is a false prophet if you reject the Torah?**

You don't find in the New Testament, the distinction between a false prophet and a true prophet. The New Testament tells us that there will be false prophets, but it doesn't tell you how to recognize them. People throw out stuff and they ultimately have to go back and retrieve it, but they go and retrieve the information and leave the testament behind. You can't do that.

We see that **there are people who make themselves a prophet.** They make themselves prophets. They make themselves teachers and evangelists and apostles.

The word *Nebuwah* is "a prediction (spoken or written)." It is translated as "prophecy" in *2 Chronicles 9:28; 15:8; Nehemiah 6:12*.

What we have as we look at this word is that there are prophesies that are spoken and then written down. So now we have prophetic books. Prophetic books are books that contain prophecy. What is challenging is when you have a prophetic book that was written 2,000 years ago and people are trying to interpret it today based upon modern events.

This is where a lot of the issues come in. I see this stuff on *Facebook*. I hear it in teachings. I hear people that are speaking and they are saying this is that. Wait a minute. Now, that is a huge stretch when you hear people talking about how this is a "Joshua generation" or how this is that generation or they are just taking the scriptures and putting names to it. You even have people who are prophesying when in truth it is prophe-LYING. That is because they are ministering to one's flesh and not to one's spirit.

There is a difference in people saying what they think people want to hear and speaking what YeHoVaH is giving them to speak. I have had them both. I have had people speak to me the word of YeHoVaH and in the same breath speak to me according to their own spirit. We have to be able to distinguish when a person is speaking by the Spirit of YeHoVaH and speaking by their own spirit. Just because somebody says, "I am sensing in my spirit," your spirit is not the Holy Spirit. "Oh, I have peace in my spirit." Well, what brings you peace?

It is the Holy Spirit that bears witness with our spirit that we are the sons of God. It is the Holy Spirit that inspires. Now the Holy Spirit and our spirit are not the same. It is the Holy Spirit that inspires or activates or impregnates or puts the word or reveals the word to us. We have to make a distinction because sometimes our spirit is not at peace. It is not at peace because we have done something to grieve the Holy Spirit.

We have to make a distinction.

We see this spoken or written *Nebuwah* in Nehemiah.

🔍 *Nehemiah 6:12*

Prophet for hire! A prophet for hire is a prophe-LIAR.

There arc people that are prophesying, "Oh, thus saith YeHoVaH. I see in the spirit that you are going to give this ministry $1,000 for a seed." Then what really gets me is when some prophets — I am not trying to mock because I think that some of this may actually be the Father speaking. But when you test a lot of it in the context and what it is associated with, it is highly suspect. When you have these televangelists in a telethon speaking to a million people or five million people or twenty million people, they say, "The Lord just showed me that there are one hundred people that are going to give $5,000." Or "He shows me that one thousand people are going to give at the $100 level. Are you one of those one thousand?"

Think about this. There are tricks and it really bothers and grieves me. When I first began to see this stuff, I was new to it. It didn't feel right, but I didn't know any better. I didn't know how to judge.

Being in the company of people who have been at this a lot longer than me, it makes you wonder if you are actually mature enough to be able to judge. As we grow and as we learn what the word actually says, you see that people in the New Testament are easily deceived. New Testament people are easily deceived; even when they try to test something.

There are two ways that you can test if something is of YeHoVaH. One, does it bear witness with the word; and two, does the Spirit bear witness with it? This is why it is important that you are able to distinguish between your spirit and the Holy Spirit. Some people operate out of their intellect and they operate out of their spirit based on what they have been taught.

When a person makes a judgment of something without actually knowing what the scripture has to say about it, that is a prejudgment. That is prejudice. They have prejudged something.

A wise man is going to hear both sides of an issue before he makes a judgment. Sometimes I have people leaving comments and making posts on videos. For instance, tongues is a popular one. Many people want to tell me that tongues is known language. They say that YeHoVaH does not have to speak to people in tongues. And I have to show them that they don't know what they are talking about. You have no clue as to what you are talking about.

People's interpretation of the Bible matters. In Pentecostalism, drinking is a sin, when it is over-drinking, getting drunk. **People look at scripture from their denominational perspective and therefore read into what the scripture is actually saying.**

When people say, "Well, the wine that Yeshua drank or made was non-alcoholic" and that in the Bible the wine is non-alcoholic, I say, "Okay. Well, Noah got drunk on grape juice." It is the first mention principle. The first time wine is mentioned is with Noah and Noah gets drunk. I have had a lot of grape juice, even the sparkling grape juice (the kind that comes in the corked bottles like champagne). With all of the grape juice that I have had in my life, I have never gotten a buzz.

Noah plants a vineyard and makes wine. This is not typical grape juice where he just squeezed the juice out of the grapes and drank it. He made something potent enough to bring him to a place of intoxication. It is the first time wine is mentioned.

Remember that we learned in the first mention principle that the first time a word is mentioned, it carries that definition throughout scripture (unless of course you look up wine in another place and it is not fermented and which you would be hard-pressed to find). It is going to be based upon theology and not on scriptural research.

The Hebrew word *Nataph* means "to ooze; (i.e. distill gradually); by implication to fall in drops; figuratively to speak by inspiration; prophecy, discourse." Some of these you will find associated with a prophecy that is given in parts. You get a piece here and a piece there. You have to marry all of these together to get some form of understanding.

Nataph

Drop	*Judges 5:4; Ezekiel 21:2; Amos 7:16*
Prophesy	*Micah 2:6, 11*

 *Ezekiel 21:2*

We see this word translated as "drop."

From these Hebrew words we see prophecy as an ecstatic vision, a burden, a divinely inspired utterance, a written or spoken prediction and a dropping down of inspired speech. You have all of these words that are associated with prophecy, but every time you see these words, it is not the word "prophecy."

Now you can see the importance of doing word studies as you are reading and trying to get an understanding of the Bible. **You can't apply English understanding to these words, because they are English words.** They come from a Hebrew origin. They originate in the Hebrew.

New Testament Greek

One of the major distinctions between the New Testament Greek words and the Hebrew (the Tanakh Hebrew) words is that oftentimes there are several words in the Hebrew that are narrowed down to just one word in the Greek.

In the New Testament, *propheteuo* means "to foretell events, divine, speak under inspiration, exercise the prophetic office; to proclaim a divine revelation, prophesy, to foretell the future, to speak forth by divine inspiration, to break forth under sudden impulse in lofty discourse or in praise of the divine counsels."

Propheteuo is translated as prophesy[6] in:

Prophesy	*Matthew 15:7* *Luke 1:67; 22:64* *John 11:51* *Acts 2:17, 18; 21:9* *1 Corinthians 14:1, 3-5* *1 Peter 1:10* *Jude 14* *Revelation 11:3*

In the New Testament you will see the word "prophesy." In Koine Greek, the concept of prophecy was solidified to the point that only one word was used to encompass it.

In the New Testament, prophesy meant to proclaim a divine revelation, to foretell the future and to break forth under sudden impulse into inspired discourse.

One of the nice things about Greek is that it has a tendency to simplify. The bad thing about Greek is a tendency to simplify.

It narrows the search, but it does not give you much room to search. That is why when you see something in the New Testament that comes from the Old Testament you cannot just rely on the New Testament research. You have to go back to where it came from. If Yeshua said something that is spoken of in the Torah, you can't just apply a New Testament definition or understanding to something that has its origin in Hebrew.

The Nature of Prophecy

Now it starts to get interesting. The nature of prophecy is basically two-fold: forth-telling and foretelling. There are as well, different degrees of prophetic inspiration.

Prophecy	
The Nature of Prophecy	
Forth-telling	Foretelling

---

[6] "Prophesy" (pro-fes-si) is the verb. "Prophecy" (pro-fes-cee) is the noun form.

Prophecy as Forth-telling

This form of prophecy is related to preaching. The prophet speaks for YeHoVaH to the people; communicating the mind of YeHoVaH for the present. **Often the past will be used to deal with the present.** This will include such things as exhortation, reproof, warning, edification and comfort. These prophecies will be a reminder.

When YeHoVaH would send the prophets to Israel, it was to remind them, to call them back to something. There were times when these prophecies will speak of things to come based upon their response to what they are calling them back to or their refusal to respond. We are going to look at quite a bit of this as we move forward.

Prophecy as Foretelling

This type of prophecy is in the form of prediction: the prophet/prophetess speaks for YeHoVaH, communicating his mind for the future. Often both past and present will be used to deal with the future. Many times the purpose of prophetic prediction is to produce present Godliness.

I emphasize some truly interesting dynamics from a male and female perspective as it relates to one who speaks for YeHoVaH. We are going to address some challenging issues with our understanding of what is really in the scriptures.

When a minister, a preacher, is preaching from the word of YeHoVaH, that is forth-telling. That is saying, "This is what the scripture says and this is how we interpret it."

Degrees of Prophetic Inspiration

Scripture reveals that there are varying degrees of prophetic unction, as follows:

The main one is:

The Spirit of Prophecy. This is defined in ***Revelation 19:10***: *"The testimony of Yeshua is the Spirit of prophecy."* The Spirit of Prophecy is the Holy Spirit's ability to come upon people (men and women) and cause them to speak forth inspired utterances. The Spirit of Prophecy is evident throughout the Bible.

1. Adam prophesied concerning his bride and the marriage estate. (***Genesis 2:20-25***)

We don't see that Adam says, "Thus saith the Lord," or "Thus saith YeHoVaH" or that the commentator says, "Now, Adam is about to prophesy" or "Adam prophesied." We simply see Adam speaking. Adam is speaking of something that has never been spoken of before.

🔍 ***Genesis 2:20-25***

What is really interesting here is that we see Adam speaking, but where is Adam getting this information from? There are some clues here because one, how does Adam know that she was made out of him? You see what he says, "This is now bone of my bone, flesh of my flesh." How does he know this?

(Genesis 2:21-22) *"And the LORD God caused a deep sleep to fall upon Adam, and he slept: and he took one of his ribs, and closed up the flesh instead thereof; And the rib, which the LORD God had taken from man, made he a woman, and brought her unto the man."*

What you don't see here is something that should be written here. I believe that we don't see much of the conversation that YeHoVaH has with Adam while he is walking with him and talking with him and dialoguing with him. We see the instruction concerning the tree, but here is the thing that we do know. If Adam is asleep, how does he know what is going on? How does he know that Eve has come from his bone and from his flesh?

YeHoVaH tells us where she came from. YeHoVaH tells us exactly what he did. It is highly possible, just as we see from the word what was done, that this was communicated. "Adam, I put you to sleep. I took from your body while you were asleep, a part of your rib, your bone and a part of your flesh. I made this beautiful creation called 'woman.' This is to be your wife. You all are to be one. You are to let nothing come between you. And all generations, when you have children, you are going to raise them up and they too will get married and they too shall become one.

You need to understand that when your children get married and become one, they are going to leave you. They are going to leave you (their Father) and they are going to leave your wife, their Mother. They will become one flesh. Then when their children are born and grow, they are going to find a wife. They are going to be married and they are going to cleave to their wives. They are going to leave their Father and their Mother. It will be this way for generations to come."

YeHoVaH is speaking this I believe, to Adam. Adam is declaring that this is the order of things from now to come. When YeHoVaH says, "Okay, be fruitful and multiply," Adam isn't going to be out there trying to make human beings out of dirt like YeHoVaH did. He is going to understand the process. I am sure that when YeHoVaH says, "Be fruitful and multiply and fill the earth, replenish the earth," there was also, "Adam, come here. Let me give you a lesson on how to do that. This is how you replenish. This is how you multiply. This is the process that you must operate and you then have to teach your children. The day is going to come when they ask you, 'Daddy, where do babies come from?'"

"This is not a story. This is not something you ought to shy away from or let someone else teach. This is something that you enter into with a clear conscience, understanding that this is how it is done. When you do this, you do this with your wife because the two of you will become one."

So there is an explanation of how procreation and regeneration is supposed to take place within the context of the instruction of YeHoVaH. With this you don't see Adam say, "Okay, I am tired of Mrs. Adam. Let me get Mrs. Adam number two," nor do you see Adam's sons nor any of the line of YeHoVaH do this.

You will find that YeHoVaH had a plan and it was for **one man and one woman to become one.** That is one man and one woman. The two (not the three, not the four) but the two shall become one.

2. Enoch prophesied of the second coming of Messiah. (*Jude 14, 15*)

Let's just take a moment and run over to Jude.

(*Jude 1:14-15*) *"And Enoch also, **the seventh from Adam**, prophesied of these, saying, 'Behold, the Lord cometh with ten thousands of his saints, To execute judgment upon all, and to convince all that are ungodly among them of all their ungodly deeds which they have ungodly committed, and of all their hard speeches which ungodly sinners have spoken against him.'"*

Just to make sure that there is no confusion, we have "the seventh from Adam." What we see here appears to be a quote from *1 Enoch*, which is also known as the *Apocalypse of Enoch*. It is important that we understand because I think for many people it has been pointed out to them, but for some, it hasn't.

Genesis 4:15-17

This is after the altercation where Cain murders his brother. This Enoch is not the Enoch spoken of in *Jude*, but we see that Cain brings forth the first Enoch. When we look at *Genesis 5*, this is why it is important to learn how to count. I am not trying to be insulting or anything, but it is important to understand chronology. It is important to understand the history. It is important to be able to read the scriptures and to really take time to think through them. Understand and don't turn your brain off. If you do, you will get misled even though the truth is right there in front of us.

We see that Cain has a son named Enoch, but if you look at Adam and then Cain and then Enoch, this Enoch would be the third from Adam.

Jude specifically says that this Enoch is the *seventh* from Adam, so where do we find that Enoch? We will find that Enoch in *Genesis 5*. He is not from Cain's lineage.

What *Genesis 5* does is take us to the beginning at Adam. Male and female he created them and blessed them and called *their* name "Adam" when they were created. So *Genesis 5* gives us some insight into *Genesis 1* and 2. We see Adam and Eve, but Adam is the one who gave his wife a name. YeHoVaH called them "Adam."

Let's fast-forward because Cain has murdered his brother Abel. Abel is dead. Cain has been exiled. Adam and his wife come together and have a son. This son is not in the image of God.

There are so many little things here that could correct wrong doctrine if we just paid attention. Adam and Eve or Mr. Adam and Mrs. Adam were created in the image and likeness of YeHoVaH. In *Genesis 5:3*, Adam lived 130 years. He begat a son "in his own likeness, and after his image," whose name was called Seth.

In verse 4 Adam didn't wait until he was 800 years old to have sons and daughters. Once Seth was born, Adam lived 800 more years. But during this 800 additional years, he had sons and daughters. When did he have sons and daughters?

The question always comes up, "Well, if Cain married, whom did he marry?" Did Cain marry and leave before Adam had other sons and daughters or are we reading the Bible like we read a book? If this is chapter 1, then what happened in chapter 1 happened before chapter 2 and what happened in chapter 2 happened before chapter 3.

We read in progression, when the fact of it is that this is not in progression. This is back and forth. Sometimes it is hard to get the mind (especially a Western/Greek mind) to think along those lines. You will hear people say, "Adam was 800 years old before he had sons and daughters or that Adam didn't have sons and daughters because that happened in chapter 5 (when Cain got married in chapter 4). There "must" have been other people. God must have created other people. Cain married some of these other people that were here that God created that he chose not to tell us about. That's because according to chapter 5, he didn't have children until after Cain got married and moved away.

You see the logic that people apply. It makes perfect sense to them.

Now I say, "Well, if it makes so much sense, who were these other people? Did YeHoVaH create them?" "Oh, they must have been the devil's seed. They must have been the angels." I am telling you that once a person gets out of the Bible, there is no stopping them now because their mind and their imagination are like the wind.

The moment that you say, "Okay, wait a minute. Let me prove what you just said is not true," like the wind, they shift and they just keep shifting. Every time you prove something wrong, they shift. "Well, what about this?" or "What about that?"

These theories are endless, which is why when I deal with people like that I just say, "You just keep shifting." They should be on Star Trek or something, the way they shape-shift.

This Enoch in *Jude* was the seventh from Adam.

The Cain/Seth Lineages

(*Genesis 4*) Adam — Cain — Enoch

(*Genesis 5*) Adam — Seth — Enos — Cainan — Mahalaleel — Jared — Enoch

We see that there is a book. People ask me, "Have you read the book of *Enoch*? The book of *Enoch* has some incredible things that answer a lot of our questions." People are trying to determine from the book of *Enoch* the whole idea of how you identify day from night and when a day starts.

They get into the book of *Enoch* and discard everything in *Genesis, Exodus, Leviticus, Numbers* and *Deuteronomy*. They just throw it out.

This is what *1 Enoch 1:9* says (It really lines up with what **Jude 14-15** says.):

"And behold! He cometh with ten thousands of His holy ones to execute judgment upon all, and to destroy all the ungodly; and to convict all flesh of all the works of their ungodliness which they have ungodly committed, and of all the hard things which the ungodly sinners have spoken against Him."

The first thing we should note is that *Jude* is quoting from Enoch himself, not from the book of *Enoch*. *Jude* didn't mention a book. *Jude* mentions Enoch and that Enoch prophesied. That is important because there is apparently some question as to the exact dating of both *Jude* and *Enoch*.

Jude is by a single author and is estimated by scholars to have been written from the mid to later half of the first century while *1 Enoch* was apparently written by several authors over a time period from about 200 B.C. to about the middle of the first century. We know that **Enoch is an apocalyptic book.**

This is important. This is where the work of people with archeological backgrounds is helpful (where you have people who understand the eras and the years). They are able to date particular writings based upon what is written; what is in the book and what is not in the book. This is how you can determine whether something was written before the destruction of the temple or after the destruction of the temple. We know that the book of *Acts* was completed before the temple was destroyed because there is absolutely no mention of it.

We note that based upon scholars that this seems to allow for at least the possibility that *1 Enoch* is actually quoting from *Jude*. When you begin to look at the dates, is *Jude* quoting from *Enoch* or is *Enoch* quoting from *Jude*? The assumption is that *Jude* is actually quoting from the book.

Understand that *Jude* mentioned Enoch. He does not mention the book of *Enoch*. Did Enoch write this book? When you look at when Enoch was born (the seventh from Adam) and the time period for the book of *Enoch*; it is conclusive that Enoch did not write the book of *Enoch* based upon when it was written (about 200 B.C.). But because it bears his name…

That is just like the Apostle's Creed. Because it has the term "Apostle's," it "must" have been written by the apostles.

Now according to several early church writers *(Clement of Alexandria, Origen and Didymus)*, **Jude 1:14** is based upon the apocryphal book called *"The Assumption of Moses."* This quote doesn't suggest that the quotations or the books they were taken from are divinely inspired. Imagine people running out and getting *The Assumption of Moses*, just like folks who have run out to get the book of *Enoch*. It only means that the biblical author found quotations to be a helpful confirmation, clarification or illustration.

Other New Testament quotations from or allusions to non-biblical works include Paul's quotations of *Aratus* (**Acts 17:28**) or *Menander* (**1 Corinthians 15:33**) and *Epimenides* (**1 Titus 1:12**). Paul quotes from these individuals. I think that people want so badly to believe that *Enoch* is a book that should be in the Bible. Most people who study the book of *Enoch* that I know of, don't even have a firm grasp of the Torah.

The assumption is that because Enoch is the seventh from Adam — you have to understand something. People can put a twist on something. Once they get this twist on it, if the scholars have agreed and everybody knows that the book of *Enoch* was written in 200 B.C. (or later) and Enoch was born several thousand years earlier, how could Enoch have written the book of *Enoch*?

There is no record whatsoever that Enoch wrote a book.

(**Acts 17:28**) *"For in him we live and move and have our being. As some of your own poets have said, 'We are his offspring.'"*

These two quotations:

1. *"...in him we live and move and have our being,"* This comes from the Cretan poet **Epimenides (c. 600 B.C.)** in his *Cretica*.

2. *"We are his offspring,"* This comes from the Cilician poet **Aratus (c. 315-240 B.C.)** in his *Phaenomena*, as well as from **Cleanthes (331-233 B.C.)** in his *Hymn to Zeus*.

Paul is quoting from these writings. That is because Paul has actually studied a lot of poetry. It is just like if a person goes to college today. They are going to study poetry and literature. They are going to study language and a variety of subjects that are part and parcel to American history. When people go into English schools and learn in the English schools and colleges, they are going to study poetry and they are going to study poets from certain eras.

You have people today who are so into poetry that they quote poetry. They can make quotes from particular books. Well, Paul learned this too. So when he is dealing with these people, he is quoting from well-known poets that they ascribe to.

It is like when I go into a foreign country. You want to learn a few words in that country so that people think, "Oh, wow. They think enough of us to learn some words to speak to us when they speak." Paul was masterful. When people talk about how he became all things to all people that he might win a few, it was not saying that Paul sat down with the heathen and ate pork chops. It is that Paul understood their culture and he learned from them. He learned of them, so he could talk to them in a language they understood.

Just like here.

You are in for a serious ride. I am seeing things for the first time. I am actually amazed at the things that the Father is allowing me to see that I did not see before and the depth of study that he is taking me into. These are things I have never taught. You will find that the things that I am pulling together and bringing together and putting into a systematic form are bits and pieces of information that are scattered all over the place. So when you go into a school of higher learning, you are not going to learn this stuff. You will learn bits over here and pieces over there. How do you put this into a perspective?

You have to understand that when it comes down to interpreting prophecy in the Bible, there are certain tools that you can apply. There are other things that are like, okay. You are going to have to wait for the revelation to come from the Almighty. There are certain things we are never going to know until he reveals them to us. It is either going to be in this lifetime or it is going to be when he chooses to reveal them to us.

How do we make the distinction?

We will find that people have been trying to interpret prophecy. They have been predicting prophecy. They have been trying to interpret prophecy from prophetic books; from books that include visions, dreams and prophecy. We have to be able to make the distinction. I believe that this particular study and these next few lessons are going to be literally life-changing when it comes to approaching the scriptures.

Class 98 Study Summary

Key Points

1. Father is revealing himself to us more and more over time in his word and by his Spirit.
2. When speaking of prophecy and prophetic books, there is a mixture of "Thus sayeth YeHoVaH" and of dreams and visions. We have to be able to distinguish the difference.
3. Prophecy is defined as an inspired utterance of a prophet, the inspired declaration of divine will and a predication of something that is to come.
4. In the Bible there are major prophets and minor prophets. A major prophet is a prophet that has more stature. The only difference between them is in their number of writings.
5. When YeHoVaH gave Israel the Torah, he said there would be people who would say, "Thus sayeth YeHoVaH" when he has not said. There will be people speaking with a false authority that is not the authority of YeHoVaH.
6. If you reject the Torah, you won't know whether a prophet is a real or a false prophet.
7. There are people who make themselves to be prophets who are not prophets.
8. There are two ways to tell if something is of YeHoVaH. First it will bear witness with the word and second, the Spirit will bear witness with it.
9. People look at scripture from their denominational perspective and therefore read into what the scripture is actually saying.
10. The first time a word is mentioned, it carries that definition throughout scripture. This is known as the first mention principle.
11. You can't apply an English understanding to Hebrew words. They aren't English words. They will have a different meaning. That is why you have to search for their meanings.
12. Some words were translated and lumped together under one word, even when they were different words. For example is the English word "prophecy." There are several Hebrew words associated with the concept of "to prophesy," but in Koine Greek there is only one word that was used to translate all of its Hebrew words. Therefore we need an understanding of word origins and their cultures to get a full understanding of our English translated Bibles.
13. Prophecy has two forms: forth-telling (speaking for YeHoVaH) and foretelling (prediction).
14. There are different degrees of prophetic inspiration. The main one is the Spirit of Prophecy.
15. The book of Enoch is a prophetic, apocalyptic book.
16. Paul quoted contemporary poets including Aratus, Cleanthes, Epimenides and Menander.
17. When it comes down to interpreting prophecy in the Bible, we must apply certain tools.

Prophecy/Prophesy

There are several words in scripture that are used to refer to prophecy. They are:

1. Chazah – Behold, look, prophecy, provide, see, to gaze at, behold with the eyes
2. Massa – Burden, carry away, prophecy, song, tribute
3. Naba – Prophesy, make self a prophet
4. Nebuwah – Prophesy, make self a prophet
5. Nataph – Drop, prophesy

Review Exercise

1. List some things defined as prophetic as we have seen in the dictionaries:

_____

_____

_____

_____

2. How do the dictionary definitions of prophecy compare to the uses of the Hebrew and Greek words translated "prophecy" in our Bible?

_____

_____

_____

_____

_____

_____

3. What are the two natures of prophecy? What makes them different?

_____

_____

_____

_____

_____

_____

4. Discuss the difference between "prophecy" and "prophesy."

_____

_____

_____

_____

_____

5. Think about and describe your experience with prophecy. How do you commonly think of prophecy? What are your attitudes toward prophecy? Have you ever prophesied or been around someone who has? Where does the interpretation of prophecy fit into your spiritual life?

_____

_____

_____

_____

_____

_____

_____

_____

_____

_____

_____

Rate the following statements
by filling in the most appropriate number.

(1 = I do not agree 10 = I agree completely)

Objectives:

1. I can define prophecy and the interpretation of prophecy.

   1. ◯   2. ◯   3. ◯   4. ◯   5. ◯   6. ◯   7. ◯   8. ◯   9. ◯   10. ◯

2. I can define words and concepts involved with prophetic writings.

   1. ◯   2. ◯   3. ◯   4. ◯   5. ◯   6. ◯   7. ◯   8. ◯   9. ◯   10. ◯

3. I can explain the two natures of prophecy.

   1. ◯   2. ◯   3. ◯   4. ◯   5. ◯   6. ◯   7. ◯   8. ◯   9. ◯   10. ◯

My Journal

What I learned from this class:

_____

_____

_____

_____

_____

_____

_____

_____

_____

_____

_____

_____

_____

Discipleship Training Class 99

The Interpretation of Prophecy (part 2)

Objectives:

As a Discipleship student, at the end of this class you will be able to:

- Define concepts from the last lesson about the nature of prophecy
- Explain authority as a function of prophetic utterance
- Describe what is meant by the ability to prophesy

We are dealing with probably the most important subject in scripture and that is prophecy and the interpretation of prophecy. We started into the interpretation of prophecy to get an understanding. As we discussed, because of the nature of this particular subject, we will be on this for a while.

Because of the major significance of prophecy and the countless problems involved with misinterpretation, we are going to spend several weeks on the subject. Prophecy is far more complex than the historical or poetical literature. You have to understand that the Bible is a conglomerate, if you would. It is filled with the historical. It is filled with poetical, information, and literature, as well as prophetic words from the Almighty. That helps us to understand or to get a better understanding of the Almighty, how he functions and what he is trying to accomplish through his people here in the earth.

The interpretation of prophecy presents one of the greatest challenges however to the interpreter in applying the science of hermeneutics. And since prophecy is also scripture, some prophecy can be interpreted by applying valid scriptural principles of interpretation.

We looked at some of the definitions.

Prophecy is defined by the *Free Merriam-Webster Dictionary* as follows:

1. An inspired utterance of a prophet
2. The function or vocation of a prophet; specifically: the inspired declaration of divine will and purpose
3. A predication of something to come

The *Free Dictionary* gives us a bit more specificity:

1. a. An inspired utterance of a prophet, viewed as a revelation of divine will
   b. A prediction of the future, made under divine inspiration
   c. Such an inspired message or prediction transmitted orally or in writing
2. The vocation or condition of a prophet
3. A prediction

You are going to find that the prophetic utterances in scripture are given. First of all you will find that in the writings, certain prophets are being communicated to by the Almighty as to what to say to a people. Then those oral communications are brought to us in writing. We see them in this book and we are privileged at times to actually be transferred to the time when the Almighty actually spoke the words.

Wikipedia says:

"Prophecy is a process in which one or more messages that have been communicated to a prophet are then communicated to others. Such messages typically involve divine inspiration, interpretation, or revelation of conditioned events to come (cf. divine knowledge) as well as testimonies or repeated revelations that the world is divine."

When we look at the Hebrew, we look at several words that are used to refer to prophecy.

1. **Chazah**
2. **Massa**
3. **Naba**
4. **Nebuwah**
5. **Nataph**

From these Hebrew words we see prophecy as an ecstatic vision, a burden, a divinely inspired utterance, a written or spoken prediction and a dropping down of inspired speech.

In the New Testament Greek, *propheteuo* means "to foretell events, divine, speak under inspiration, exercise the prophetic office; to proclaim a divine revelation, prophesy, to foretell the future, to speak forth by divine inspiration, to break forth under sudden impulse in lofty discourse or in praise of the divine counsels."

We also looked at the nature of prophecy. **The nature of prophecy is basically two-fold: forth-telling and foretelling.** There are as well, different degrees of prophetic inspiration.

We looked at forth-telling. That is to speak what the Almighty has said. When we speak and we read the scriptures and when we read the prophecies, we are reading what is there. We are speaking forth what is written.

To foretell is to be shown by the Almighty something that is about to happen or that is in the distant future that will happen. This form of prophecy is related to preaching. The prophet speaks for YeHoVaH to the people; communicating the mind of YeHoVaH for the present. Often the past will be used to deal with the present. This will include such things as exhortation, reproof, warning, edification and comfort.

One of the things that you will find is that YeHoVaH always seemingly said to the people through the prophets to "remember." To remember is to look back. It is something that has been said; something that has been done that they are to remember.

Oftentimes Father would remind them of the way they have come so that he would be justified in his response. The time will come, which is why the gospel of the Kingdom must be preached to the ends of the earth. Every person will be responsible. Every person will be responsible and it is our responsibility to speak forth what the Father has given us to speak forth to a world headed in the wrong direction.

This type of prophecy is in the form of prediction. The prophet/prophetess speaks for YeHoVaH; communicating his mind for the future. Often both past and present will be used to deal with the future. Many times the purpose of prophetic prediction is to produce present Godliness.

We looked in the last lesson as Paul was speaking. We identified that Paul not only quoted from the scriptures, but Paul quoted from other sources. Peter acknowledged the fact that Paul's writings sometimes were difficult to understand or to be understood and also how people took what Paul wrote and twisted it.

In the last lesson we looked at the fact that Paul not only quoted from the prophets of the Bible, but he also spoke or quoted from the prophets of other belief systems.

It is interesting that Paul is not quoting their prophecies as divine scripture. But as the Bible says, Paul "became all things to all people that he might win a few." Paul learned the customs, the culture and the understandings of the people with which he communicated. Paul had an innate ability to go into a community. Part of his training, part of his learning — Paul was a very learned individual. He was knowledgeable in various languages as well as various customs. He went into a particular environment and was able to communicate to the people through the understandings they had.

We see some of Paul's work in how he was able to speak to the Roman leaders. We see how he was able to speak to Roman authorities and how he was able to pit the Pharisees against the Sadducees. He understood the denominational understanding of the Pharisees and he used that to his advantage. He understood the denominational understanding of the Sadducees and he knew where they disagreed and when they would gang up on him. Paul had the ability to speak to one group in a way that he knew so that the other group would be in stark disagreement. So now he had them pit each other against themselves where they would take the focus off of him. Paul was very, very cunning.

Paul also quoted from other sources and we find these quotes in Paul's writings.

In the last lesson we looked at some of those. You can review lesson 98. Today we are going to look at some more.

*(**1 Corinthians 15:33**) "Do not be misled: Bad company corrupts good character."*

Where is this in scripture? It isn't. Paul is quoting from the Greek comedy that is written by the Greek poet Menander and whose writings the Corinthians would know. The application of the quotation is that those who are teaching that there is no resurrection (verse 12) are the "bad company." They are corrupting the "good character" of those who hold to the correct doctrine.

So here Paul is quoting from a Greek poet. He is not quoting from scripture. This is so important for us to understand, because Paul does this in various places within his writings.

Understand that Paul was also a Pharisee. He was knowledgeable in Pharisaic law. Paul also had an understanding of Sadducee law. There were times when Paul would say, "It is written in the law," but we can't find this in the Torah. People think that whenever Paul used the term "law," that he was speaking about the Torah.

Here is the thing about the law or the Torah. When a quote is given in reference to the Torah or from the Torah, we should be able to find the reference in the Torah. We will look at some of this.

In the last lesson we identified that Paul quoted from several sources, not just from the scriptures. We also asked then as we will ask now, when Paul quoted in *1 Corinthians 15:33* — I have taught this to my children. I think that many parents have used this term. "Beware of the company you keep. Bad company corrupts good character." We are trying to teach you good character, but if you are hanging out with bad company, they are going to corrupt you.

The assumption is that because Paul said it that it is in the Bible, but it is not a quote from the scriptures. It is a quote from some other source.

When we looked at *Jude* quoting from Enoch who prophesied, he is not quoting from a book. It is a quote that Enoch prophesied.

The question becomes, because Paul quoted this, does this quote suggest that the quotations or the books that they were taken from are divinely inspired? Absolutely not. The Talmud is not divinely inspired. It is the commentary of men as it relates to scripture. Paul used quotations from sources that were not divinely inspired and we need to take note of that.

(Titus 1:12) *"Even one of their own prophets has said, 'Cretans are always liars, evil brutes, lazy gluttons.'"*

The quotation is from the poet Epimenides (a sixth-century B.C. native of Knossos, Crete), who was held in high esteem by the Cretans. Several fulfilled predictions were ascribed to him. Now, just like you had the prophets of Baal, you have prophets who are from Crete; who are Cretan prophets.

There are people today who are saying that there are some of these musicians who are writing songs that seem to be prophetic. The world has their prophets. Hip-hop has their prophets. Some have said that Prince was prophetic and Michael Jackson was prophetic, and many others who were prophetic, all the way back to the early '40s, '50s and '60s — even Elvis.

These individuals wrote things that were inspired, but not inspired by the Holy Spirit. There are things that people subject themselves to such as alcohol, drugs and other things. Some have even come out publically and said that they have sold their souls to the devil for success.

In the Bible we know that even when Elijah confronted prophets, there are prophets who are out there that are not prophets of YeHoVaH. And yet they say things that seemingly are fulfilled and therefore they have high esteem among the people of that group. Here we see that the Cretans had a prophet.

Noah was a preacher of righteousness.

(2 Peter 2:5) "And spared not the old world, but saved Noah as the eighth person, a preacher of righteousness, bringing the flood upon the world of the ungodly;"

Understand something. There were other people named Noah in the Bible and there were other floods. People who live in flood zones have to get flood insurance. Some of them have memories of floods of the past. There are some areas that hardly ever flood. When they do flood, there is a lasting memory because it is a very unusual situation or circumstance or event.

Peter here wants to make sure that people are not confusing Noah with some other Noahs during some other era. Therefore he classified him as the eighth person. Noah was a preacher of righteousness.

Abraham was spoken of as a prophet by YeHoVaH to Pharaoh. He told Pharaoh to restore Abraham's wife because Abraham was a prophet.

(Genesis 20:7) "Now therefore restore the man his wife; for he is a prophet, and he shall pray for thee, and thou shalt live: and if thou restore her not, know thou that thou shalt surely die, thou, and all that are thine."

We note that one of the words meaning "prophet" is **Naba.** The word here is **Nabiy**.

Isaac and Jacob had the Spirit of Prophecy upon them as they blessed their sons. When you talk about laying hands on their children and speaking over them; that is a wonderful thing. There are times when Father will inspire you to lay hands and to speak and he gives you the words to speak. So the Spirit of Prophecy was upon Isaac and upon Jacob. They spoke by divine revelation concerning their sons and what would be their outcome down through the generations; even with their descendants. (*Genesis 27; 48; 49; Hebrew 11:20, 21*)

(Hebrews 11:20-21) "By faith Isaac blessed Jacob and Esau concerning things to come. By faith Jacob, when he was a-dying, blessed both the sons of Joseph; and worshipped, leaning upon the top of his staff."

Here we remember when Isaac blessed Jacob. Through the workings of his Mother, he deceived his Father into thinking that he was Esau and he gave Jacob the blessing. You should note that there is a distinction because when Esau came, he said, "Don't you have a blessing for me?" And Jacob said, "Well, I don't," but he spoke some things over Esau.

Jacob laid his hands on Joseph's sons and in what YeHoVaH did — this is why I say to you that YeHoVaH doesn't have grandchildren.

I know that we as human beings have grandchildren, but note what happens here. Jacob takes his son, who now has two sons. These two sons would have been Jacob's grandsons. Jacob takes his grandsons and pronounces a blessing over Ephraim and Manasseh and elevates them to sonship on the same plain as the other sons or brothers of Joseph.

So now Jacob's grandsons are like his sons with sonship status. He elevates them from grandsons and brings them into sonship status. Today we have Ephraim and Manasseh on the same plain as Judah, Naphtali and Benjamin.

Joseph prophesied of the Exodus from Egypt (*Genesis 50:24, 25; Hebrews 11:22*).

(Genesis 50:24, 25) "And Joseph said unto his brethren, 'I die: and YeHoVaH will surely visit you, and bring you out of this land unto the land which he sware to Abraham, to Isaac, and to Jacob.' And Joseph took an oath of the children of Israel, saying, 'YeHoVaH will surely visit you, and ye shall carry up my bones from hence.'"

When Joseph died, there were several years (many, many years) that the children of Israel were in harsh bondage. That is because a new Pharaoh arose who did not know Joseph. Joseph knew prophetically because Abraham had spoken to Isaac and Isaac had spoken to Jacob and Jacob spoke to Joseph. This is prophecy that YeHoVaH had given to Abraham way back in *Genesis 12*. Joseph is holding onto what was given in *Genesis 50*. Generations later he is saying, "The Almighty is going to deliver you from this place. He is going to take you into the land that He swore to Abraham, to Isaac, and to Jacob."

Joseph is dying. He has knowledge of what is going to happen. He is saying to them, "When that day comes (because I am just as sure that that day is coming), the Almighty who spoke this does not lie. He watches over his word to perform it. It will not return to him empty. When the Almighty fulfills his promise, his word, his prophetic word that he spoke to Abraham, here is how you are to take care of me. I want you to take my bones out of this place."

(Hebrews 11:22) "By faith Joseph, when he died, made mention of the departing of the children of Israel; and gave commandment concerning his bones."

In *Numbers 11:24-30*, YeHoVaH took the Spirit that was upon Moses and placed it upon the seventy elders of Israel and they prophesied.

Numbers 11:24-30

I want to take a moment and look at some of these. As we are talking about this subject of prophecy and interpretation, we need to look at some of the examples.

We live in a time of individuality and independence. It has been from the beginning that Father established leadership. The thing about leadership is that no one is given power over another person that is dictatorial. Even Moses who was called by the Almighty to deliver the children of Israel was not given the authority to be a dictator.

He was given the authority to speak for YeHoVaH. The thing about leadership (and we are going to get into that in a few lessons) is that leaders are not dictators, but they do walk in authority.

People will either submit to that authority or they won't submit to that authority. When you submit to the authority that the Father has placed in your life, then the benefit of submitting to that authority is now yours to enjoy. If you refuse to submit to the authority that Father has placed in your life, then you will not see the benefits that the Father is trying to get to you.

No person can make you submit to that authority. Submission is an individual's response to a recognized authority and the desire to see the blessings of that authority manifesting in their lives.

YeHoVaH did not give the elders his Spirit. Notice what it says in verse 25. YeHoVaH had put his spirit upon Moses, but he took some of the Spirit that was on Moses that he had put on Moses and placed it upon the elders. What he was doing by taking the Spirit that was upon Moses and placing it upon the elders was bringing the elders under Moses' authority.

Whenever those who were under Moses' authority rebelled against Moses, YeHoVaH said, "They are not rebelling against you. They are rebelling against me." **When we rebel against the authority that the Father has placed in our lives, we are not rebelling against the authority in itself. We are rebelling against the one who placed that authority in our lives.**

This is why *Hebrews 13* says, "Obey them that have rule over you." That does not make them your ruler, but it does give them rule over you. They watch for your soul. They are watching. It is like a shepherd, not a hireling. It is like a shepherd who watches over the sheep. When the hireling sees a wolf coming, the hireling runs. A shepherd is going to stand there and defend those sheep against any intruder or predator. The shepherd will put his life on the line to protect those under his authority.

We live in a day of independence and individuality. "Who made you ruler over me?" "Who died and made you God?" "Who died and made you king?" Any leader who tries to force their authority upon people is now moving into a place where the enemy has a place to operate.

We need to understand authority. Authority is not a dictator. We have to submit, just like husbands and wives. There are foolish men out there who think they can rule their wives. Some wives put up with that for a minute and then say, "You aren't my Daddy. You're my husband. We're partners." When this partnership ceases to be a partnership, the partnership is dissolved and it is called "divorce."

Any man out there who is trying to rule his wife or who is trying to be a dictator will find that they can't. They will find that if a wife refuses to submit to that dictation, she is free to leave. Some men get violent and try to force submission. That will cause you to go to jail because you have no right to put your hand on or to be violent toward another person who refuses to submit to you.

"You are supposed to submit to me." "Oh, yeah?" "Yes!" And you might be right, but it is *my choice* to submit to you just because you are my husband or my boss. It is just like some of you who say, "I quit" and you leave your job. Or when some of you say, "I am not longer going to be a member of this ministry" and you leave that ministry. What you are saying is, "I no longer submit to the authority that you have to this job. You are no longer my boss." And as far as a wife or husband, they are saying "We are done."

Moses was a leader appointed by YeHoVaH. The elders were appointed under Moses' leadership. When those elders rebelled or those who were under Moses' leadership rebelled, it cost some of them their lives. For others, it cost them serpent bites and for others, it caused their carcasses to be wasted in the desert unable to enter into the land of promise that was promised by the Almighty.

The Almighty did not break his promise. By taking their children into the Promised Land, he fulfilled the promise he made to Abraham.

We read about Eldad and Medad. They were written among the elders, but they were not with them when the Spirit was taken off of Moses and placed upon them. Even though they were not there, the Spirit that was taken off of Moses also rested upon them.

Here Moses put up a wish, if you would; a petition. What he is saying is, "If I had my way about it, all of YeHoVaH's people would be prophets." This is a very powerful, powerful statement. You see, Moses from day one did not want to be responsible for these people. When YeHoVaH tried to get Moses to go into Egypt to get them, he tried to talk YeHoVaH out of the calling.

YeHoVaH said, "Well, if you don't want to answer my calling, I'll just kill you and find somebody else." He was not about to let Moses go. As a matter of fact, even after Moses answered the call, the Bible says that there was an angel of YeHoVaH who was prepared to kill Moses. But because of what his wife did in circumcising his son, the anger of YeHoVaH was quelled. He repented. He didn't follow through, if you would.

So Moses is saying, "I do not want to be responsible for these people." Real leadership really does not want the job. These people who have ambition to rule over people don't have a clue as to what they are getting themselves into.

Let me tell you something about people. People will let you rule over them as long as they are getting something out of it. It is when YeHoVaH calls you to say things to people that they don't like, that they don't want to hear. Now they are ready to hang you up on a stake.

The real prophets of YeHoVaH are going to speak for YeHoVaH, not to itching ears. The false prophets and the hireling prophets are going to prophe-LIE. They are going to prophesy for money. They are going to do what they do to benefit themselves.

The true prophets of YeHoVaH will speak for YeHoVaH even if it brings the death penalty at the hands of those that YeHoVaH is trying to communicate with. And I've got to tell you, of all of the mess that I have had to endure, to stand and to proclaim week after week after week and to speak what YeHoVaH is putting into my heart to speak, I endure. I endure the attacks I get, even from people who supposedly love me. There are emails and phone calls and people calling and cussing me out on the phone. People write to me and leave nasty messages that I'm "under a curse." I'm "under the law." I'm "straight from hell." I have "my theology mixed up." I have to endure this mess and keep moving.

Then there are those who have tapped into Judaism and tradition and hype. You have folks who are hype masters and who are always pitching hype. They are coming up with schemes and all kinds of other things to get people on board. We have to plow and plow and say things that people may not want to hear. We have to avoid this and not go into that and say things that cause people to look at other people with one eyebrow raised.

I am not out here to try to throw anybody under the bus, but the proof will put you under the bus. If you don't want to hear it, you either fall on that rock (that word) or that word falls on you. Wisdom is crying out and trying to get people's attention. People reject wisdom until they get into trouble. Then they cry out for wisdom and wisdom does not hear them.

It is like, "I tried to tell you." You have heard that old saying, "You made your bed, now lie in it." There are people who are on a path of destruction. YeHoVaH says, "I love you too much to watch you go down this path of destruction. Repent! Repent! Repent! Turn, turn, turn!" And people say, "I am not going to repent. I am not going to turn!" Then when they are down on their faces and bleeding with nowhere to turn they say, "Oh, God! Help me! Help!"

I imagine there are people who say stuff like, "You're a Christian. You're supposed to help me." Oh, yeah? Where do you get that from?

When you look at the children of Israel, you wonder how many years they cried out before YeHoVaH actually responded to the cry. There were hundreds of years of bondage, seventy years of captivity and exile from the land. "Oh, God! Help me! Help me!" YeHoVaH says, "I warned you. I told you. If you diligently hearken to obey these commands, all of these blessings will come upon you. If you do not hearken to obey these commands, all of these curses will come upon you. What part of 'all of these curses' don't you understand?"

Now that people are experiencing the curses. They are going through difficulties and hardships and you have these bleeding heart Christians who are talking about how, "You ought to be nicer. You ought to…" Listen to where you come from.

Don't you know the word? No. I'm not here to beat people up, but I'm not going to compromise the word because somebody doesn't want to hear it. Let them do what their ancestors did — close their ears.

Believe it not, that is what the Pharisees and the Sadducees did. They closed their ears and began to cry out. "We don't want to hear that! Kill him! Crucify him!" It was just like they did to all of the prophets.

YeHoVaH raises up prophets to a generation. He sends them to the people and they end up crucifying them.

Let me tell you something. I am under no delusions of grandeur. I know my standing in the place of the prophets before me, just like Yeshua said to his disciples.

(Matthew 5:10-12) "Blessed are they which are persecuted for righteousness' sake: for theirs is the kingdom of heaven. Blessed are ye, when men shall revile you, and persecute you, and shall say all manner of evil against you falsely, for my sake. Rejoice, and be exceeding glad: for great is your reward in heaven: for so persecuted they the prophets which were before you."

When people revile you, it is not a pretty sight. Persecution is not something that you throw a party for. They are calling you names. They are calling you a "cult." They are calling you a "false teacher" or a "false prophet." They are calling you all kinds of not so nice things.

I had someone write me about a response they had received from the Christmas message. The person went on the attack and then wrote "I haven't watched the teaching." They are responding but they haven't even watched the teaching. It is like, "Why are you saying that my theology is all screwed up or that I am some person who doesn't know? Why are you saying that I am under the law or that I am under some curse but you haven't watched the teaching yet?"

"I'll watch it and maybe I'll learn something."

Maybe you will. I have never understood why people respond without even hearing it. I have had people just go off. They look for reasons to go off.

Let me tell you something. Rejoicing in this situation is easier said than done. It is hard to rejoice when you are under persecution. It is hard to rejoice, especially a person like me. I love to be liked. I think most of us like being liked. We don't like people who have learned to be hated. Now they think that everybody hates them and they thrive on that. I like to be liked. People who love the Almighty for the most part, want to be liked.

When people say nice things about us, we like that. We don't let it go to our head. But when people spew venom and just come at you with all kinds of negativity, this is what the prophets dealt with.

Imagine one raised up by YeHoVaH and sent to YeHoVaH's people to tell his people what they should have already known and should have already been doing. They are sent to tell his people, "You are not doing what I told you to do. You need to turn. You need to repent. You need to get your act together. You need to start living according to my word or let me tell you what is going to happen. You think you have it bad now."

The Spirit that was upon Moses, YeHoVaH put upon the elders. He said that he wished that all of YeHoVaH's people were prophets. I can kind of feel Moses at this point. Here it is on a couple of occasions (at least) that Father wanted to destroy his people and start over.

In one particular case he said, "Moses, let me at 'em." Moses petitioned the Almighty on behalf of this hardhearted, stiff-necked, rebellious people. It was even to the point where YeHoVaH says, "Your people which YOU brought out of Egypt." He disowned them, in other words. He says, "They are not MY people, Moses. They are YOUR people." He said, "Let me kill all of them and start over." Moses said, "Don't do that. What will the nations say?"

So Moses says, "If all of YeHoVaH's people were prophets." Do you know what that means? That means now that — I love this. I absolutely love this. That means now that when people want to hear from YeHoVaH, they don't have to come to me. They can go to him themselves.

This is the heart of YeHoVaH; that all of his people are prophets. He says that when he pours out his Spirit, his sons and daughters will prophesy. **You will have the ability to hear the voice of the Almighty, to learn his voice, to walk by his voice and to be led by his Spirit.** This is what Moses is saying, "I wish all of your people were prophets." They won't have to wear me out with all of this counsel and with all of this "need to know" and "what do you mean by thats."

But until that day comes, YeHoVaH has people that he has placed in authority to speak for him. And then you have people who reject that authority. They fail to submit to that authority. They continue that stiff-necked, hardhearted, rebellious spirit as it was in the day of Moses.

Let me tell you something. Submitting to authority does not make you weak. It does not make you incompetent. It does not make you less of a person than the authority that you submit to. As a matter of fact, it takes great courage, great strength and great faith to submit to authority.

When Yeshua had the centurion who came to him and told him about his servant, Yeshua says, "I will come to your house." The centurion said, "No! You don't have to come to my house. I am a man of authority and I understand authority. All you have to do is speak the word and it shall be."

When you understand authority, submitting to that authority does not make you less of a person. As a matter of fact it validates the authority that you have.

The devil wants to pervert people's minds to think, "Oh, you think you are better than me." No, no. Absolutely not. You have to understand that with the authority comes (get this) *the* Authority.

When one has been given authority from heaven, one has authority in heaven to command things. And because of that authority, heaven backs up that authority. When people walk in false authority, they don't have the authority of heaven. Instead, they give place to the enemy.

⌕ *1 Samuel 19:20-24*

In this passage, the Spirit of Prophecy fell upon several groups of messengers as well as upon King Saul. When you look at this, Saul was king, but the point is that even though the king was the sole legal authority over the people, the voice of YeHoVaH was with the prophet.

Now, the kings could have the prophets put to death. The prophets could not have the kings put to death, but the kings could have the prophets killed. Do you see this? If the king was wise, he would heed the voice of YeHoVaH spoken through the prophet. The king did not have to listen to the prophet. The king was the sole authority.

What made the distinction between a Godly king and an evil king was YeHoVaH's instructions. The ungodly kings did what they pleased and didn't care or yield or give heed to anybody other than themselves. The righteous king, the holy king knew that there was one greater than themselves and that he had prophets. When those prophets came and spoke, they knew that those prophets spoke for YeHoVaH Almighty who put them in the position of authority that they operated in.

A good king listened to the prophets. A bad, evil king killed them.

When the power of YeHoVaH, the authority of YeHoVaH is revealed, it is so important. That authority, that Spirit; that which YeHoVaH has placed upon those whom he has chosen to be his spokesperson now begins to flow upon those who yield and submit to the authority.

They don't have to. You don't have to. It is amazing in this Messianic community, that people are so — it is almost like there is such rebellion and such hardhearted, stiff-necked people that they don't want anybody telling them what to do. As a matter of fact, they want to tell the prophets what to do. They want to tell the apostles and the elders what to do and they seemingly have no remorse and no restraint whatsoever.

That is your right. You are free to say whatever you want to say, but let me tell you something. Free speech ain't free. You will be held accountable for your words, every one of them. Some people have a tendency to just say whatever comes to their mind. They think that they can say anything to anybody any time they want. That is because they have freedom of expression and freedom of speech. They say, "You are not my Daddy" and "You are not my king." There are even people who say, "You are not my husband," but they don't listen to their husband. It is amazing.

Then you have these others who are out there trying to force their authority upon other people. I would say to you that you need to stop that. There is no authority other than the authority that YeHoVaH has given.

If you walk in that authority, that doesn't mean that anyone has to submit themselves to that authority. Yeshua says it this way. "Whoever gives a glass of water to a prophet will receive a prophet's reward."

When you recognize a prophet, you understand the authority that the prophet comes in. When you recognize authority, you understand the authority that is there. You either submit to that authority or you rebel against that authority. When you rebel against that authority, you will pay the price.

It may not be by the authority, but it will be by the one who gave the authority in the first place.

Remember that the authority is given by the authority. When people rebel against those in whom he has given that authority, they are not rebelling against that person. They are rebelling against him and he knows. You can leave. You can go. You can say, "I am outta here," but let me tell you something. Just like David who understood that no matter where he went, he was there; YeHoVaH is there. He said that if he went to the depth of the sea or to the highest mountain, he is there. You can get away from them whom he has sent, but you can't get away from him.

It is important for us to understand prophets and prophecy and the interpretation thereof. You also need to know that there is a difference between the gift of prophecy and the office of prophet. Every one of YeHoVaH's people is supposed to prophesy. That does not make you a prophet. There are people whom because they have the ability to prophesy, think that if they lay hands on a few people, that means that they have a healing ministry. All of us have a healing ministry.

These signs shall follow them that believe. If you are a believer, you have a healing ministry. If you are a believer, you have a prophetic ministry. But that doesn't make you a prophet or a prophetess.

The Ability to Prophesy is a Promise

We find that promise in *Joel 2* and we find that promise being fulfilled in *Acts 2*. In the book of *Joel* we read:

(Joel 2:28-29) "And it shall come to pass afterward, that I will pour out my spirit upon all flesh; and your sons and your daughters shall prophesy, your old men shall dream dreams, your young men shall see visions: And also upon the servants and upon the handmaids in those days will I pour out my spirit."

This is the promise. The ability to prophecy is a promise. Every believer has the ability to prophecy — every one of you. If you have the Spirit of YeHoVaH, the Spirit of Prophecy should manifest. But in order for the Spirit of Prophecy to manifest in your life, you have to recognize and receive this ability as the promise. It is a promise just as much as any promise of Abraham.

People say, "I am an heir. I am Abraham's seed. I am grafted in." YeHoVaH's promise to prophesy is just as valid as any promise in the Bible. If you are going to stand on any promise of YeHoVaH's, the promise to prophesy is a promise directly from YeHoVaH.

We are going to pick this up in the next lesson when we get into the interpretation of prophesy, looking at the promise to prophesy, the ability to prophesy, the gift of prophecy and the offices of prophets and prophetess. We are going to look at that too. I think you are going to be amazed and astonished at the things that are going to be unveiled in these teachings.

Class 99 Study Summary

Key Points

1. The nature of prophecy is basically two-fold: forth-telling and foretelling. To forth-tell is to speak what the Almighty has said. To foretell is to be shown by the Almighty some future event that is to come and to speak that to the people.

2. In *1 Corinthians 15:33* Paul is quoting from a Greek poet. He does this several times in his writings. He quotes his contemporaries, but that doesn't make those quotes scripture.

3. When we rebel against the authority that the Father has placed in our lives, we are rebelling not against the authority in itself. We are rebelling against the one who placed that authority in our life. We are rebelling against the Almighty.

4. We need to understand authority. We are not to rule over one another. We are to submit to authority. When you understand authority, it doesn't make you less of a person. It validates the authority that you have.

5. The true prophets of YeHoVaH speak for him even under pain of death.

6. The Spirit that was upon Moses, YeHoVaH put upon the seventy elders. This was a corporate filling of the Spirit.

7. You have the ability to hear the voice of the Almighty, to learn his voice and to be led by his Spirit.

8. When the Almighty pours out his Spirit, sons and daughters will prophesy. The ability to prophesy is a promise.

9. When one has been given authority from heaven, one has authority in heaven to command things and because of that authority, heaven backs up that authority. Heaven has no obligation to back false authority or authority that has not been given.

10. If you are a believer, you have a healing ministry.

Review Exercise

1. The first century was hip-deep in prophets. How would someone figure out if a prophet was a prophet?

_____

_____

_____

_____

_____

_____

2. Bible prophets had authority problems. We know that every last one of them was killed. What does this say about YeHoVaH's people?

_____

_____

_____

_____

_____

_____

3. How do you feel when someone challenges or worse, denies your authority in whatever area? Describe a time that occurred. Indicate what the area of authority was, who gave you the authority and who it was that confronted your authority. What was the outcome?

_____

_____

_____

_____

_____

_____

_____

_____

_____

_____

_____

Rate the following statements
by filling in the most appropriate number.

(1 = I do not agree 10 = I agree completely)

Objectives:

1. I can define concepts from the last lesson about the nature of prophecy.

    1. ◯   2. ◯   3. ◯   4. ◯   5. ◯   6. ◯   7. ◯   8. ◯   9. ◯   10. ◯

2. I can explain authority as a function of prophetic utterance.

    1. ◯   2. ◯   3. ◯   4. ◯   5. ◯   6. ◯   7. ◯   8. ◯   9. ◯   10. ◯

3. I can describe what is meant by the ability to prophesy.

    1. ◯   2. ◯   3. ◯   4. ◯   5. ◯   6. ◯   7. ◯   8. ◯   9. ◯   10. ◯

My Journal

What I learned from this class:

_____

_____

_____

_____

_____

_____

_____

_____

_____

_____

_____

_____

_____

_____

_____

_____

_____

_____

_____

Discipleship Training Class 100

The Interpretation of Prophecy (part 3)

Objectives:

As a Discipleship student, at the end of this class you will be able to:

- Define the gift of prophecy
- Explain what the office of a prophet is and what it means
- Describe how scripture itself prophesies
- Identify evidence that Yeshua was a prophet

Prophecy is something that we should all do. Every last one of us should be able to prophesy. Prophesying is the manifestation that the Holy Spirit has been given to us. Unlike what many would say, the manifestation or the evidence of the Holy Spirit residing in our lives is the ability to speak in other tongues.

Well, the Bible teaches that when the Spirit is poured out upon all flesh, sons and daughters will prophesy. Young men will see visions. Old men will dream dreams. This outpouring of the Holy Spirit is going to be upon all — sons, daughters, handmaidens, servants, all those who are far off and all that the Almighty will call. That is a promise.

We find that prophecy (again) must not be confused. The gift of prophecy must not be confused with the office of prophet. We looked at *Joel 2*. Today we are going to take a look in *Acts 2*.

Acts 2

Look at verse 16. In *Acts 2* we see the fulfillment of what Joel is talking about. Here is where we have to understand prophecy and the proper interpretation of prophecy. Prophecy has to be properly interpreted because if it is misinterpreted, then doctrines and theological views that are inaccurate will emerge and take hold within society.

Again, Joel said that the sign of the outpouring of the Holy Spirit will be prophesying. Sons and daughters will prophesy. We read that in the last lesson. Peter comes along in *Acts 2* and says:

(Acts 2:15-16) *"For these are not drunken, as ye suppose, seeing it is but the third hour of the day. But this is that which was spoken by the prophet Joel;"*

A huge misunderstanding has evolved from what Peter said; comparing what Peter said to what has preceded what he is saying. What has preceded what he is saying and what has occurred is that the Holy Spirit had been given, as we find in *Acts 2:1-2.*

Now with "this house," if you look at the word "house" there, we in our Western understanding see a dwelling place. We see a place where people live. And this is what has caused people to think that they must have been in an "upper room." The "house" that is spoken of here, the House of YeHoVaH is what is being referred to here. It is the House of YeHoVaH.

We note that in *Acts 1* there were 120 people. There were 120 in this environment. Peter would stand in the midst of them. If you understand Hebrew culture, where the men stay and where the women stay are going to be separate quarters. When we look at where Peter, James, John and those individuals were staying, the men lived there. These were living quarters, but here it is talking about the House of YeHoVaH.

As David would say, "Let us go up to the House of YeHoVaH." The House of the Lord, if you would. Here Peter is interpreting what is taking place. They were in one accord. They were all filled; all of the house. It filled all of the house where they were sitting.

(Acts 2:3-4) *"And there appeared unto them cloven tongues like as of fire, and it sat upon each of them. And they were all filled with the Holy Ghost, and began to speak with other tongues, as the Spirit gave them utterance."*

Here is where individuals now say, "See? Here is the evidence of the filling of the Holy Spirit because they spoke in tongues." That is partially true. It is certainly partially true.

(Acts 2:5-6) *"And there were dwelling at Jerusalem Jews, devout men, out of every nation under heaven. Now when this was noised abroad, the multitude came together, and were confounded, because that every man heard them speak in his own language."*

Those who were filled with the Holy Spirit spoke in tongues, but those who were from faraway places heard those that were speaking in tongues in their own language. So what you have are tongues and interpretation of tongues. You have speaking in tongues and you have interpretation of tongues.

Now, those who stand on the fact that tongues is the evidence of one being filled with the Holy Spirit, obviously they stop at verse 4 and don't continue. You stop at a particular verse or you go to a particular verse and make the argument — "See! There it is! When they were filled with the Holy Spirit, they spoke in tongues." Yes, they did.

But in verse 6, it says that they heard. Every man heard in their own language. Now what we see is that this was not some gibberish. This was not somebody tarrying at the altar to get some language that no one understands.

In verse 7 and following, it tells us the tongues that they spoke in.

🔍 *Acts 2:7-11*

"They are speaking in tongues, but we are hearing it in our own language, from where we were born." It goes on to tell us where these individuals were born (verses 9-11). They not only heard them speaking in tongues, but they interpreted what was being spoken in their own language. It appears that there were many languages. And distance-wise, almost up to 1,000 miles away, these individuals had come up to Jerusalem for the Feast of Shavuot.

What you actually see here is tongues and the interpretation of tongues. Paul in *1 Corinthians 14* tells us:

(1 Corinthians 14:5) *"I would that ye all spake with tongues but rather that ye prophesied: for greater is he that prophesieth than he that speaketh with tongues, except he interpret, that the church may receive edifying."*

What he is saying is that if you speak in tongues and there is the interpretation of tongues, people understand what you are saying. This takes it out of gibberish with no one understanding, to tongues with understanding. So you have the interpretation of tongues.

The Gift of Prophecy

This is mentioned in *1 Corinthians 12:10* as one of the manifestations of the Spirit. Prophecy can be defined as the God-given ability to speak forth supernaturally as the Spirit gives utterance.

(1 Corinthians 12:10) *"To another the working of miracles; to another prophecy; to another discerning of spirits; to another divers kinds of tongues; to another the interpretation of tongues:"*

You see that within the manifestations you will have tongues with interpretation. Prophecy can be revealed as being an operation of the Spirit in the New Testament community of believers.

Guidelines are given when the manifestation is operational within a congregational gathering. When prophecy is in operation, there are guidelines and there are rules. When tongues are in operation, there are guidelines and there are rules. In places where there are no guidelines and rules being adhered to, you have chaos. You have everybody doing their own thing.

Believe me. I have been a lot of places that are chaotic. People think that everybody is speaking in tongues. No one can interpret and somebody walks in who does not have a clue as to what is going on. They are thinking that these people are nuts. Some of us have been in places where people have been speaking in tongues and where there has been no interpretation of tongues and they look and sound like nut cases.

Not only can the prophets speak, but you can all prophesy according to these verses.

🔍 *1 Corinthians 14:1-3, 5, 29-33*

That is every believer according to *Joel 2* and *Acts 2*. When the outpouring of the Holy Spirit is given, the evidence is that you will prophesy. We have looked at prophecy as foretelling and forth-telling. When we begin to talk about prophecy, when it comes to prophesying, **prophesying is one speaking by inspiration of the Spirit that which is being revealed by the Almighty.** They are not coming up with stuff. They are speaking what YeHoVaH is giving them to speak.

In the Bible here, Paul says to desire that. Pentecostalism is teaching people to run all over the place looking for tongues. They teach people to learn how to speak in tongues instead of teaching people to desire the actual biblical manifestation of the Holy Spirit, which is prophecy. This is because of the misinterpretation.

(1 Corinthians 14:2) *"For he that speaketh in an unknown tongue speaketh not unto men, but unto God: for no man understandeth him; howbeit in the spirit he speaketh mysteries."*

When you speak in tongues, you are speaking to the Almighty. This is a conversation between you and the Almighty. It is not a conversation for you and I. You are speaking to the Almighty. Understand something. There is you speaking to the Almighty and then there is the Almighty speaking to you. We need to understand that, because you can speak in a tongue to the Almighty. But when the Almighty is speaking to you, that is the gift of tongues.

There is going to be the interpretation of tongues if it is a public setting. If it is a private setting, then it is just you and the Almighty. We are going to see that where there is no interpretation in a conversation between you and the Almighty, then you speak quietly to the Almighty. Don't be interrupting us with your conversation with the Almighty so that we have no clue as to what is being discussed.

It is like being at the table with two people who are speaking a language that you don't understand. Have you ever been in that situation? You are sitting here in the company of folks and they are speaking to you. They are speaking to one another and then they get into a conversation in a foreign language and dialect. You don't have a clue as to what is going on. It makes you want to say, "If you all want to have a private conversation, take that conversation out of my earshot or speak English!" We really want to say, "Speak English!"

(1 Corinthians 14:3-4) *"But he that prophesieth speaketh unto men to edification, and exhortation, and comfort. He that speaketh in an unknown tongue edifieth himself; but he that prophesieth edifieth the church."*

Now in verse 5:

(1 Corinthians 14:5) *"I would that ye all spake with tongues but rather that ye prophesied: for greater is he that prophesieth than he that speaketh with tongues, except he interpret, that the church may receive edifying."*

When someone is having a conversation at your table in an unknown language, you have no clue as to what is being said. They may be speaking praises of you. They may be saying nice things about you or they may be saying the opposite. The problem is that you don't know what they are saying. But when they speak in a language that you understand, you now know what is being said and you feel part of the conversation and not alienated.

⌕ *1 Corinthians 14:29-33*

Let's backtrack a little bit to verse 26 to set this up.

(1 Corinthians 14:26-28) "How is it then, brethren? when ye come together, every one of you hath a Psalm, hath a doctrine, hath a tongue, hath a revelation, hath an interpretation. Let all things be done unto edifying. If any man speak in an unknown tongue, let it be by two, or at the most by three, and that by course; and let one interpret. But if there be no interpreter, let him keep silence in the church; and let him speak to himself, and to God."

There is a difference between being silent and not speaking. He is saying here to let that person speak in private. Let that person speak quietly because it is a conversation between him and Elohim. It is like there should be a whisper, not some rambunctious tongue trying to impress the assembly and here you are having a conversation with the Almighty. If you go to have a conversation within our earshot, then let there be interpretation so that we understand what is being said.

There are rules. Now to verse 29 and following.

*(1 Corinthians 14:29-33) "Let the prophets speak two or three, and let the other judge. If anything be revealed to another that sitteth by, let the first hold his peace. For **ye may all prophesy** one by one, that all may learn, and all may be comforted. And the spirits of the prophets are subject to the prophets. For God is not the author of confusion, but of peace, as in all churches of the saints."*

Every last one of you can prophesy. Let's just do it in order. Let's not have everybody jumping up saying, "I got a word!" Then you have three or four people prophesying at the same time. It sounds like gibberish. Have you ever been in a conversation where you have two or three people trying to speak, even in a language you understand? I can only listen to one person at a time. I can't listen to three conversations. Some people can, but you don't get the whole thing. You get bits and pieces. If you walk away from a conversation with bits and pieces of a conversation, then chances are you did not hear correctly. You have bits and pieces.

What he is saying is operate in the gifts. Operate in the manifestations just like you would operate in the natural. Operate in the spiritual things with the same respect and regard as you would if you were having a natural conversation with people if you want to understand what you were communicating.

When it comes down to prophecy, there is some confusion here. We are talking about the interpretation of prophecy. **The Bible says that we are not to despise prophesying.** You will find that most Messianics despise prophesying. The reason why people despise prophesying is because there has been a lot of prophe-LYING. There have been all kinds of people out there who are speaking, "The Lord has said" and he hasn't spoken. "Thus saith the Lord." They all ought to go and sit down somewhere.

This is why you should even be able to judge the prophesies. As we see with the rules, if there are two or three at the most, then let the other ones judge to see if what is being spoken is really of YeHoVaH or if somebody is just making something up.

I am going to tell you that when you are in the presence of prophets and there is a legitimate Spirit of Prophecy, you will find that people who don't typically normally prophesy, will begin to prophesy because the Spirit of Prophesy has filled the place.

We see this with Saul and with David. Saul was mistaken for the prophet. He sent individuals down there to confront some things and they got in the company of the prophets and started prophesying. He sent some more folks and they started prophesying. He sent some more folks. Then he said, "Wait a minute. I'll go myself." Then he ended up naked and prophesying. People said, "Is Saul a prophet?" In the company of prophets, you prophesy. When you come into the company of legitimate prophecy and the Spirit of Prophecy, you will find yourself prophesying.

Don't despise it.

(1 Thessalonians 5:17-21) *"Pray without ceasing. In everything give thanks: for this is the will of God in Christ Jesus concerning you. Quench not the Spirit. Despise not prophesying. Prove all things; hold fast that which is good."*

In everything gives thanks. It took awhile for me to learn the value of giving thanks to the Almighty. People who give thanks to the Almighty for everything that happens in their lives are people who understand that nothing happens in their life without the permission of the Almighty.

If the Almighty is allowing certain things to happen in our lives, that means that he is trying to get us someplace. He is trying to teach us something or trying to get us away from something. He is either trying to teach us something, trying to get us someplace or trying to get us away from something. We attach to things in a physical, emotional or natural way. There are things that we attach ourselves to that please our natural man, but which grieve the Almighty.

The Almighty has given specific instructions that certain things are not to be done and yet because people are led by emotions, they get themselves entangled in things. When they get entangled, they develop these ties, these soul ties, these bonds that become bondage.

It is really disturbing sometimes to watch what are so-called Christian movies, Christian plays and things that are done within church environments.

You come to find that many people are sleeping around, fornicating, committing adultery and lying. You have individuals who are having children and they are ministering. They are psalmists. They are praise leaders and worship leaders.

People have a tendency to overlook these basic abominations before the Almighty. They have rejected the abominations that the Almighty says because they are contained in the Old Testament. There are valid reasons why people want to disregard or discard the Old Testament.

That is because the Old Testament is filled with YeHoVaH's Laws that point out what lawlessness is.

"I don't want to know what lawlessness is. I just want to walk in love," so they disregard all of that "law" stuff. Like Paul says, "How in the world are you going to know what sin is if you don't know what the law says?" "I don't want to know what sin is. I'll determine what sin is. Sin will be the stuff I don't like." That is basically what it is. "I don't like broccoli or spinach. That is an abomination." And yet with the abominable things like shrimp and lobster and crab and swine and honey-baked ham it is, "Oh, I love that." The things that YeHoVaH calls abominable, people love. The things that people call abominable, the Father does not (unless of course we are on the same page as the Father).

But when it comes down to giving thanks, when you have committed your life to the Almighty, there are things that he allows to happen that is for the purpose of preparing us for where he is calling us to. It is hard to be compassionate if you have not been in situations that require compassion. The Bible tells us that he who has been forgiven much, they love much. People who have been forgiven little, love little.

That does not mean that you have to run out there and commit transgressions. That occurs simply from living. You have people who love the Almighty. They want to serve him with all of their heart, mind, soul and strength; but who make stupid mistakes. They get caught up in emotions. You have people who want to help people. The Father is saying, "No, don't help that person." That is somebody who has consistently rejected wisdom that has been crying out.

The Bible says in *Proverbs* that wisdom cries out in the marketplace. Wisdom is crying out all over the place, but you reject wisdom. Then calamity comes upon you and then you cry out for wisdom. Wisdom will now ignore you. It will not respond.

There are people who have consistently disregarded the way of the Almighty. They have run from him. They come to a place where they really haven't repented. They just want help. I am down on my luck. I want help. I want to get back up on my feet. Why? So you can continue to run.

You help them get on their feet and they do exactly what you knew they were going to do. They run completely in the opposite direction and now they need help again. You bail them out. They run some more.

You will find that some people who are Christians go through stuff. They say they are believers. Then they get mad at the Almighty. They just quit fellowship. They are saying, "I still love the Lord. I just don't want to be around his people."

Let me tell you something. This is how you know that the love of YeHoVaH is in you; when you love his people. When you start getting away from his people and start hanging out with people that are not his people, then who are you really loving? Your actions are telling you who you love. What people say with their mouths does not mean a whole lot to me anymore. I used to believe people and what they said. I now say, "I believe you, but I want to see your actions. I want to see your words. I don't want to hear your words. I want to see them."

"Are you walking by sight brother?" No, I am not walking by sight. I am like John. John says, "You say you repent. Bring fruit worthy of repentance. Show me your repentance. Show me your faith." Faith is something visible. Faith is not just words. It is an action.

Do you see this? Despise not prophesying. You have people despising prophecy and claiming to be Torah-observant. How are you going to despise prophecy without despising the one who gives it? "I don't need that gift from God. I don't need tongues from God. I don't need that from God. I just need this, this and this (and that is fine). Who are you to determine what you need?

He knows what you need before you ask. If he didn't think you needed these things, I don't believe our loving Father would have given us things we don't need. We may not understand the need for them, but he knows the end from the beginning. He knows what we need and he supplies all of our needs. How dare we despise something; declaring we don't need it when he is the one who is giving it and saying, "Hey, yes you do. You are rebellious, stiff-necked and hard-hearted."

That is not the will of the Father for you. The will of the Father is that in everything you give thanks. Okay? I have been in places where they don't prophesy correctly. If you understood the Spirit of Prophecy, the gift of prophecy and the work of a prophet, then you now should be able to judge whether or not and test the spirit to see if these things are of YeHoVaH.

With some things, the only way you will know is whether they come to pass.

The Office of a Prophet

Philip had some daughters.

🔍 *Acts 21:8-9*

We know that this was not Philip who was one of the apostles. This is Philip who was one of "the seven." These seven are the *diakonos,* the deacons.

We are going to look at the office of a prophet. Abraham was the first man to bear the title. Remember when we talk about the first mention principle, that there is the first time a word is mentioned, but there is also the first time that the word is demonstrated.

The first person who prophesied was Adam. Adam prophesied:

(Genesis 2:23-24) "*...bone of my bone, flesh of my flesh, for this cause shall a man leave his father and his mother, cleave unto his wife and the two shall become one flesh.*"

That was prophetic.

Enoch prophesied, we read in *Jude*. Abraham was the first person to bear the title "prophet."

(Genesis 20:7) *"Now return the man's wife, **for he is a prophet**, and he will pray for you and you will live. But if you do not return her, you may be sure that you and all yours will die."*

That is the kind of relationship you want to have with the Almighty — where he now gets in people's faces while you are outside of the gate trying to figure out how to get into the gate. You are out there praying. You are in right standing with the Almighty. You are asking the Almighty to make a way out of no way. The whole time the Almighty has the person on the inside who has the authority to open the gate. He has him up against the wall, saying, "Listen. You better open that gate and let my servant in or I am going to mop the floor with everybody inside of this gate."

That is the kind of relationship you want. You don't need to make threats. When the Father says, "No, son. Just step back. I've got this." You just relax. Let him fight your battle. "The battle is not yours. It is mine and I can do a lot more than you will ever do." We need to learn to rest in the Almighty.

This goes back to *Thessalonians* when he declares "give thanks in all things." When you trust the Almighty, you put your life in his hands. And even though by your natural sight things don't look like they are lining up, you don't have a clue that the Father outside of your peripheral view is fighting on your behalf. All you know is that because you stood and when you have done everything you know to do to stand, then the doors open. Then you say, "Yes. That's my Elohim. He is always fighting on my behalf." Or you can get into your flesh, which I advise you not to do. Don't walk in the flesh. Walk in the Spirit.

The word there is **H5030** — ***nabiy***, naw-bee'; from **H5012**; a prophet or (generally) inspired man:--prophecy, that prophesy, prophet.

We are going to **H5012** — ***naba'***, naw-baw'; a primitive root, to prophesy, i.e. speak (or sing) by inspiration (in prediction or simple discourse):--prophesy(-ing), make self a prophet.[7]

The last prophet before Yeshua was John the Baptist/Yochanan the Immerser.

(Luke 7:26-27) *"But what went ye out for to see? A prophet? Yea, I say unto you, and much more than a prophet (**proteses**, prof-ay'tace). This is he, of whom it is written, Behold, I send my messenger before thy face, which shall prepare thy way before thee."*

G4396 — ***proteses***, prof-ay'-tace; from the compound of **G4253** and **G5346**; a foreteller ("prophet"); by analogy an inspired speaker; by extension a poet: -- prophet.

The last prophetess before Yeshua was Anna.

G4398 ***prophetis***, prof-ay-tis, feminine of **G4396**, a female foreteller or an inspired woman:--prophetess.

-----

[7] You certainly don't want to make yourself a prophet, but there are people who did that. They made themselves a prophet.

Anna was a prophetess. This is the feminine of the word "prophet." A prophetess is a female foreteller. A prophet is a male foreteller.

> *(**Luke 2:36**) "And there was one Anna, a prophetess, the daughter of Phanuel, of the tribe of Aser: she was of a great age, and had lived with an husband seven years from her virginity;"*

Yeshua was The Prophet

> *(**Acts 7:37**) "This is that Moses, which said unto the children of Israel, '**A prophet** shall YeHoVaH your Elohim raise up unto you of your brethren, like unto me; him shall ye hear.'"*

Moses is speaking prophetically concerning the Messiah, but he is also speaking concerning the prophets who would come. Every prophet that spoke for YeHoVaH we had to listen to and obey or it would cost. When the prophets came and began to speak to the people concerning the things that they had done, the things that the Father is requiring of them to do, the Bible says that they killed the prophets. The prophets went through hell (if you would) trying to get YeHoVaH's people to return. When you have people who are bent on doing their own thing and trying to force YeHoVaH into their will versus submitting to his will, then you will have people who will use scripture to justify their actions, even though their actions are wrong.

> *(**Acts 7:38**) "This is he (Moses), that was in the church in the wilderness with the angel which spake unto him in the mount Sina, [Sinai] and with our fathers: who receive the lively oracles to give unto us:"*

This has a lot to do with the interpretation of prophecy. Many teach today that the "church" was born at Pentecost. They say that when the Holy Spirit was given, the church was born. Well, interestingly enough, here in the Greek we have this term. We are going to find that every time we see the word "church" in the New Testament, we find that it is related to the Greek word *ekklesia*. It is the same thing here.

> *(**John 7:37-40**) "In the last day, the great day of the feast, Jesus stood and cried, saying, 'If any man thirst, let him come unto me, and drink. He that believeth on me, as the scripture hath said, out of his belly shall flow rivers of living water.' (But this speak he of the Spirit, which they that believe on him should receive: for the Holy Ghost was not yet given; because that Jesus was not yet glorified.) Many of the people therefore, when they heard this saying, said, 'Of a truth this is **the Prophet**.'"*

The people of YeHoVaH were looking for *The Prophet*, which would be the Messiah. The term was used interchangeably depending on the church or synagogue or congregation or family that a person was brought up in. One would say "the Prophet" and another would say "the Messiah," just as we are going to see here. They are one and the same.

Here is the difference. They knew that there were prophets of old. There were many prophets who came, but there would be one Messiah. There were many Messiahs, but this Messiah would be the one who speaks for YeHoVaH, like Moses said. He will speak for YeHoVaH and those who did not listen, it would be required of them. In other words, when the Prophet speaks, you hear and obey.

The Prophet would be the Messiah. He would be the one who would speak for YeHoVaH. He would also be the one who would deliver his people. The prophets of old were not deliverers. They simply came and spoke "Thus saith YeHoVaH." This particular prophet would be the deliverer who would deliver Israel and who would save his people from their lawlessness.

The Hebrew writer informs us that YeHoVaH now speaks to us by his Son.

(Hebrews 1:1-2) *"God, who at sundry times and in divers manners spake in time past unto the fathers by the prophets (**profetes**), Hath in these last days spoken unto us by his Son, whom he hath appointed heir of all things, by whom also he made the worlds;"*

I am taking this in an order. John was the last prophet before Yeshua, but he was not the last prophet. He was the last prophet before Yeshua. Anna was the last prophetess before Yeshua, but she was not the last prophetess.

Yeshua Declares His Authority

We see in *Matthew 28* that Yeshua declares all authority in heaven and in earth. Then we find this in *Ephesians*:

(Ephesians 4:4-8) *"There is one body, and one Spirit, even as ye are called in one hope of your calling; One Lord, one faith, one baptism, One God and Father of all, who is above all, and through all, and in you all. But unto every one of us is given grace according to the measure of the **gift of Messiah**. Wherefore he saith, 'When he ascended up on high, he led captivity captive, and gave gifts unto men.'"*

This word "gift" is *dorea*. The word "gifts" is *doma*.

This is important. We are going to see gifts that are also going to be *charis* or *charisma*. These are the gifts associated with the Holy Spirit. The gifts associated with the Holy Spirit are *charis/charisma*. This is the manifestation of the Holy Spirit. But YeHoVaH through Yeshua is not giving *charisma*.

There is the gift of the Father, which is the Son. There is the gift of the Son, which is known in Pentecostal and Charismatic circles as apostles, prophets, evangelists, pastors and teachers.

There is the manifestation or gifts of the Holy Spirit which we know are prophecy, wisdom, knowledge, faith, miracles, healing and the like.

As we look at these words:

G1431 *dorea*, do-reh-ah'; from {1435}; a gratuity

G1435 *doron*, do'ron; a present; specially a sacrifice:--gift, offering, gift.

What we see here is that Yeshua would be a sacrifice. He himself is a gift. When Paul talks about the wages of sin is death but the gift of YeHoVaH is eternal life, he is talking about Messiah. When we read in *John* and John says, "For YeHoVaH so loved the world that he gave," that is the gift of Messiah. He gave his only begotten Son. This is the gift. He is the gift of the Almighty.

Here we find:

G1390 *doma*, dom'ah; from the base of G1325 ; a present:--gift.

(Ephesians 4:9-11) *"Now that he ascended, what is it but that he also descended first into the lower parts of the earth? He that descended is the same also that ascended up far above all heavens, that he might fill all things.) And he gave some, apostles; and some, prophets; and some, evangelists; and some, pastors and teachers;"*

We are seeing the gifts that he is giving. He is giving apostles. Understand something. I purposely stated that John was the last prophet before Messiah. Paul is not talking about prior to Messiah. He is talking about what Messiah gave. Messiah gave gifts. These gifts were apostles and prophets. The word "prophets" here is the same word used to describe the prophets of old. In the New Testament Greek it is ***profetes***.

It is not some New Testament prophet that has a totally different meaning and function. This prophet will walk in the office of a prophet just like John. The apostle will walk in an authority. The prophet will walk in an authority. The evangelist will walk in an authority. The pastor will walk in an authority. The teacher will talk in an authority. These authorities are given to them by the one who has all authority.

We have to learn how to look at the fruit of individuals because this is how you are going to tell the tree. There are false pastors and there are true pastors. The only thing that is going to help you distinguish between the true pastor and the false pastor is the fruit. You will know a tree by its fruit. The only thing that is going to distinguish a false apostle from a true apostle, a false prophet from a true prophet, a false evangelist from a true evangelist, a false pastor from a true pastor and a false teacher from a true teacher, is the fruit.

Who are they speaking for? Are they speaking for themselves? Are they speaking for their denomination? Are they speaking for their institution? Is the doctrine that they are propagating denominational or are they teaching people to prepare for the return of the Messiah? Are they making apostates?

Yeshua said to the Pharisees that they scoured the world over to find one proselyte. By the time they were done with him, they were twice the son of hell as they were before they found them. Before they found them, they were just a son of hell. Now they are twice the son of hell. Wow. You just made bad worse.

This is what denominations are making. They are making bad worse. People are joining churches. People are joining institutions. People are joining organizations. Just because your name is on the roll of some institution does not mean that your name is written in the Lamb's Book of Life.

That is the book you want to be in.

Understand something. Yeshua is saying, "There were the prophets that prepared YeHoVaH's people. The prophet's job, the priest's job was to teach people the distinction between what is holy and what is profane, what is good and what is evil. That is the role of the prophet. That is the role of the priest. It is to teach people the difference between the holy and the profane and to call it out. When people are moving in a profane direction, YeHoVaH sends a prophet and says, "Hey, you are going the wrong way! Repent! Return and get back on track!"

That is the role of the prophet. It is the role of the apostles, prophets, evangelists, pastors and teachers that Yeshua gives. He says, "There are people who are going to be coming out of all of these institutions and they are going to be coming out of the world. And they are not going to have a clue as to how they are supposed to live." They are used to people telling them what to do, telling them when to get up and where to go. That is because our society, our world has trained us to do that.

From the moment we are born, our society begins to indoctrinate us to be model citizens, law-abiding citizens according to manmade rules and regulations. We are sent to institutions to conform, to be "educated" or indoctrinated. We are to be good workers in somebody's factories, in somebody's jobs and to go to higher learning. That determines whether you are a blue collar or white collar. It determines whether you work the factory floor or whether you are in management.

Then you have the elite institutions and the Ivy League. That determines how high in management you go or whether or not you actually own the business. Then you have all of these fraternities and sororities with secret societies that help one another by secretly manipulating the system. The people who have pledged to that brand of sorcery or to that brand of demonic activity or to that brand of demonic behavior; we are going to help you.

People don't realize that about the fraternities and sororities. It is amazing that many of them have Greek names. These names are after some mystic deity. They are pledging. They are talking about how they are a Christian. They are talking about how "I believe in YeHoVaH." You are taking pledges with Masons and secret societies and fraternities and sororities and you are pledging allegiance to some flag.

The only flag you should be pledging allegiance to (and they don't have one), is the flag, the banner of heaven. Your primary allegiance is to the Almighty and not to this country, not to any other country, not to any world leader and not to any world government.

Don't pledge your allegiance to any flag. What does that mean? That means that God becomes secondary to country. It is country first and God second. People say "God first and country second." No. It is country first. People are going to war to fight.

I don't have a problem with war. But no soldier of the Kingdom entangles himself in civilian affairs or in worldly affairs.

You have people manipulating things and manipulating society and trying to rule and govern and usher in some "one world government." They are trying to tell this country what they can have. We have all of these missiles, but we are "safe." We are not going to push the button, but we don't want you to have one because you just might push the button. You are unstable.

They sell this junk down people's throats because they have pledged some allegiance.

YeHoVaH gave these apostles, prophets, evangelists, pastors and teachers for the perfecting of the saints.

(Ephesians 4:12-14) "For the perfecting of the saints, for the work of the ministry, for the edifying of the body of Messiah/Christ: Till we all come in the unity of the faith, and of the knowledge of the Son of God, unto a perfect man, unto the measure of the stature of the fullness of Messiah: That we henceforth be no more children, tossed to and fro, and carried about with every wind of doctrine, by the sleight of men, and cunning craftiness, whereby they lie in wait to deceive;"

Every time there is a new moon prediction or somebody comes up with a new means of calculation, they are running from this camp to that camp and then to that camp over there. The enemy is constantly figuring out ways to get people off of YeHoVaH's calendar, off of YeHoVaH's reckoning of time, off of YeHoVaH's Torah and off of his commands and his instructions, with some weird way of interpreting these things. They become unstable and it is all because of the sleight of men and cunning craftiness; which tells me that HaSatan is behind it.

YeHoVaH through Yeshua says, "We are going to establish a government. There are apostles, prophets, evangelists, pastors and teachers. They don't work for themselves. They work for me." Their responsibility is to prepare people for his return. They have to perfect the saints. The saints have to now begin to look at their lives and see all of the issues and areas in their lives that do not line up with the word. The prophets, apostles, evangelists, pastors and teachers are going to teach the people the difference between the holy and the profane; the good and the evil. They will encourage and inspire people to choose good over evil, the holy over the profane, to live a holy life and to be holy as he is holy.

(Ephesians 4:15-16) "But speaking the truth in love, may grow up into him in all things, which is the head, even Christ: From whom the whole body fitly joined together and compacted by that which every joint supplieth, according to the effectual working in the measure of every part, maketh increase of the body unto the edifying of itself in love."

We are building each other up, not tearing each other down.

A prophet was a person who was given the distinctive ministry of representing God before man. They did so by moving under the "prophetic mantle" that came upon them.

The prophet was God's mouthpiece or spokesperson through which the word of God flowed whether forth-telling or foretelling. There were many men and women of God throughout scripture that held this office.

The Prophecy of Scripture

(2 Peter 1:19-21) "We have also a more sure word of prophecy; whereunto ye do well that ye take heed, as unto a light that shineth in a dark place, until the day dawn, and the day star arise in your hearts: Knowing this first, that no prophecy of the scripture is of any private interpretation. For the prophecy came not in old time by the will of man: but holy men of God spake as they were moved by the Holy Ghost."

What is he saying here? He is not saying that you can't privately interpret the prophecy. He is saying that scripture didn't come by some man. Those who spoke under the inspiration of the Holy Spirit is how we got the scriptures.

There were false prophets also among the people.

(2 Peter 2:1-3) "But there were false prophets also among the people, even as there shall be false teachers among you, who privily shall bring in damnable heresies, even denying the Lord that bought them, and bring upon themselves swift destruction. And many shall follow their pernicious ways; by reason of whom the way of truth shall be evil spoken of. And through covetousness shall they with feigned words make merchandise of you: whose judgment now of a long time lingereth not, and their damnation slumbereth not."

You have Christians on Christian TV talking about the Feasts of YeHoVaH for the sole purpose of raising offerings. "Bring your tabernacle offerings." You have these fundraisers that these television networks have (i.e. TBN, TCT, Inspiration). They bring these fundraisers. They scour through the scriptures and find passages where people are to bring Firstfruits and to bring their offerings and their sacrifices. They twist the scriptures and bring them into some context where now people are putting hundreds of thousands of dollars in these coffers, but they are not keeping the feasts.

How are you going to bring a feast offering and not keep the feast?

Instead you celebrate Christmas and Easter. That is not a feast of the Bible.

These guys get on TV and make these wonderful presentations of the people of old. Now you have new people who don't even want anything to do with feasts. They are bringing feast day offerings as if YeHoVaH is going to bless that.

If you are going to give a feast offering, at least keep the feast.

(2 Peter 2:4-9) "For if God spared not the angels that sinned, but cast them down to hell, and delivered them into chains of darkness, to be reserved unto judgment; And spared not the old world, but saved Noah the eighth person, a preacher of righteousness, bringing in the flood upon the world of the ungodly; And turning the cities of Sodom and Gomorrah into ashes condemned them with an overthrow, making them an ensample unto those that

after should live ungodly; And delivered just Lot, vexed with the filthy conversation of the wicked: (For that righteous man dwelling among them, in seeing and hearing, vexed his righteous soul from day to day with their unlawful deeds;) The Lord knoweth how to deliver the godly out of temptations, and to reserve the unjust unto the day of judgment to be punished:"

You don't have to run and hide in the hills. You don't have to build bunkers to withstand some nuclear holocaust. When it is your time to go, you are going. Whether you get scorched by the nuclear radiation or you die in the bunker safe from the radiation, when your number is up, you are leaving here. When thinking about running to the mountains and preserving your life; he that preserves his life shall lose it.

The expression "prophecy of the scriptures" is used to refer to the prophetical books of the Old Testament. **Because the scriptures are the inspired word of God, the prophecy therein must be regarded as inspired and infallible revelation.**

(2 Timothy 3:16-17) *"All scripture is given by inspiration of God, and is profitable for doctrine, for reproof, for correction, for instruction in righteousness: That the man of God may be perfect, thoroughly furnished unto all good works."*

When he is talking about "all scripture," there is no New Testament. He is talking about the scripture that was at the time of the writing. That is why when I refer to the New Testament, I refer to it as the Bible. It is the Bible, the *Acts* of the apostles, the gospel narratives, the epistles of Paul and James and John.

The scripture is the word that came from YeHoVaH's mouth. I say to people that Paul taught scripture. He wrote letters and his letters contained scripture. That does not make his letters scripture. But the letters that contain scripture are filled with scripture and all the scripture in his letters is scripture.

But when Paul says, "I, not the Lord," what is he saying? He is saying, "He didn't say this, so don't try to get me as some false prophet. I am not a false prophet. I am letting you know that he didn't say this. He didn't even tell me to say this, but I am giving you my opinion."

Is Paul's opinion scripture? Some people want to think so.

Class 100 Study Summary

Key Points

1. Prophecy must be properly interpreted or false doctrines and false theological views will emerge.

2. There is a huge misunderstanding surrounding the "house" described in *Acts 2:1-2*. People believe it is a dwelling place or an "upper room." But the "house" described therein is really talking about the "House of YeHoVaH." It is talking about how those who were gathered were of his household and were gathered with one accord.

3. In *Acts 2* they were speaking in tongues but others were hearing what was being spoken in their own natural language.

4. Prophecy can be defined as the God-given ability to speak forth supernaturally as the Spirit gives utterance.

5. There are guidelines that the Father has given us for when tongues manifest. We are not to speak them in a public place if there is no interpretation.

6. The Bible says that we are not to despise prophesying.

7. Those who love the Father will not mind being chastised or corrected. Those who do not love him will walk away from him when things get tough.

8. Father knows what we need even before we ask him. However we are to ask him and it is his will that in all things we give him thanks and praise.

9. The first person who ever prophesied in the Bible was Adam.

10. Allow YeHoVaH to fight your battles. We need to learn to rest in the Almighty. When we do that, he promises that he will fight our battles and he is faithful.

11. The gifts that are associated with the Holy Spirit include "charis" or "charisma." This is the manifestation of the Holy Spirit.

12. The Father gave us the gift of his Son, Yeshua, but Yeshua also gives gifts of men. He gives us apostles, prophets, evangelists, pastors and teachers.

13. We have to learn how to look at the fruit of individuals because this is how we will know who is of YeHoVaH and who is not.

14. The role of apostles, prophets, evangelists, pastors, teachers and prophets is to prepare YeHoVaH's people. We are to teach people the distinction between what is holy and what is profane; what is good and what is evil.

15. Our primary allegiance is not to any flag. It is to the Almighty.

16. People try to bring "feast" offerings when they don't even keep the biblical feasts.

17. Christmas and Easter are not feasts of the Bible. They are manmade traditions.

18. Because scripture is the inspired word of God, the prophecy therein must be regarded as inspired and infallible revelation.

Review Exercise

1. Yeshua tells us that many false prophets will come to lead Yah's people away. How will you be able to discern a false prophet?

_____

_____

_____

_____

_____

_____

2. What differentiates the office of prophet from the gift of prophecy?

_____

_____

_____

_____

_____

_____

3. What is the danger of improper interpretation of prophecy?

_____

_____

_____

_____

_____

_____

_____

Rate the following statements
by filling in the most appropriate number.

(1 = I do not agree 10 = I agree completely)

Objectives:

1. I can define the gift of prophecy.

    1.◯ 2. ◯ 3. ◯ 4. ◯ 5. ◯ 6. ◯ 7. ◯ 8. ◯ 9. ◯ 10. ◯

2. I can explain what the office of a prophet is and what it means.

    1.◯ 2. ◯ 3. ◯ 4. ◯ 5. ◯ 6. ◯ 7. ◯ 8. ◯ 9. ◯ 10. ◯

3. I can describe how scripture itself prophesies.

    1.◯ 2. ◯ 3. ◯ 4. ◯ 5. ◯ 6. ◯ 7. ◯ 8. ◯ 9. ◯ 10. ◯

4. I can identify evidence that Yeshua was a prophet.

    1.◯ 2. ◯ 3. ◯ 4. ◯ 5. ◯ 6. ◯ 7. ◯ 8. ◯ 9. ◯ 10. ◯

My Journal

What I learned from this class:

_____

_____

_____

_____

_____

_____

_____

_____

_____

_____

_____

_____

_____

_____

_____

_____

_____

_____

_____

_____

Discipleship Training Class 101

The Interpretation of Prophecy (part 4)

Objectives:

As a Discipleship student, at the end of this class you will be able to:

- Define gender as it relates to the prophetic office
- Identify various prophetesses, women who were prophets, in scripture
- Describe the work of prophets in the New Testament
- Explain what is meant by the prophet as seer

My goal is (as I pray it is your goal is) to glorify the Father in our lives. These teachings are helping to get his word out. You will have the tools that the theologians have — those who are teaching and preaching. You will now be able to take these tools and apply them in your own study. You will begin to see the word as it was intended to be seen.

We are bringing these teachings to you from a Hebrew Roots/Messianic perspective so that you will see his word in light of the Torah from *Genesis* all the way through the book of maps.

We left off in the last lesson talking about the gift of prophecy and about the move into the office of prophet. We instructed, informed and hopefully inspired you to understand that there is a difference between the gift of prophecy and the office of prophet. You cannot confuse the two.

We noted that the expression "prophecy of the scripture" is used to refer to the prophetical books of the Old Testament. **Because the scriptures are the inspired word of YeHoVaH, the prophecy therein must be regarded as inspired and infallible revelation.**

We use the term "Old Testament" because that is a commonly used term among people of today. But we know that there is no "Old" and "New" Testaments. There is, from *Genesis* to *Revelation,* a continual revelation. It is all YeHoVaH's word. You can't separate the old from the new. The idea of giving it the term "Old Testament" is to indicate that it is old and no longer needed. It indicates that the New Testament is new and that is what people are looking for and what people want. There is no distinction. The only thing is that Yeshua has come to show us how to live the Old Testament out.

(2 Timothy 3:16-17) "All scripture is given by inspiration of God, and is profitable for doctrine, for reproof, for correction, for instruction in righteousness: That the man/anthropos (human being) of God may be perfect, thoroughly furnished unto all good works."

I want you to pay attention to the word "man." Typically here in the West and in most other countries there is a distinction between the words "man" and "woman." However in this particular verse, what you need to look at is the word used here. That is the word *anthropos*. We get the word "anthropology"(the study of humans) from this.

Anthropos is a human being. The human being is the best way to see this. The reason why I wanted this word to be brought out for what it is, is that if we look at it from a Western perspective, we use the term "man." Then it separates man out from woman. Once you separate man from woman — you will find that the Bible for the most part, is skewed or geared or spoken of in a masculine form. The terminology that is used in the Bible which refers to man oftentimes does not include woman unless the word woman is actually there.

There are places in the Bible when the term "man" includes both male and female; or the human being without gender and that is important, especially here in *Timothy*.

The question is, is it only profitable for doctrine for men? Is it only profitable for reproof, for correction, for instruction in righteousness for men? Because it says here the "man" of God. But what about the woman of God? Does the woman of God not need to be perfect and thoroughly furnished unto all good works?

When you look at the context of what is being said here, you will automatically see that this is not just talking about the male. It is talking about the human. That is all of YeHoVaH's people and that is important for where we are going.

The Ministry of the Prophets

There are certain terms that when people hear them or when people see them, they automatically think of gender. Well, I have a surprise for you.

Designations of the Prophets

In all of the various periods of Israel's history in the Old Testament, there appears to be no greater or grander ministry than that of the prophets. The prophets were noble and holy men and women of God. Isn't "prophet" male? Shouldn't the term prophetess — which refers to female?

The term "prophetess" is a female prophet. That is what it is.

They were the representatives of YeHoVaH to Israel. They were declaring his word and his mind and his will to the nation in times of prosperity or adversity. These prophets were known under the following designations:

1. The Men of God
2. The Women of God

(Numbers 12:6) *"And he said, 'Hear now my words: if there be a prophet among you, I YeHoVaH will make myself known unto him in a vision, and will speak unto him in a dream.'"*

Now the phrase says, *"will make myself known unto <u>him</u> and speak unto <u>him</u> in a dream."* The fact is that YeHoVaH has women prophets. This verse doesn't say, "I will make myself known unto them." It says, "I will make myself known unto him." A person who is anal in their theology will say, "See? That says 'him.'" It is just like some would take what Paul says: that a bishop must be the husband of one wife. So that automatically means that since females can't have wives, that it must be a male. Well, again we are going to look at the scriptures. We are going to look at them not just from a word study, but also from the Spirit of YeHoVaH himself.

The men prophets are well-known and many books are ascribed to them from *Samuel* to *Malachi*.

New Testament Prophets

Here is another thing we are going to get into, because many people make fun of the idea that there could actually be prophets in today's time (as if John the Baptist was the last prophet). As I noted, John/Yochanan the Immerser was the last prophet before Yeshua. Anna was the last prophetess before Yeshua that we see. There is a distinction between *before* Yeshua and *after* Yeshua.

Now many will say that because they don't understand their Bible, that after Yeshua, there were no more prophets. Prior to Yeshua there were. After him there were not.

The Bible specifically speaks of New Testament prophets.

(Acts 11:27) *"And in these days came **prophets** from Jerusalem unto Antioch."*

Acts 11:27 is many years after the resurrection. Now, it doesn't mention their names here, but there are places in the New Testament where the names of prophets are actually mentioned. We are going to look at some of those so that you are not ignorant concerning the word.

I know that there are a lot of ignorant Messianics out there that are stuck in a time and an era. And then through that ignorance they say things that people who don't know any better buy into. Now you have two people who are ignorant. The first ignorant person convinced the second person who may have had some understanding and who may have received revelation had they not been exposed to the ignorant teacher.

Ignorance doesn't mean "stupid." Ignorant simply means one who lacks knowledge in a particular area. I am not trying to call anybody ignorant or stupid or to make fun of anybody. The fact is however, that if you are saying things based upon a lack of knowledge and people buy into it, then they too will have the same knowledge that you have. This means that both of you will lack knowledge.

The way Yeshua addressed this in his day is that you have blind guides leading the blind people and they both end up in a ditch. If you are following someone who is blind, then you are going to end up where that blind person is.

If you are following someone who is ignorant or who lacks knowledge, then you are going to end up where that person is — in the same camp. You will be saying some of the same things until you are enlightened.

Many of us should know this. We were in places before we became enlightened and decided that we would no longer follow the ignorance of these individuals any longer.

Look at the verse from *Timothy* in context.

(Acts 13:1) *"Now there were in the church that was at Antioch certain prophets and teachers; as Barnabas, and Simeon that was called Niger, and Lucius of Cyrene, and Manaen, which had been brought up with Herod the tetrarch, and Saul."*

This is some serious controversy or should I say that it is a controversial passage or verse that we are going to spend just a moment on.

Notice that in verse 27 of chapter 11, it talks about prophets coming from Jerusalem. Some prophets came from Jerusalem. How many of you know that there were prophets in Antioch too? They came from Jerusalem up to Antioch.

In *Acts 13:1* they were in the church that was at Antioch. It was the *kahilah*, the Messianic community where there were certain prophets and teachers. Here it is giving us names.

Barnabas was Bar nabas, *naba, nabiy, bar* — son. *Naba* = prophet. Barnabas means "son of a prophet." Then there was Simeon that was called Niger. In some translations they use Niger. But the actual translation (which is of Latin origin), Simeon was what he was called. His name was Simeon, but they called him "Niger." The word here means "Black." Simeon was Black. And it could mean that the term "Niger" was used way back here in *Acts 13* in the first century.

You be the judge of that. Simeon was his name, but they called him something else. The word itself means "Black." When we look at this word in the Greek, we note that it is of Latin origin. It is a Greek word, but it originated in Latin. The term "Niger" is pronounced neeg'-er. That is how you pronounce it. It means "Black."

[G3526] *Niger*,--neeg'-er; of Latin origin; Black; Niger, a Christian: -- Niger.

His name wasn't Niger. He was called "Neeger." His name was Simeon.

> **Niger** (ni-juhr). Latin nickname meaning "Black." Surname of Simeon, one of the teacher-prophets of the early church at Antioch. Blacks were a common sight among the populations of Egypt and North Africa in the Hellenistic period. — *Holman Bible Dictionary*

Notice that the *Holman Bible Dictionary* says that Blacks were a common sight in the period among populations of Egypt and North Africa. Now unfortunately in most of the arts and depictions that we see, we find that a lot of these individuals are of a Caucasian persuasion.

The historians have tried to write people of color right out of the book, when the fact is that all of the people of Eastern/Middle Eastern descent were certainly not of Caucasian persuasion (even though there were some). I don't agree with folks who say, "Well, all of the Jews were Black." I have to say that there were mixed multitudes. The history of this country and many around the world is that people have a tendency to look at things that are black as demonic.

Like Black magic is bad magic but White magic is okay. The only time that black is good is when you are not in the red.[8] It seems that when this term is used, it is always used with a negative connotation. There are some who are bold enough to say, "Hey, wait a minute." The fact of the matter is that we know that all of the people of the book are not as they are depicted in art. If we are to be honest and open and truthful in our interpretation of scripture, we know that YeHoVaH has people of every nation, every color, every tongue and every ethnicity who call upon his name.

Here they were in Antioch. They were in Jerusalem. They were all over the known land and there was Lucius of Cyrene and Manaen, which had been brought up with Herod the tetrarch; and Saul.

(Acts 15:32) *"And Judas and Silas, **being prophets also themselves**, exhorted the brethren with many words, and confirmed them."*

Right now I have shown you three biblical passages after the resurrection that are identifying prophets. How can people come to the conclusion that prophets are no longer? Or that John the Baptist was the last prophet as if there were no prophets in the New Testament? They say they didn't need them. Well, why didn't they? We are going to keep reading.

We see Judas and Silas. This is not Judas of Iscaria or Judas Iscariot as he is known in the King James Version. We see Judas and Silas being prophets also themselves.

(Acts 21:10) *"And as we tarried there many days, there came down from Judaea a certain prophet, named Agabus."*

We see that there was a prophet named Agabus. Other prophets were named Judas and Silas. There were prophets named Barnabas and Simeon who also taught. Then there was Lucious of Cyrene and Manaen. All of these individuals were known and identified in the New Testament scripture as prophets.

Paul writes:

(1 Corinthians 14:37) *"If any man think himself to be a prophet, or spiritual, let him acknowledge that the things that I write unto you are the commandments of YeHoVaH."*

We see here that Paul identifies that there are prophets. He says that if there are any prophets here who I am writing to, then you should be able to acknowledge the things that I am writing to

---

[8] I am not trying to push a Black ministry. If you are in the red, you are going in the wrong direction financially. But if you are in the black, you are alright. That is the only time.

you. You should be able to judge what I am writing here and determine whether or not what I am saying is of the commands of YeHoVaH.

Morally and ethically speaking, the prophets were indeed men and women of God. They were following, declaring and upholding the ways of God. We are talking about the interpretation of prophecy. You have to understand that prophecy came from prophets. Old Testament prophecy came from prophets. There were New Testament prophecies that also came from prophets.

The Women of God

Although there are several women prophetesses mentioned in the Bible, there are no prophetic books authored by women in scripture. This is what has been communicated. We don't necessarily dispute that. However there are books out there that are not necessarily identified as canon. In other words, they did not meet the tests and are discarded. But even though there are women who have no prophetic books ascribed to them, there are many women prophets.

(Exodus 15:20) *"And **Miriam the prophetess**, the sister of Aaron, took a timbrel in her hand; and all the women went out after her with timbrels and with dances."*

The only reason the term "prophetess" is there is because Miriam was a female. Miriam was a female prophet.

(Judges 4:4) *"And **Deborah, a prophetess**, the wife of Lapidoth, she judged Israel at that time."*

She was not only a prophet, but she was also a judge.

(2 Kings 22:14) *"So Hilkiah the priest, and Ahikam, and Achbor, and Shaphan, and Asahiah, went unto **Huldah the prophetess**, the wife of Shallum the son of Tikvah, the son of Harhas, keeper of the wardrobe; (now she dwelt in Jerusalem in the college;) and they communed with her."*

You can be in lots of conversations and never hear of Hulda who was a prophet or that because she was a female she was considered a prophetess.

(Isaiah 8:3) *"And I went unto the prophetess; and she conceived, and bare a son. Then said YeHoVaH to me, 'Call his name Maher-shalal-has-baz.'"*

This is an unknown prophetess. It is believed to be the wife of Isaiah. We don't know her by name, but we know her husband and we know her child. Either Isaiah is committing adultery or fornication (which I doubt) or this is his wife. All scholars agree that this is his wife.

It was not an immaculate conception. YeHoVaH did not say, "Isaiah! What have you done?" He did not rebuke Isaiah; which again confirms that this is his wife.

The last person mentioned by the title "prophetess" is Anna; however the prophetess is a female prophet. Therefore as long as the office of prophet exists, so will there be female prophets. That is not too hard to gather. Some would dispute and argue that, because they demand and feel less than a man to think that they are not or cannot dominate.

I don't know where men get this idea that they must dominate when YeHoVaH never gave man dominion over another man. He certainly didn't give him dominion over women. But men have taken this dominating, domineering attitude in their approach to YeHoVaH's creation. They support this misinterpretation of scripture (or the lack thereof) because they are using principles and tools that are not necessarily valid tools when it comes down to hermeneutics.

(Luke 2:36) "And there was one Anna, a prophetess, the daughter of Phanuel, of the tribe of Aser: she was of a great age, and had lived with an husband seven years from her virginity;"

In other words, her husband that she married is the one she gave her virginity to. For seven years they were married until her husband died.

(Luke 2:37-38) "And she was a widow of about fourscore and four years, which departed not from the temple, but served YeHoVaH with fastings and prayers night and day. And she coming in that instant gave thanks likewise unto YeHoVaH, and spake of him to all them that looked for redemption in Jerusalem."

Anna was an old woman. We see here that she was more than likely 84-years old. She looks at him and she speaks of him and she is literally prophesying.

(Luke 2:39-40) "And when they had performed all things according to the law of YeHoVaH, they returned into Galilee, to their own city Nazareth. And the child grew, and waxed strong in the spirit, filled with wisdom: and the grace of God was upon him."

It is interesting that when you begin to look at it, *"And she coming in that instant gave thanks likewise unto YeHoVaH."* Who is she giving thanks to? The infant child?

You will notice that the thing about the New Testament is that it is hard to distinguish "the LORD" from "the Lord."

(Luke 2:41-42) **"Now his parents went to Jerusalem ever year at the feast of Passover.** *And when he was twelve years old, they went up to Jerusalem after the custom of the feast."*

Here is an example of a family going up to the feasts. Some people would look at **Deuteronomy 16:16** where it says that all males are required to appear. They make the argument that this means all males and that the females don't have to come. Of course with Judaism, only the males who have been bar mitzvahed and who become sons of the commandments are required to come.

But here we have the example of how this commandment was more than likely lived. That is because his parents (that is, his Mother and Father) went to Jerusalem every year; not just this particular year.

The Bible says that they went every year. And when he was twelve years old, they went up to Jerusalem. Some people would read that they only went up when he was twelve. No, they went up every year.

Chances are that Yeshua went up to Jerusalem when he was eleven for the feasts and also when he was ten and when he was nine and eight and seven. We see that they certainly traveled up to Jerusalem when Yeshua was in her womb. He was born just a stone's throw away from Jerusalem in Bethlehem. They came and he was dedicated in Jerusalem.

Every year based upon this passage, we see that his parents went to Jerusalem. They went every year at the Feast of the Passover. Is that the only time they went up? "Well, see, it doesn't say that they went up at all of the other feasts." There are many things that the Bible doesn't say.

Do you see how people have a tendency to interpret and to read into things that aren't there? Do you see how they ignore things that *are* there?

They went up every year. It just so happened when he was twelve-years old that they went up to Jerusalem after the custom of the feasts. The custom of the feasts is that three times a year they were to go up. So if his parents were honoring the commands, they didn't just go up for Passover. They went up for Passover. They went up for Shavuot and they went up for Sukkot. It was three times a year as the custom of the feasts; the command of YeHoVaH.

When the King James puts it in there as after the custom of the feasts, they have a tendency to try to make you think "Jewish customs" not "commandments of YeHoVaH." You have to watch this stuff because the word of YeHoVaH was given to us. But it was penned and translated and in some ways, hidden behind words. You can't turn off your common sense. People who have no knowledge of the Torah are easily deceived with the idea that that is a Jewish custom and not a commandment of YeHoVaH.

We have to point these things out so that people can get it.

(Ephesians 4:11) *"And he gave some, apostles; and some, prophets; and some, evangelists; and some, pastors and teachers."*

Who is "he?" He is Yeshua. Before he ascended, he gave some gifts. He gave gifts unto men is what the Bible says. He gave gifts unto men. Well, what are these gifts that he gave? What he is saying here is that he gave men as gifts. It reads that he gave gifts unto men, but what he did was give gifts. He gave men as gifts. It is as if he gave apostles, not like he gave some to be apostles. What he did was that he gave apostles. He gave prophets. He gave evangelists. He gave pastors and he gave teachers.

If you don't know whether you are an apostle, prophet, evangelist, pastor or teacher, that doesn't mean that you aren't. As some people develop their relationship with the Almighty, he says, "Now here is what I have called you to be. And what I have called you to be; therein lies your purpose."

You see, when the Father spoke to me several years ago, I was sitting in a Charismatic Pentecostal Church. I heard, "I have called you to be an apostle." I did not need to go up to

Jerusalem and check with Peter. I heard his voice. It took me four, almost five years of truly wrestling with that. The way that I overcame it (as some of you know my story) is that I have a son. When this son was born, Father said, "Call his name Apostle."

That is how he got his name. He got his name because I was wrestling with my call. My son's name is Apostle Arthur Bailey. I did not just come up with something. I remember the first time I said to a fellow in my community what my son's name was. He went off on me. "How dare you call your son 'Apostle?'"

Do you have to feed him or buy him clothes or pay his bills? What makes people do some of the things that they do?

What Father was saying was that I would have to get over this. Now you are going to hear this every day. Apostle Arthur Bailey. It is "Apostle Arthur Bailey" every time I hear or call his name and it is "Apostle" every time his Mother calls his name. It is like Father is saying, "Get over it. Get over it and get on with it."

Today I have people with that same spirit. They say, "How dare you call yourself Apostle?" I didn't. I would have easily ignored it, not wanting to deal with it. That is because I knew the moment that I embraced what the Father is calling me to; I knew exactly the kinds of spirits that I was going to have to deal with.

But like the Apostle Paul says, it is like, "Look at my fruit." It is like Yeshua said when John sent his disciples, "Are you the one?" He said, "Look at my work."

My work should speak. I am not out here trying to make apostles, prophets or evangelists or pastors or teachers. I am simply trying to recognize those whom the Father has called to be such and to help equip them and prepare them for the work of ministry that he has called them to because they are going to be accountable to him.

My job is to do what I have been called to do and to lead them to do what they have been called to do. If my part is to help them find their part, then that is my part.

It was he (Yeshua) who gave some apostles and some prophets and some evangelists and some pastors and some teachers. We just simply recognize and identify the call that he gave to an individual.

Paul's teaching emphasized the prophetic gifting, prophesying and prophets.

(Ephesians 4:9-10) *"(Now that he ascended, what is it but that he also descended first into the lower parts of the earth? He that descended is the same also that ascended up far above all heavens, that he might fill all things.)"*

1 Corinthians 14:1-5

In this passage we see what the Bible says. He says to desire spiritual gifts. He wants you to desire that you may prophesy. How many of you desire that? How many Messianics are desiring to prophesy or are we too busy bashing prophetic ministry? The very things we bash are the things that the Father has really called us to. If you remember, the sign of the outpouring of the Spirit (according to Joel manifested in *Acts 2*) is that in the last days he is going to pour out his Spirit upon all flesh. Sons and daughters will do what? They will prophesy.

Prophesying is the work of the Spirit operating in our being. There is forth-telling and there is foretelling. There is speaking what YeHoVaH has said and that is allowing YeHoVaH and the Holy Spirit to come upon us according to Messiah. We shall be reminded. First of all, the Holy Spirit is going to teach us. The Holy Spirit is going to remind us of the things that he taught and the Holy Spirit is going to show us things to come.

When the Holy Spirit shows us things to come and we are speaking those things that are in the distance based upon what the Holy Spirit showed us, how many of you know that that is prophesying?

That is what prophesying is. That is the work of the Holy Spirit. The work of the Holy Spirit is to show us things to come, not to scare us. Yeshua said, "The things that I reveal to you in secret, you get on the mountain top and shout them out!" That is prophecy. That is prophesying.

These are his words. These are not some crooked preacher, some prophe-LIAR, or some false prophet. I don't know why people confuse Yeshua's words and then make them of no effect because of some jack-leg prophet out there who is prophesying for money or whatever the reason they are prophesying. "Now you see what that prophet did? That is the reason I don't believe in prophesy."

I see who your god is. I see who you are looking at for guidance and direction. I don't care if a thousand false prophets show up and start prophe-LYING all over the country and all over the globe. **That doesn't nullify YeHoVaH's word.**

Yet for many people it does exactly that. Stop being ignorant! Don't be a fool! Don't allow the work of the enemy to cause you to despise the very things the Father says. "Do not despise prophecy." If you despise prophecy, you cut off the work of the Holy Spirit.

You become dependent upon men to tell you what the Holy Spirit says when the Father wants to have this direct relationship with you to show you things to come. But because you have been exposed to some false prophet, you shut the true Prophet off. Now you are dependent upon men, which is not what YeHoVaH wants.

It is a dirty job, but somebody has to do it. I have been called to bring it forth and that is what apostles do. Apostles break ground. They stir things up. They call people and they lead people and they challenge. They go into places where others fear to go.

It is like the Father just takes all the wiring out of the brain of the apostles and prophets and says, "I don't want you to think. Just speak what I give you to speak and don't worry about it. I have your back."

But there are too many people who have watched too many false teachers. Now they have concluded that all teachers are false. There are too many people who have seen too many false preachers, too many false apostles, too many false prophets and too many televangelists that are talking about $58 miracles. And they have concluded that all televangelists and all prophets and all apostles are crooked.

That is exactly where the devil wants you. You will find yourself doing the very thing that Paul writes to us and says not to do, based upon the inspiration of the Holy Spirit. Do not forbid, do not despise prophecy and do not forbid the speaking in tongues.

"Oh, there you go with that tongues stuff." Can't prophesy, can't speak in tongues. What can you do?

"Just keep the Sabbath." You go right ahead. The Sabbath is a small portion. The Sabbath is the doorway. You come in the door through the Sabbath. There is a whole lot more besides the Sabbath and the feasts. Folks are only interested in keeping the Sabbath and making sure that they go to the feasts.

Come on. You better grow up.

Paul says that when a person speaks in tongues, nobody understands him, but wait a minute! What about those folks who say, "Well, tongues is a known language." Well, if it is a known language, then somebody should understand every time somebody speaks in tongues. But Paul says that nobody understands them. Come on!

So now they are calling Paul a liar. He says that nobody understands when you are speaking in tongues unless there is the gift of interpretation. Now a person says, "Well, he is talking about known languages." Well, it is a known language so you don't need an interpretation. See? That is what I am saying. You don't need an interpreter if it is a known language.

Somebody understands it. Paul says that when you speak in tongues, when you speak in an unknown tongue, you don't speak unto men but unto Elohim; for no man understands.

(1 Corinthians 14:39) *"Wherefore, brethren, covet to prophesy, and forbid not to speak with tongues."*

Now he goes from desiring "spiritual gifts that you may prophesy." And now he goes into this whole idea of coveting. Wait a minute. Coveting is bad! No, coveting is not bad. Coveting someone else's stuff is bad. Coveting another man's ox and his ass and his wife, that is bad. But here he is saying "covet to prophesy."

Covet! Desire it so badly that you can actually find yourself moving toward it. Covet to prophesy and don't forbid speaking with tongues. Yet people say, "Oh, no. We don't speak in tongues here." "Oh, you forbid speaking in tongues? What Bible are you people reading? You have one of those 'funny' Bibles."

Prophets were first called seers because of the visions, insight and foresight they received from YeHoVaH for his people.

(1 Samuel 9:9) *"(Beforetime in Israel, when a man went to inquire of YeHoVaH, thus he spake, 'Come, and let us go the seer: for he that is now called a Prophet was beforetime called a Seer.)'"*

A seer — the word is:

H7200 *ra'ah*, raw-aw'; a primitive root; to see, literally or figuratively (in numerous applications, direct and implied, transitive, intransitive and causative):--advise self, appear, approve, behold, certainly, consider, discern, (make to) enjoy, one who has experience, gaze, take heed, indeed, joyfully, lo, look (on, one another, one on another, one upon another, out, up, upon), mark, meet, be near, perceive, present, provide, regard, (have) respect, (fore-, cause to let) see (-r, -m, one another), shew (self), sight of others, (e-) spy, stare, surely, think, view, visions.

A prophet is what is called a "seer." According to what Yeshua says, one who has been given the Spirit will see things. They will see things afar off. They will see things coming before everybody or anybody else sees it. Father says this: "I don't do anything in the earth, nothing. There is nothing that is done in the earth before I first reveal it to my servants the prophets."

The Father says that the prophets are his friends. He tells them what he is going to do before he does a thing. And when he speaks to them, he speaks to them face-to-face.

"Say this to these people. Here is what you say. Here is where you go. Here is what you say to them. Here is how you go and here is how you come back."

He gave them specific instructions to go and to speak to a people who did not want to hear what YeHoVaH had to say. Imagine that. YeHoVaH had to raise somebody up. He had to literally raise someone up and send them to a people. Have you ever had to go?

There is a term, a phrase here in the West that people say. "Don't shoot me. I am just the messenger." Basically what they are saying is, "I know I am bringing you something you don't want to hear. Don't kill me. I am just the messenger. I am not the one who originated the message. The message was given to me to bring to you."

Most of the time when the Father would send a prophet, it was for correction. Correction is not pleasant when it comes. Some of you have been angry at me because of what I have said. I know it. I feel it. That is why I am forcing and speaking at the top of my lungs. Believe it or not, there is a timid "me" that does not want to say certain things because I know the moment that I say it, people are not going to hear YeHoVaH's words.

They are going to hear the words of Arthur Bailey. They are not going to run off and say, "YeHoVaH says." They are going to say, "Did you hear what that Bailey said?"

As if "Bailey" is speaking for Bailey. I am comfortable not even standing here. I can be doing something else somewhere else. I did not call me to do this, but since I have been called, I am going to do what I have been called to do. That is because I know what it is like to run from the Almighty. He corners you.

Let me tell you something. If you have ever been cornered by the Almighty, he will put a fear into your heart that you will never, ever, EVER be afraid of another man. "What are you going to do to me? Oh, thank you, Jesus! I am done and I am outta here." They would be doing me a favor (well, not really).

When it is time to go, I am gone. Until then I have been called to do a job that very few people will even accept. It is like *Mission Impossible* for real, because you are preaching and teaching to people who don't want to hear it. These are folks who have listened to ignorant people and who have held onto ignorant doctrines even though you show them what the scriptures say. They something like, "I don't know. I have to study that for myself." We are studying right now!

We are turning a corner and we are going down a road. In these recent times I have had so many individuals who have been upset. They want to correct me. I got a phone call the other day from an apostle. He saw me on the *Church Channel*. He wanted to call me. I am going to call him back. He asked me to. "How can I use the name 'Jehovah" with a 'Y'?" This is what he asked and "Don't I know that it is 'Jehovah' with a 'J'?" I am calling him back.

These are the kinds of things I deal with. If I showed you some of the letters that I receive and the things I get, it is like, "Man, don't you all have something better to do than to pick on YeHoVaH's servant?" Like that is going to stop him. No.

YeHoVaH says, "I am going to show you something and when I show it to you, I want you to tell my people. You need to tell them something, friend. They are not going to want to hear it. I also need to let you know that the ones that I sent before you, a lot of them didn't make it back. I need you to know what you are up against." They persecuted all of the prophets. When you experience persecution, just know that you have ticked them off.

It is not you who has ticked them off. It is the message that I am giving you that is going to tick them off. They are going to want to stone you, cut you and drag you to pieces. They are going to scream at you at the top of their lungs and try to act like they don't hear you. They are going to persecute you for his name's sake. And what you ought to do when you face that persecution is to rejoice and be exceedingly glad because you are in good company.

The prophets were the interpreters of the Law of YeHoVaH. They interpreted the history of Israel in accordance to the word of YeHoVaH.

(Isaiah 43:27) "Thy first father hath sinned, and thy teachers have transgressed against me."

The word "teachers" here means "interpreters."

H3887 *luwts,* loots; a primitive root; properly, to make mouths at, i.e. to scoff; hence (from the effort to pronounce a foreign language) to interpret, or (generally) intercede:--ambassador, have in derision, interpreter, make a mock, mocker, scorn(-er, -ful), teacher.

The word here is that your teachers (the ones who are responsible for interpreting) have transgressed. There is a fellow we know of in the book of *John* who was a teacher of Israel. Yeshua said, "You are a teacher of Israel and you don't know these things?"[9]

Many in denominations are teaching what the denomination teaches. I have said before that I have been in denominations where people did not believe what the denomination was teaching, but they wanted to be part of the denomination. They taught things they did not agree with and they lived something else.

That is unfortunate. The Bible calls them "hirelings." They are preachers for hire, prophets for hire, apostles for hire. Oh, yeah. You hire them and they will come in and they will give everybody prophesies for $50 or $100. There are $500 prophesies and $1,000 prophesies. What can you afford? How much money have you got?

They even have websites. You can go to the website and make a donation and they will send you a prophecy in the mail, in your email.

Prophets were the divine messengers sent by YeHoVaH; bearing the message of YeHoVaH to the nation. They delivered these messages faithfully.

(Malachi 3:1) *"Behold, I will send my messenger, and he shall prepare a way before me: and Adoni, who ye seek, shall suddenly come to his temple, even the messenger of the covenant, who ye delight in: behold he shall come, saith YeHoVaH of hosts."*

The prophets were also called "The Servants of YeHoVaH."

(Jeremiah 44:4) *"Howbeit I sent unto you all my servants the prophets, rising early and sending them, saying, 'Oh, do not this abominable thing I hate.'"*

What did he do? Here is a prime example. When you look at what they did to Jeremiah and what they tried to do to Jeremiah, Jeremiah knew full well. That is because YeHoVaH said, "You are going to go to a people. They are not going to like what you have to say. They are not going to want to hear what you have to say. Here are some of the things that they are going to do to you. When you speak to them, don't look at their faces. If you have to, close your eyes and speak. If you look at these people, then guess what? They are going to be looking like demons. They are going to be gnashing. They are going to give you some of the ugliest stares and looks with their arms crossed. When you look at their faces, it is going to scare you and make you want to back up. It will make you get timid and not say what you have to say. Now, you are going to want to sweeten things up. You will want to make them sound all nicey-nice so that they are palatable and they taste good and are easy to swallow." YeHoVaH told him. "None of that."

The prophets had to go to the people of YeHoVaH and speak for YeHoVaH. They had to say, "Thus saith YeHoVaH. The things that you are doing are abominations. Stop it!"

---

[9] That of course was Nicodemus that Yeshua was speaking to.

The most common designation is that of prophet. As we lay all of these things out, hopefully when you see and hear these prophecies, they will begin to make a little bit more sense. These men and women who are prophets, were public expounders and preachers of the word of YeHoVaH. They spoke under inspiration of the Spirit.

(Hosea 12:10) *"I have also spoken by the prophets, and I have multiplied visions, and used similitudes, by the ministry of the prophets."*

"Holy men of YeHoVaH spake as they were moved by the Holy Spirit."

G444 *anthropos*, anth'-ro-pos; man-faced, i.e. a human being:--certain, man.

You will notice that in certain parts of scripture, it identifies animals that have certain types of faces. This is not animal faced. Here *anthropos* is man-faced, or human being.

They prophesied through preaching and prediction. They represented YeHoVaH's word to Israel. They upheld the righteousness of the holiness and mercy of YeHoVaH and Divine Sovereignty over the nations and reproved the sinfulness of men.

The sinfulness of men was lawlessness; whenever the people deviated from his law. Here is the thing that convinces me when a people don't want to be blessed. When I am saying "blessed," I am talking about having the Almighty's protection and the Almighty's provision. Think about this for a moment.

YeHoVaH gave his law to his people so that his people may live a long life, a prosperous life and so that they would enjoy the land flowing with milk and honey that he delivered them out of the hand of Egypt to bring them into. He promised them that if they lived according to his commands, they would live long in the land. They would have wells they did not dig, houses they did not build and vineyards they did not plant. They would be protected from their enemies. They would be raised high above all of the nations of the world. They would be lenders and not borrowers. They would not be slaves to anybody. They would be on top, never beneath. They would be the head and never the tail. They would be blessed in the city and in the country and blessed in the field. Everything they put their hands to would be blessed.

The only stipulation is that you keep my commandments. If a people want to be blessed, they would keep the commands of YeHoVaH. Let me tell you something. YeHoVaH wants you to be blessed more than you want to be blessed. When the people began to deviate from the commands, YeHoVaH said, "Wait a minute. Don't you know what you are doing? You are walking away from the blessing!" Why would you walk away from the blessings to a curse? Why would you leave freedom to go into bondage?

The world turns that around. Why would you leave bondage and be free? Why would you leave the bondage of grace that requires absolutely nothing and where you can violate God's laws all day long to go back under bondage (which is actually freedom)?

The people of YeHoVaH left the freedom that was contained in the law, the perfect law of liberty (as James puts it), to go into bondage by violating the commands of YeHoVaH. They walked away from freedom. They walked away from deliverance. They walked away from the blessings. They went into the curse.

YeHoVaH says, "Wait a minute! I never called you to be cursed! I called you to be blessed." So now he raises up a prophet and sends him to the people to say, "Walk away from the curse. Come back into the blessings." They killed that prophet.

That is a people that does not want the blessings. We live in a nation of people who don't want the blessings of YeHoVaH. They are convinced that the blessings are curses. They are trying to make their own way.

That is the sinfulness of men, the lawlessness of men. They uphold the denominational law, exalting it above the Law of YeHoVaH. They exalt the traditions of men, the traditions of the elders, the traditions of the denominations. They are exalting that above the Law of YeHoVaH. And they are thinking that if they give their tithes and offerings, they are going to somehow become debt-free.

If we give the tithes and offerings and the wealth of the wicked that is laid up for the just, imagine that. The wealth of the wicked is laid up for the just and you claim to be the just. Yet you don't have the wealth of the wicked. I wonder why.

Is it possible that you may be justified (as you think) because you believe in Jesus? But the just shall live by faith? Faith in what? Faith in his instructions.

In the next lesson we are going to get into the prophetic office. We will be looking at the development of the prophetic office. As we move into this arena, we are going to begin to see how prophecies are given, how they unfold and how we today are to interpret the prophecies that have been given to us.

Class 101 Study Summary

Key Points

1. The men and women of God who were prophets of old were declaring YeHoVaH's word, his mind and his will to the nation in times of prosperity and adversity. We are to do the same thing today.

2. Ignorance does not mean "stupid." It means one who lacks knowledge in a particular area. The way Yeshua addressed this in his day was to say that (spiritually) blind people had blind guides leading them. If you follow someone who is "blind," both of you will end up in the ditch (the pit). Once you become enlightened, you can no longer follow a blind guide.

3. The word "Niger" was pronounced "nee-ger" and was the nickname of Simeon, one of the teacher-prophets of the early church at Antioch. This Latin name means "Black." Blacks were a common sight among the populations of Egypt and North Africa in the Hellenistic period.

4. Most of the arts and depictions that we see of Yeshua and his apostles are of people from a Caucasian persuasion; when the reality is that culturally and ethnically people were very different. Historians seem to have tried to write "people of color" out of the history books.

5. In his writings, Paul identifies that there were prophets among those to whom he was writing. These prophets were morally and ethically upholding the ways of God.

6. Men are never to dominate women. That is not how things were established at creation, but there are men who would argue that fact. The reason they argue is because they are using faulty hermeneutics to interpret scripture. YeHoVaH made men and women equal.

7. People have a tendency to interpret and to read into things that aren't there and to ignore the things that are there.

8. Our work should speak for itself. People should be able to tell that we are of the Father by our fruit.

9. Our job is to do and to lead others to do what they are called to do. Our job is to equip others to prepare them for the work of ministry to which they are called.

10. Prophesying is the work of the Spirit operating in our being.

11. When you speak the word and people get upset by it, it is not you that has necessarily upset them. It is the Holy Spirit that is convicting them.

12. The prophets of old were the interpreters of the Law of YeHoVaH. They interpreted the history of Israel in accordance to the word of YeHoVaH.

13. Many people in denominations are teaching what their denomination believes. They are not necessarily teaching what the word really says.

14. YeHoVaH gave his Law to his people so they could live a long, prosperous life and enjoy the land flowing with milk and honey that they were promised. He promises us that if we are obedient that we will likewise be blessed, but we have to keep his commandments.

15. The wealth of the wicked is laid up for the just. If you give tithes and offerings, you should see the manifestation of his blessings including prosperity in finances and in other areas.

Review Exercise

1. Is there a conflict between the reality of women as prophetesses and Paul's admonition that women be silent in church? Why or why not?

_____
_____
_____
_____

2. Why are prophets referred to as "seers" and what does that entail?

_____
_____
_____
_____

3. Some people come from family, locality or religious backgrounds that foster discomfort with the idea of women as prophets/prophetesses. Drawing upon instances from your own life and spiritual walk, briefly describe your attitude toward women as prophets.

_____
_____
_____
_____
_____

4. Are you desiring to prophesy? What does that look like?

_____
_____
_____
_____
_____
_____

Rate the following statements
by filling in the most appropriate number.

(1 = I do not agree 10 = I agree completely)

Objectives:

1. I can define gender as it relates to the prophetic office.
    1. ○ 2. ○ 3. ○ 4. ○ 5. ○ 6. ○ 7. ○ 8. ○ 9. ○ 10. ○

2. I can identify various prophetesses; women who were prophets, in scripture.
    1. ○ 2. ○ 3. ○ 4. ○ 5. ○ 6. ○ 7. ○ 8. ○ 9. ○ 10. ○

3. I can describe the work of prophets in the New Testament.
    1. ○ 2. ○ 3. ○ 4. ○ 5. ○ 6. ○ 7. ○ 8. ○ 9. ○ 10. ○

4. I can explain what is meant by the prophet as "seer."
    1. ○ 2. ○ 3. ○ 4. ○ 5. ○ 6. ○ 7. ○ 8. ○ 9. ○ 10. ○

My Journal

What I learned from this class:

_____

_____

_____

_____

_____

_____

_____

_____

_____

_____

_____

_____

_____

_____

_____

_____

_____

_____

_____

Discipleship Training Class 102

The Interpretation of Prophecy (part 5)

Objectives:

As a Discipleship student, at the end of this class you will be able to:

- Explain the development of the prophetic office in the scriptures
- Define Moses as a prophet
- Label the Old Testament prophets after Moses, classifying writing and non-writing prophets

As we have noted, one of the primary reasons why there is so much division is because of how prophecy has been interpreted by the different religious groups. That is why there is so much misunderstanding. Based on this misinterpretation, principles are applied that may not necessarily be the right principles.

As we are closing out our Discipleship Training, we are going to go through these classes concerning prophecy. I don't want to skip anything.

We began to look at the development of the prophetic office. We looked at scripture that warned us not to despise prophecy. We looked at scripture as it related to the inspiration of prophecy and how it came about and we began to look at the development of the prophetic office.

We also discussed some of the men who were prophets. We identified that prophetesses were women who were prophets. By taking on the title of "prophetess"; a prophetess is a female prophet. We identified that no books were written by female prophets, although we did look at several prophecies that were given. We identified those individuals.

We went through the New Covenant/New Testament/Brit Chadasha and identified the prophets that are throughout the book of *Acts*. We identified several individuals who are named by name and who are identified as prophets or prophetesses (females) who prophesied in the Brit Chadasha.

As we move on in this lesson, we are again going to be looking at the development of the prophetic office. It is important to see the rise and development of the prophetic office. There are two focal points which are seen in the prophets Moses and Samuel.

The Prophet Moses

The Letter of the Law: Moses stands unique among the Old Testament prophets because of what he represents before YeHoVaH and the nation of Israel. It was he who received the law from the Almighty.

It is unfortunate that today there are many who still exalt Moses above Messiah. Moses is the one they follow. Rabbinic teaching alludes to Moses. They have taken the authority of Moses. On the flip side are those who follow Paul. Messiah is caught in the middle. He is the Prophet that we were warned to listen to and to take heed to. We were warned that whatever he spoke, we were supposed to do.

This is the very thing that the people of Israel said to the Almighty when they said, "No longer speak to us." They told Moses to receive the word from the Almighty and whatever the Almighty said, they would do. We know they didn't.

Today you have people who are adhering to the rabbinic writings surrounding the teaching of Moses. Then you have individuals who confess to follow Messiah, but in essence they follow Paul as if Paul taught something different than what Messiah taught.

We have noted that Paul was an avid teacher of Torah. We noted that he did not teach contrary to Messiah. Nevertheless, neither Moses nor Paul paid the ultimate price for any of us. It was Messiah who shed his blood. It was Messiah who is the Prophet. It is Messiah who is the one that Moses spoke of. We are going to look more at his ministry through the prophets.

Moses was a prophet who received the Law of YeHoVaH on Mount Sinai. He actually became the *foundational ministry*. All succeeding prophets were tested by the law given to Moses. That is how we knew. That is how the people of old knew. That is how we know today. Any prophet today who comes that is speaking contrary to the Torah, contrary to the Messiah, tells us that they are a false prophet. We have been warned that many will come.

YeHoVaH communicated with Moses face to face. He became a type of Messiah who was "like unto him." (***Numbers 12:6-8; Exodus 33:11; Deuteronomy 18:15-18; Acts 3:22-23; Isaiah 8:16-20; Luke 16:29***) These scriptures are here for your research, so you can look these things up for yourself.

The Prophets Samuel to Malachi

The Spirit of the Law: It is under Samuel that we see a distinct development in the prophetic office. The scriptures clearly mark Moses and Samuel as key men in the prophetic ministry. The people had abandoned the law. They (by the Spirit) came and began to call people back to the law.

(Acts 3:22) *"For Moses truly said..."*

(Acts 3:24) *"Yea, and all the prophets from Samuel and those that follow after..."*

(Acts 13:20) *"And after that he gave them judges about the space of 450 years, until Samuel the prophet..."*

Samuel was the last of the Judges and the first of the line of the prophets. Thus, from *Samuel* to *Malachi* we have the ministry of the prophets. It seems evident from the scriptures that Samuel (under the direction of YeHoVaH) gathered young men who were hungry after YeHoVaH into "schools of the prophets."

We note that the Bible has been written with a male bias. Therefore of the terms, "he" is predominate when it refers to individuals. The "he" that is used causes individuals to argue that, "This is referring to a male." We have already identified that there are terms "man." The definition *anthropos* as noted in the last lesson in the Brit Chadasha was related to prophets. When it related to individuals, it was "human beings" or "man-faced;" which was neither male nor female, but mankind.

These things are important. I believe that one of the reasons why religion is in the state of confusion that it is, is because it has not necessarily embraced the fullness of what the Almighty has. It is the same thing with what is related to as the five-fold ministry gifts. There are many today who believe that there is no need for apostles or prophets or evangelists. They believe that all we need today are pastors and teachers.

The thing is that when the Almighty has set a plan, when the Almighty has given an instruction, we are not to deviate from that instruction.

As we noted, He gave these things to us. He gave these apostles, prophets, evangelists, pastors and teachers. He gave these manifestations of his Spirit to us. He gave all of these things for us for the perfecting of the saints, to build up the body of Messiah.

We can't just throw things away and decide what we are going to take and reject all of the other things. This is how denominations are established. "We don't believe that. We don't believe this. Here is what we believe." They are all in a sense opposing one another. As the scripture would say, they are "swallowing camels but straining at gnats." They are looking at the minute things instead of looking at the whole of things.

From *Samuel* to *Malachi* we have the ministry of the prophets and yet the ministry of the prophets continued on throughout, even until today.

John was actually the last prophet (as we noted) before Messiah. He was the voice crying out in the wilderness. He is believed to have been prophesied by *Malachi* (as Yeshua says) for those who can receive it. John was that Elijah.

I have been asked, "Are those 'schools of the prophets' still valid today?" You have to understand that there is a lot of scrutiny that individuals have because of abuses and because of straying from the commands. Because of the establishment of different religious and denominational religions, the word has been addressed and approached from a variety of angles.

We will get into a little bit more of that today. Right now there is a lot of confusion and we are trying to clear some of these things up. The attacks that come based upon those confusions are to the point where if people were to just back up for a moment and relax and search the scriptures, it would work itself out. As I have shared with you time and time and time again, when you get into confrontations with people, oftentimes it is not about what the scriptures teach. It is about what a person believes. People argue doctrine. They don't argue scripture. How can you argue scripture if you don't know the scripture? And if you know the scriptures, you would not be arguing some of the arguments that you argue.

People are arguing based upon what they believe regardless of what the Bible says.

"Well, I don't believe that." Well, who cares whether you believe it or not? That is what the Bible says. "Well, that is not how I understand it." Well, how do you understand it? I mean, does your understanding change what the Bible clearly teaches?

Again, people are not taught scripture. They are taught doctrine and because of doctrine, it blinds them to what the scripture actually says. We have taken tests where we have read the scriptures. We see that people read from a doctrinal perspective with blinders on.

When you read the Bible, if you already believe that you know what the Bible says, that is what you read when you read the Bible, even though it doesn't even say that.

You have to take the blinders off. You have to take the denominational glasses off. You have to take a fresh look at the scriptures and then look at what it actually says versus what people say that it says.

That is how many of us got deceived for so many years into Sunday worship. It is how we were deceived into Christmas and Easter and a whole lot of other traditions that are so closely guarded and held that if you talk about it or speak against it, you will feel the venom of religion in full force.

"Where is that in the Bible?"

"Well…"

"Why are you so passionate about something that isn't even written?"

People are.

The prophets in the schools of the prophets received education and instruction out of the Law of Moses. They were taught how to respond to the Spirit of YeHoVaH in worship and in prophecy. *(1 Samuel 19:20)*

You might say to yourself, "Why does a prophet need to go to the school of a prophet?" Well, if you remember, Samuel struggled. When Samuel first began to hear the voice of YeHoVaH, he knew not the voice. He did not know the voice. Eli, a backslidden priest said to him, "The next time you hear that voice, just say 'Here am I. Speak, Lord. Here am I.'"

Now Samuel, through that bit of instruction, begins to have dialogue with an entity he didn't know. He was simply following the instruction of Eli.

When I began to hear the voice of YeHoVaH, I didn't know what it was. I had no clue who was speaking to me. I am hearing voices as far as I know.

"Maybe I need to be on some *Ritalin* like some of the other children who hear voices." Fortunately for us, there was no *Ritalin* in those days or some of the other mind-altering drugs they are putting children on to calm them down. You don't go around telling people that you hear voices.

There are people who hear voices. They don't know how to discern these voices that they are hearing, or how to identify what it is. I know people today that have dreams. And as I have shared with people, **not every dream comes from YeHoVaH**. After listening to some of the dreams, I know that dream did not come from YeHoVaH.

But they think that because they are saved, because they are walking with YeHoVaH, this must be a dream from YeHoVaH. Obviously it is not.

Prophets needed to develop their ministry. They needed to understand how YeHoVaH operated. They needed to learn the Torah. They needed to practice in an environment, in a school, in a company where they could be adjusted and corrected and encouraged.

(1 Samuel 19:20) "And Saul sent messengers to take David: and when they saw the company of the prophets prophesying, and Samuel standing as appointed over them, the Spirit of YeHoVaH was upon the messengers of Saul, and they also prophesied."

The company of the prophets, the sons of the prophets (as it is identified in some versions).

Who appointed Samuel? You see, Samuel was called. But just as Samuel was called as a child, there were many, many others who were called and who didn't know what to do with those gifts. Part of what I have been called to do is to help develop those gifts.

I have helped people develop those gifts once those gifts have been identified. There are people who don't even know they have been called to certain callings. As I am communicating with them, the Father would tell me, "This is why you are dealing with this. This is why you are having this kind of challenge."

Identifying the giftings — Paul was one who could impart gifts, impart spiritual gifts. He was one who could actually anoint and appoint.

Messiah gave gifts unto men, so it is a matter of identifying it. One of Samuel's responsibilities as one who was appointed over these individuals was to help them to develop their ministries. When we look at some of these references, there were so many prophets in these schools. Yet we only hear of a handful of them (major prophets, minor prophets). Although they are mentioned within the scriptures, because they don't have books that are associated with their names, they would be considered somewhat obscure.

Here it is. Samuel is appointed over them and the messengers of Saul also prophesied.

The scriptures speak of these centers where the sons of the prophets would gather together in preparation for ministry. It seems that schools of the prophets were found in four locations:

1. Ramah (*1 Samuel 19:18-24*)
2. Bethel (*2 Kings 2:3*)
3. Jericho (*2 Kings 2:5, 7, 15*)
4. Gilgal (*2 Kings 4:38; 23:1*)

These were places where there was a school. Let's just take a moment and look at these places.

🔍 *1 Samuel 19:18-24; 2 Kings 2:3; 2 Kings 2:5, 7, 15; 2 Kings 4:38; 23:1*

Naioth is a more specific location within Ramah. We also see that there were the sons of the prophets or the school of prophets at Bethel and at Jericho. There are at least fifty of them at Jericho. That is not to say that that is all there were, but it says that fifty men of the sons of the prophets went and stood by Jordan.

These prophets somehow are now receiving the word of YeHoVaH. Remember that the Bible says that YeHoVaH does nothing in the earth unless he first reveals it to his servants, the prophets.

Here we see that he is revealing it. They are telling this Elisha that his master is going to be taken away.

We see the sons of the prophets also at Gilgal.

It appears that the dominant purpose in the establishment of these schools of the prophets was to call Israel back to the law. We see now that there are schools where the prophets went.

Locations of schools of the prophets

You would think that if a prophet is a prophet, why do they need a school? Just speak for YeHoVaH. Much of what has to be done (just as Elisha was trained by Elijah) is okay, the prophet's apprentice watches the prophet and how the prophet does what the prophet does.

Just as Yeshua, who was the Prophet, called twelve men and told them to follow him, he said to them, "The things that I do, you shall do." There are people today who don't believe that they need anyone to teach them. Basically no one can teach them anything. They take the idea. The scripture says that there is safety in the multitude of counsel and we are to gather many, many different teachers. As I was sharing with a sister and have shared with others, if you have teachers who are teaching you opposing things, what they are teaching you to be is stagnant.

The disciples of John the Baptist, Yochanan the Immerser, were not following John on Wednesday and following some other Immerser on Thursday and then following Yeshua on Friday and following the Rabbis on Saturday and following the Sadducees on Sunday. They followed John.

How do you keep from being misled? Well, let me tell you something. If you are following different teachers, you are already misled. Why? If one is teaching you one thing and another is teaching something contrary to that, then what you have in your spirit is confusion. This causes you to be stagnant. If one person is teaching you about healing and another person is teaching against healing or if one person is teaching about spiritual gifts and another person is teaching that it is done away with and you don't see any of this in the midst of you, then you are not going to do any of that. You are not going to believe it is possible. You have opposing views.

You are caught between two opinions or two doctrines. Am I saying that we should just all follow Bailey? No. I am not saying who you should follow, but here is how you will know who is leading you. Are they teaching you what the scriptures say or are they teaching you from the other books? What are you being taught?

Let's look at the production. What are you producing? I am not trying to get followers. That is not what I am saying. What I am saying is that throughout scripture we see where individuals submitted themselves to leadership from Abraham, Moses or the prophets. They had schools of the prophets and sons of the prophets. Yeshua, Paul and now us. We live in a day where people don't feel that they have to follow anybody or whoever they follow, they don't necessarily trust.

I can see why people would be like that, but that is unproductive. You are going to have to follow someone. What you have to do is make sure they are leading you straight.

Until you are faithful with that which belongs to someone else, it is going to be difficult for you to have that which is your own. We all need mentoring. We all need discipleship. We all need the instructions and the demonstrations of the power of the word displayed in front of us. We see this pattern throughout the word.

The prophets' responsibility was to call Israel back to the law. That is a good thing right there. When you begin to think about the teachings; if someone's teaching opposed the law, then that should be a sign. They are not teaching what Yeshua taught because Yeshua didn't come to abolish the law or the prophets.

If individuals are teaching you the rabbinic traditions, then that is contrary to what Yeshua taught. He says, "Do not call any man Rabbi. Beware of the leaven of the Pharisees. Beware of the leaven of the Sadducees. Beware of the leaven of Herod."

We have all of these warnings and yet people tend to ignore the warnings. Then they wonder why they get sidetracked or they are off in some field somewhere trying to find their way back.

As Moses received the law and gave the law to the people of YeHoVaH, the true prophets of YeHoVaH never contradicted the letter of the law. They upheld it and called YeHoVaH's people to return to his law.

Prophets in Relation to the Kings

Not only do we see the beginning of the prophetic office in Samuel, we also see the beginning of the kingly office. It was the prophet Samuel who anointed both Saul and David to their kingly ministries.

Prophets had great roles among Israel's leaders. They were the ones who sanctioned. Now unfortunately the pope today; in certain places, they are the ones who basically swear. They do not necessarily appoint leaders, but they sanction leaders as the supposed mouthpiece of the Almighty.

In the Bible, it was the prophets. The prophets were also responsible for calling the kings and for calling those who were in leadership to come back to the commands when they strayed away from the commands.

From this period until the captivities of the House of Israel and the House of Judah, there is a distinct relationship between the prophets and the kings. Most of the kings of Israel and Judah had a prophet that YeHoVaH had sent to them.

YeHoVaH's purpose was to influence the government of the nation as a whole through the king by means of the prophetic word. The prophet represented the word of YeHoVaH to the kings. The kings were judged according to their acceptance or rejection of the prophetic word.

In previous periods, men inquired of YeHoVaH through the priest, but now inquiry of YeHoVaH was primarily through the prophet. Thus most of the kings were privileged to have the ministry of the word of YeHoVaH through the prophets.

- Saul and David had the ministry of Samuel. (*1 Samuel 9-10, 16*)
- David had Nathan and Gad as prophets. (*2 Samuel 12; 24:11*)
- Solomon had the prophet Nathan. (*1 Kings 1:38*)
- Rehoboam had the prophet Shemiah. (*1 Kings 12:21, 22*)
- Ahab had Elijah and Elisha. (*1 Kings 17:11, 19:16*)

The kings of the Houses of Israel and Judah had prophets sent to them. These are referred to as the major and minor prophets. They are spoken of in the opening verses of the books of the major and minor prophets. For examples, see *Isaiah 1:1-2; Jeremiah 1:1-2, Hosea 1:1-2; Micah 1:1.*

(Isaiah 1:1-2) *"The vision of Isaiah the son of Amoz, which he saw concerning Judah and Jerusalem in the days of Uzziah, Jotham, Ahaz, and Hezekiah, kings of Judah. Hear,*

O heavens, and give ear, O earth: for the LORD *hath spoken, 'I have nourished and brought up children, and they have rebelled against me.'"*

(Jeremiah 1:1-2) "The words of Jeremiah the son of Hilkiah, of the priests that were in Anathoth in the land of Benjamin: To whom the word of the LORD *came in the days of Josiah the son of Amon king of Judah, in the thirteenth year of his reign.'"*

We see similar things in *Hosea* and *Micah*.

Understanding the character and times of the kings of Israel and Judah is necessary for an understanding of the nature of the word of YeHoVaH through the respective prophets of that period.

Classification of Prophets

The prophets were classified under two groupings. This is where it gets interesting with non-writing prophets and writing prophets.

Non-Writing Prophets

There are a number of prophets mentioned in scripture who were not involved in the writing of scripture. They ministered in the realms of guidance, forth-telling, foretelling and in words of wisdom and knowledge.

We noted some of those prophets who spoke. They were "sons of the prophets" (as they were referred to) and who spoke to Elisha telling him, "Did you know your master is going to be taken away from you today?" We don't know what their names are.

YeHoVaH confirmed their ministries with signs and miracles. In the Old Testament there were men like Aaron, Nathan, Gad, Abijah, Elijah and Elisha. In the New Testament there were men such as John the Baptist, Agabus and Silas.

Writing Prophets

Out of the prophets YeHoVaH chose certain individuals to be inspired writers of scripture (*2 Peter 1:20-21*). These prophets wrote scripture in different styles: historical, poetical and prophetical.

- **Historical** — Some prophets were primarily involved in writing history. Moses was involved in writing the Pentateuch and Samuel in writing the books of *Judges* and *1* and *2 Samuel*.
- **Poetical** — Some prophets were inspired to write poetry. Two such men were David (who wrote many of the *Psalms*) and Jeremiah (who wrote *Lamentations*).
- **Prophetical** — Many prophets were inspired to record their visions and prophecies. Daniel, Ezekiel and Zechariah especially were prophets of visions. These they received and recorded under inspiration as infallible prophecy; foretelling the future and destiny of the nations.

You will note that in pretty much all of the denominations, there are many who have tried to interpret Daniel's writings. They have tried to interpret Ezekiel's and Zechariah's writings. Oftentimes this is one of the challenges. It is hard for me sometimes to deal with people who are trying to interpret prophecies; especially from prophets who prophesied hundreds of years ago. Many individuals try to interpret today's prophecies through modern events.

Every generation does this. One of the things that I have done, is read. My son asked me, "Dad, what hobbies do you have?" My hobby is reading. I mean, I read. I read anything. I read the labels on bubble gum. I get into a waiting room and I just grab a book and start reading. I like reading and I like research. I like finding the origins of things. Some of the things that I read (for instance) have to do with how many times the end of the world has been prophesied.

I am telling you. This has been going on for at least 500 years. It was going on (if we look at scripture) in the context of scripture. We will see that there were individuals in Paul's day. If you read *1* and *2 Thessalonians* you get the impression that there were individuals back in the day of Paul's writings who expected the end of the world to come during their lifetime, during the first century.

Each century after that, each generation after that, individuals have predicted based on current events or based on their understanding of *Daniel* and *Ezekiel* and *Jeremiah* and *Zechariah.* They have been predicting end time events for millenniums.

Every year and every generation there arises someone who wants to predict the end of the age, the end of time. They want to look at modern events and current events. I mean, how many scenarios have we heard concerning who the Anti-Christ is? How many scenarios have we heard concerning the "mark of the beast?" There are more than we can count of what the mark is going to be. People spend days and weeks and months and years debating this issue. They are no closer today than they were a thousand years ago.

We can spend our time trying to figure out what the mark is or we can spend our time trying to figure out what the Messiah wants us to do.

I would rather spend my energy trying to figure out what I am supposed to be doing than eating all of this stuff that people are sending me to birth fear. There are too many fearful people saying, "Did you see this? This is a must-read. The end is near!"

I see stuff like that. Those are fear mongers. The Father has not given us a spirit of fear, so why are those who claim to be his people promoting fear? If he hasn't given us this spirit of fear, then why are you promoting fear?

When you die, you are dead. Then there is the judgment. You can either live afraid to die or you can live knowing that you are going to die one day and welcome death. Death is not the end. It is the transition. We are here to live our lives as fully as we possibly can. There is no fear here for real.

The prophets were called. As we look at their prophecies, does that mean that we don't think about them and take them to heart? Oh, absolutely. Daniel's words are important. Ezekiel's words are important. Zechariah's words are important.

I will tell you whose words are more important than all of them put together and those are Messiah's words. What he said is the one that we are supposed to be listening to. When he identified things that were spoken by the prophet Jeremiah or the things that were spoken about by any of the prophets, he was trying to teach us something from the prophets. We need to recognize that. He is the one that we need to really pay attention to.

The prophetical books of the Old Testament have been referred to as the major and minor prophets. This distinction refers only to the volume of their contents.

Major Prophets

Isaiah	Jeremiah[10]	
Jeremiah	Ezekiel	Daniel

Minor Prophets

Hosea	Jonah	Haggai
Joel	Nahum	Zechariah
Amos	Habakkuk	Malachi
Obadiah	Zephaniah	

All of these books include both forth-telling and foretelling with greater emphasis on foretelling.

Classification of Written Prophecy

In the writings of the prophets there can be found three major classifications of prophetic revelation. They are: Local Prophecy, National-Destiny Prophecy and Messianic Prophecy.

Local Prophecy

These are prophecies that were for a specific locality. This refers to instances when the prophet speaks to his own generation about their spiritual condition and YeHoVaH's desires for them. He is speaking to a particular people about what YeHoVaH was requiring of them. For instance, one of the prophets (Jonah) was sent to Nineveh. He was sent to speak to the Ninevites concerning what the Almighty was going to do to the Ninevites. That was a local prophecy. It has absolutely nothing to do with us. It was for that people at that particular time. The king of Nineveh called a fast. He called the people to fast and to seek the Almighty. Basically they came to a place of repentance where the wrath of the Almighty was thwarted. That was a specific prophecy dealing with a specific location with a specific people at a specific time.

---

[10] He is believed to have written Lamentations.

Examples of Local Prophecy: *Isaiah 40:18-31; 55:6-7; Jeremiah 26; Micah 6:8.* These prophecies obviously included timeless principles applicable to all generations. The Father is still requiring that we do justice and love mercy.

National-Destiny Prophecy

This was prophecy that spoke to the national future of Israel and what YeHoVaH was going to do. National-Destiny Prophecy is when the prophet speaks concerning the future history of nations. That future history is sometimes for a time; like when the Almighty would tell the children of Israel that they are going to go into captivity and they are going to go into captivity for a specific time. He also talked about the two houses and what is going to happen; and even the end from the beginning. He tells them what is going to be the outcome of Israel.

Some examples of National-Destiny Prophecies: *Isaiah 11:11-16; 43:1-28; Jeremiah 30; Ezekiel 27* and *Romans 9, 10* and *11*.

Isaiah 11:11-16

There is so much there, but I just want you to see prophecies that deal with the destiny, the national destiny.

Messianic Prophecy

This is when the prophet speaks concerning Messiah and the ekklesia or called out ones. This is viewed primarily as prediction. This is a case where the prophet may use various elements of past history, the present local situation and even the future national destiny to foretell the ultimate phase of YeHoVaH's purpose in the Messianic era. This goes all the way back to *Genesis*.

Messianic Prophecy encompasses all that relates to Messiah and the ekklesia or called out ones; from his first coming through his second coming.

It is interesting that with some prophecies, if you read them and you take time to read them and not be in a hurry and if you can ignore the marks that are there, some of these prophecies become clear. They clearly speak of the first and the second coming.

It was spoken of by Peter as "the sufferings of Messiah and the glory that should follow."

1 Peter 1:1-16

Notice that Peter's letter is addressed like many of the letters that are written. If Paul is writing to the Church of Ephesus or the congregation or ekklesia or the called out ones or the *kahilah* of Ephesus, that is who he is writing to. Peter here is writing: *"to the strangers that are scattered through Pontus, Galatia, Cappadocia, Asia, and Bithynia."*

What Peter is actually saying is that we once were his, but we fell away. Now he has brought us back. It is almost like saying, "We have been born again, again." We were begotten, and now we are begotten again.

Peter is saying that there is a salvation that is coming. People sometimes struggle with the idea. I know that the Calvinists came up with the philosophy that "how do you explain this salvation thing?" Are we saved? When do we get saved? The Calvinists came up with the philosophy that we are saved, we are being saved and we shall be saved.

Again, Peter is saying that there is a salvation coming. **What Yeshua said to us in** *Revelation* **is that those who endure to the end shall be saved.** This salvation that we put our hope in is going to come at the end, but **the prerequisite for that salvation is endurance.**

You can't quit. You can't give up. If you give up, if you don't endure to the end, then guess what? You won't be saved.

What do I mean? Well, is it the end yet? It is an endurance to the end. I am not talking about works. I am talking about what the Bible says.

There is a seal. The seal is the Holy Spirit. We have been marked. We have been sealed by the Holy Spirit. But how many of you know that you can grieve the Spirit? You can resist the Spirit. You can "not" be led by the Spirit (not as in "cannot," but as in not being led as an option). You can walk away from the Spirit.

You have to endure to the end. You have to be led by the Spirit. You have to walk in the Spirit. If we walk in the Spirit, we will not fulfill the desires of the flesh, so we are living a holy life. This is what Peter is getting to.

We have to endure. We have to live. We have to look at all of this mess around us and all of the garbage and the junk that the world is throwing at us and not give in. Some of it, I am going to tell you right now. Some of this stuff that they are throwing at us doesn't look wicked. It looks pleasurable until you get caught up in it.

The next thing you know, you hear the clank-clank of that prison cell. A person who has an addiction, a person who has sold their soul; you didn't know you were giving your soul to the devil when you first took that hit on that marijuana cigarette. You didn't know you were giving your soul to the devil when you first started sniffing that white powder or drinking that liquor. That wasn't the plan. The plan was simply to enjoy oneself. The plan was simply to have a little fun.

The next thing you know, the fun becomes work. The work became an addiction. So now people start working for their addictions to satisfy the cravings of their flesh. That is what an addiction is. It is when you crave something to the point where you will do whatever it is you need to do to get it. You don't care about anything else. But it didn't start out that way.

This is why you can't give place to the devil. You just don't know. I have story after story, after story. The only thing that keeps me from sharing some of them is the confidentiality. But there are things that people do that they give themselves to. When it comes down to it, all it takes is one time for a child to be abused. You can't undo that. Some things you just can't undo. Once a person has crossed that line, it is not like I am just playing footsies with the devil. The devil doesn't play.

When we were children, we used to shoot marbles. We had how we are going to shoot for "funsies." If you win all of my marbles because we are shooting for funsies, you have to give them back. Then you could shoot marbles for keeps. That means that whatever you win is yours. The devil doesn't play for funsies. He plays for keeps.

This is why the Bible explicitly says to give no place to the devil, none. Don't even think about it. Peter is saying, "He's all around us like a roaring lion. He's seeking whomever he may devour." He doesn't come to invoke fear as much as he comes to bring a temptation.

Let me tell you something. Those who fear YeHoVaH recognize the temptation before it even gets up to them. They see it coming. They are trained to look for it and to resist it.

You are going to see. This was a Messianic Prophecy. There is something that you have to have in your heart first.

How do you gird up the loins of your mind (verse 13)? These are metaphors. You are going to find as we begin to look in the word, that there are many metaphors like bind the word around, let them be as frontlets between your eyes, bind them on your hands. That doesn't mean to go out and get leather straps and phylacteries, but people take metaphors and try to bring them into reality and the next thing you know, you have a tradition.

Verse 13 is talking about the second coming. In other words (verse 14) you have come out of that. Now look to the coming, the return.

Messianic Prophecy may be divided into three groupings based on three stages of fulfillment:

1. The First Coming of Messiah

These prophecies deal mainly with the birth, growth, ministry, sufferings and exaltation of Yeshua. Most of the Old Testament Messianic Prophecies pertain to the first coming of Messiah and its related events.

Some examples are: *Genesis 3:15; Deuteronomy 18:15-18; Psalms 2, 8, 22* and *40; Isaiah 7:14; 9:6; 40:1-8; 52:14; 53:-12; 61:1-4; Jeremiah 31:31; Micah 5:1-2; Zechariah 11:12-13; 13:9.*

Let's take a look at the first one. In the beginning, YeHoVaH had already planned this thing out even before there was the beginning. I learned a long time ago about philosophical debates. These are conversations you can get deep into when you have smoked a little marijuana. "Why did God put the tree in the garden? Didn't he know they were going to eat? Why did he make man in the first place? Why did he give him a woman who is going to eat from the tree and cause them to get kicked out? Was it Adam's fault or was it the Creator's fault?" You get into a lot of these philosophical debates, especially when you don't have a whole lot of other things to do, like the word.

It is important. As I was mentioning earlier, if you don't have the fear of the Almighty in you, you will not recognize the works of the enemy. **In order to recognize the counterfeit, you have to be intimately acquainted with the real.** YeHoVaH is the real. He is the real.

When Adam and Eve ate from the tree, they said these words, "We hid because we were naked and we were ashamed." YeHoVaH's response was, "Who told you that? Who told you that you were naked?"

We don't see the devil or the serpent saying, "Hey, did you guys know you all were naked?" No, we don't see those words in the *Genesis* account, but we see the Almighty ask a question: "Who told you that you were naked?" You are listening to someone who is saying something to you that I have already said, but they have put a twist on it. The Bible says that they were both naked and they were not ashamed.

Now we see that the Almighty is about to pronounce judgment. He says,

> **(Genesis 3:15)** *"And I will put enmity between thee and the woman, and between thy seed and her seed; it shall bruise thy head, and thou shalt bruise his heel."*

This word "enmity" is a flat-out hatred. **We should hate sin. We should hate the things that YeHoVaH hates.** The things that he despises, we should despise. If we don't have a hatred for the things that YeHoVaH hates, we will find ourselves moving into a position of tolerance and acceptance and compromise.

Then the enemy begins to redefine YeHoVaH to us. They "love" each other. "Doesn't the Bible say that God is love? And if we love him and love our neighbor it is really all about love. If two people love each other, isn't that what the Almighty is about, regardless of whether they are two men loving each other or two women loving each other? It's really about love, right?"

The enemy begins to redefine the Almighty. He begins to reintroduce an old conversation with a new spin. This causes us to look at it just like he did with Adam and Eve. "Wait a minute. Did he really say that?" You see, he knows that when you do this, that this is what is going to happen. He doesn't want that to happen.

This is what some of the individuals do who try to philosophize. They try to give an answer for why the Almighty doesn't want people to do certain things, when the scripture doesn't say that is why he doesn't want you to do that.

I am not here to try to explain stuff that he hasn't explained. Like the Adventists wanted to figure out a way to keep some parts of the law without accepting the law. So the part about the clean and unclean food becomes not really a command. It is rather that we just look at it as dietary the right thing to do. What you have just done is you have figured out a way to keep a part of the law that you want to keep without addressing it as the law. "After all, we are not under the law."

"Well, if you are not under the law, then why are you keeping the dietary parts?"

"Because that is just eating healthy."

"So are you telling me that this portion of his commands are good, but the rest of it is not?"

This is what people do. They take what they want and discard the rest. They put a twist and a spin on it so it is not necessarily the law. It is something else.

YeHoVaH doesn't play those games.

If we look at where it says this, this enmity that he puts between you and the woman and between the woman's seed and your seed, is a flat-out hatred for the things that YeHoVaH hates.

Now, you have to understand something. YeHoVaH hates homosexuality, but he is not zapping homosexuals. YeHoVaH hates adultery, but he is not killing adulterers. He is saving his wrath for the children of disobedience that he will mete out at the judgment.

In the meantime he is giving all mankind space to repent, and that is the call — *REPENT! For the Kingdom of Heaven is at hand.* The love of the Almighty is that he is not pouring out his wrath on you right now, but that means that you have to repent because his wrath is being held up. There is a day that he is going to unleash it in full force and you don't want to be in that line.

So now, today is the day of salvation. Today is the day of deliverance. Today is the day of repentance and that is the good news.

He is offering you a chance to be begotten again.

Class 102 Study Summary

Key Points

1. One of the primary reasons why there is so much division is due to how prophecy has been interpreted by different religious groups.
2. Moses was the one who received the letter of the law from the Almighty. It is unfortunate that even today there are those who exalt Moses above the Almighty, as if it is Moses' law. They are following the letter of the law, but they don't have the Spirit of the law (Holy Spirit).
3. By the Spirit of the law, under Samuel we see a distinct development in the prophetic office. People who had abandoned the law were being called back to the law.
4. The Bible has been written under a male bias. There are few women mentioned in the Bible, but of those who are, their roles are not expounded upon.
5. John the Baptist (Yochanan) was the last prophet before the Messiah came.
6. People are not being taught scripture. They are taught denominational doctrines.
7. Every dream that you have does not come from YeHoVaH.
8. If individuals are teaching you the rabbinic traditions, then that is contrary to what Yeshua taught.
9. Prophets had great roles among Israel's leaders. They were the ones who sanctioned. They spoke to the kings, the rulers. The kings of the House of Israel and Judah had prophets sent to them to speak the words of the Almighty. A good king heeded their wisdom. A wicked king killed them.
10. There are writing prophets and non-writing prophets. The writing prophets are those who wrote scriptures. The non-writing prophets are mentioned in scriptures, but we do not see anything they wrote in the scriptures.
11. Of the writing prophets, some were involved in writing history, some were involved in writing poetry and some were inspired to record their visions and prophecies.
12. For centuries people have been trying to predict end times prophecy using the writings of *Daniel, Ezekiel, Jeremiah* and *Zechariah.*
13. Yeshua said in *Revelation* that those who endure to the end will be saved. This salvation is what we put our hope in, but the prerequisite for that salvation is endurance and obedience.
14. In order to receive the real, you have to be able to recognize the counterfeit.
15. We should hate sin. We should hate the things that YeHoVaH hates.
16. Today is the day of deliverance. Today is the day of repentance. That is the good news.
17. Messianic prophecies pertain to the first coming of Messiah and its related events including his birth, growth, ministry, sufferings and exaltation.

Classifications of Prophetic Revelation

There are three major classifications of prophetic revelation. They are:

1. Local Prophecy – These are prophecies meant for a specific locality.
2. National-Destiny Prophecy – This was prophecy that spoke to the national future of Israel and what YeHoVaH was going to do.
3. Messianic Prophecy – This is when the prophet speaks concerning Messiah and the ekklesia or called out ones. It is viewed primarily as prediction.

Review Exercise

1. Why is it said that Moses' prophetic ministry is the foundational ministry?

_____

_____

_____

_____

_____

_____

_____

2. Complete the missing information on this prophecy classification sorter:

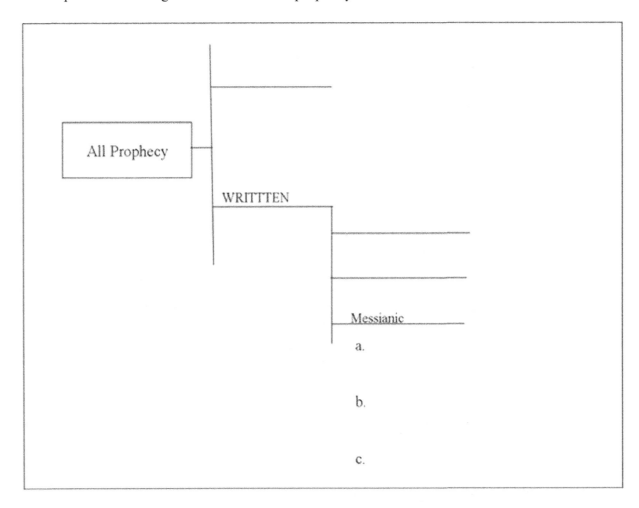

(NOTE: You will need to reference Lesson 103 to complete this chart.)

3. Samuel was instrumental in the growth of the prophet office. Why?

_____
_____
_____
_____
_____
_____
_____
_____
_____

4. Name the three literary styles of written prophecy and note an example of each.

a._____
_____
_____
_____
_____
_____

b._____
_____
_____
_____
_____
_____

c._____
_____
_____
_____
_____
_____

Rate the following statements
by filling in the most appropriate number.

(1 = I do not agree 10 = I agree completely)

Objectives:

1. I can explain the development of the prophetic office in the scriptures.

   1.◯ 2.◯ 3.◯ 4.◯ 5.◯ 6.◯ 7.◯ 8.◯ 9.◯ 10.◯

2. I can define Moses as a prophet.

   1.◯ 2.◯ 3.◯ 4.◯ 5.◯ 6.◯ 7.◯ 8.◯ 9.◯ 10.◯

3. I can label the Old Testament prophets after Moses; classifying writing and non-writing prophets.

   1.◯ 2.◯ 3.◯ 4.◯ 5.◯ 6.◯ 7.◯ 8.◯ 9.◯ 10.◯

My Journal

What I learned from this class:

_____

_____

_____

_____

_____

_____

_____

_____

_____

Discipleship Training Class 103

Interpretation of Prophesy (part 6) — Principles of Interpreting Prophecy (part 1)

Objectives:

As a Discipleship student, at the end of this class you will be able to:

- Define the classifications of written Messianic prophecy
- Explain interpretive principles as they apply to the interpretation of prophecy

As we look at prophecy, we got into the first coming of Messiah and prophecies that deal mainly with the birth, growth, ministry, suffering and exaltation of Yeshua. We noted that most of the Old Testament Messianic prophecies pertain to the first coming of Messiah and to its related events.

Let's look at *Jeremiah 31*. It is interesting as we look at what *Jeremiah* shares with us. What is really interesting in this particular verse is the language. Make sure you search out those passages listed near the end of class #102. It is important that as we look at biblical prophecy, that we look at some principles on how to interpret these prophecies.

(Jeremiah 31:31) *"'Behold, the days come,' saith the* LORD*, 'that I will make a new covenant with the house of Israel, and with the house of Judah:'"*

This is one of those prophecies that people are very familiar with (for the most part). I did a teaching on the *Renewed Covenant*[11] that actually deals with this particular passage. This is one of those teachings that I really encourage people to get. It really goes well with the teaching *You Must Be Born Again.* These two teachings are really very good companions for one another.

But here in *Jeremiah* it is a Messianic prophecy. Actually if you look at it closely enough, you will see that it is two-fold. You will notice that the language deals with the House of Israel and the House of Judah. That is because during Jeremiah's time the House of Israel and the House of Judah were separate. There was a division. These are now two houses; the House of Israel and the House of Judah.

Pay attention now.

---

[11] See all of our video teachings and books at *www.ArthurBaileyMinistries.com.*

(Jeremiah 31:32) *"'Not according to the covenant that I made with their fathers in the day that I took them by the hand to bring them out of the land of Egypt; which my covenant they brake, although I was an husband unto them,' saith the LORD:"*

At that time there was only one house, the House of Israel. The House of Israel now has become two under Jeremiah's prophecy. Jeremiah is prophesying that Israel is going to be divided. Under Solomon, when Solomon died, Israel was divided into two kingdoms — the Southern kingdom and the Northern kingdom. That was the House of Israel and the House of Judah. From that time on, Israel and Judah had separate kings.

(Jeremiah 31:33) *"'But this shall be the covenant that I will make with the house of Israel; After those days,' saith YeHoVaH, 'I will put my law in their inward parts, and write it in their hearts; and will be their Elohim, and they shall be my people.'"*

Now, if you notice the language, there is a change. There is a change in the language in this verse and if you don't pay attention, you will miss it. He starts out by saying, "I'm going to make a New Covenant with the House of Israel and the House of Judah." Now there is a change.

He is going to make a New Covenant with the House of Israel and the House of Judah, but now there is only one house, the House of Israel. The House of Judah and the House of Israel are now going to become one house again. This is what Messiah is going to do. He is going to bring both together. It is going to be one. It will be the House of Israel.

Here he is saying that this is the covenant made with the House of Israel AFTER those days.

"Behold the days come" is looking at two houses, but after those days it is going to be one house. That will be the House of Israel. Notice also that Israel will not be brought into Judah. In other words, it will not be the House of Judah. It will not be the House of the Jews. **All of Israel is not going to become Jewish. It will be the House of Israel. It will consist of all of the tribes.**

Unfortunately today when people think of Israel, they hear "Israel," but they think "Jewish." That does serious damage to the Messianic kingdom. The Messianic kingdom will not be filled with Jews. You don't have to convert to Judaism. You don't have to become a Jew. You don't even have to think Jewish.

I don't understand why so many today are trying to look Jewish, sound Jewish or are trying to act Jewish when the fact of the matter is that Judah and Israel will become one house. It will not be the House of Judah. It will be the House of Israel. This is what Jeremiah is prophesying.

(Jeremiah 31:34) *"'And they shall teach no more every man his neighbor, and every man his brother, saying, Know the LORD: for they shall all know me, from the least of them unto the greatest of them,' saith the LORD: 'for I will forgive their iniquity, and I will remember their sin no more.'"*

Notice what is going on. He is going to put his law in their inward parts. This is not a new religion. This is not a Gentile religion. This is not what it is talking about. In many Seminaries and Bible Colleges and churches, they are teaching about the different ages. They are teaching about the age of the church, the church age, the age of the law. The church age is the age of grace.

All of this is *replacement theology.* It has no place in scripture and yet it is being taught as scripture. Now all of Israel has become Jewish and if you are part of Israel, you are now a Jew. This is another form of replacement theology.

You have the church replacement theology where now all of the Jews have to become Christians and you have Judaism replacement theology where all of Israel now has to become Jewish.

This is what is going on in the land today. In order for a person to make aliyah, in order for a person to become part of the commonwealth of Israel, they now have to convert to Judaism and denounce Messiah. This is not the plan of YeHoVaH, but this is exactly what is being played out and some would attribute this to biblical prophecy.

I will tell you how it associates with prophecy. The way it associates with prophecy is that YeHoVaH is going to bring that down. He is going to bring it all down. Israel as we know it today will not be the Israel in the fulfillment of scripture. It will not be the land of the Jews. It will be the House of Israel.

Those of you who want to get caught up in Zionism, I am telling you that you are wasting your time. You are wasting your energy. You are wasting your money because that is not the plan of YeHoVaH.

Messianic Prophecy, continued

We were talking and are continuing with Messianic prophecy. It is divided into three groupings based upon three stages of fulfillment.

The first coming is the first.

2. The Ekklesia or Called out Ones

These prophecies deal mainly with that which was to be the fruit of Messiah's sufferings, even the glory of the ekklesia or called out ones. (*Ephesians 3:21*) There are many Old Testament prophecies which deal with the coming of the Gentiles into the Kingdom of Messiah.

The ekklesia has been wrongly interpreted as "the church." When you read in the Bible, you will see the term "church" when in actuality it is "the called out ones," the *ekklesia* (in the Greek).

One of those prophecies was literally prophesied that when you begin to look at the interpretation of prophecy, that things will look like they do today.

Some examples of Messianic prophecy concerning the ekklesia or called out ones are: *Isaiah 9:6-7; 26:1-4; 35:-10; 54:1-17; Jeremiah 31:33; Joel 2:28-32; Zechariah 2:10-11; Malachi 1:11.*

Let's look at *Joel 2*. Many people are familiar with Joel. Peter certainly quoted Joel in his response to those who were saying that those who were of Messiah were drunk when they began to be filled with the Holy Spirit.

🔍 *Joel 2:28-32*

When you read Joel, what you are going to find is that what happens on Shavuot in *Acts 2* is a fulfillment of *Joel* that shall come to pass <u>afterwards</u>. Something is going to happen "before-wards." After this happened, YeHoVaH is going to do such and such. He is going to pour out his Spirit upon all flesh.

The Pentecostals intepreted this to speaking in tongues. They believe that when the Holy Spirit comes, the evidence of the Holy Spirit is going to be speaking in tongues. This is a false interpretation, a wrong interpretation, a misinterpretation. Now you have people seeking spiritual gifts instead of seeking YeHoVaH, who through Yeshua gives the gift of the Holy Spirit and all that comes with it.

Now you have people tarrying and desiring the gift of tongues, when nowhere in the Bible does it say to desire the gifts of tongues. As a matter of fact, the one who even spoke on spiritual gifts and who wrote to us said, "Tongues are the least of the gifts. I would rather that you prophesy." That is the fulfillment of the prophet Joel, not speaking in tongues except that there is interpretation.

Read *1 Corinthians 14* and look at what actually happened in *Acts 2*. There were tongues and those who were there from all of the different nations and who heard them in their own language — interpretation. Tongues and interpretation equals prophecy (fulfillment of *Joel*).

3. The Second Coming of Messiah

These prophecies deal primarily with Messiah's return to consummate that which he initiated in his first coming. This is what we are looking to. Those of us who are his (of Messiah) are looking for him and living our lives in a way expecting that one day he is going to come. We don't know the day. We don't know the hour, but we do know that he is coming.

We look to and anticipate his coming. In the meantime we are casting out devils, laying hands on the sick, prophesying and taking the good news of the Kingdom to the whole world — not that gospel about Jesus, but the gospel that Yeshua preached.

Some examples of second coming prophecies are: *Genesis 49:10; Isaiah 2:10-22; 13:6-16; 24:1-23; 30:26-33; 34:1-17; Daniel 2 and Daniel 7; Joel 3; Zechariah 14; Malachi 4:1-4; Matthew 24; Mark 13; Luke 21; 1 Corinthians 15: 1 Thessalonians 4:14-18; 2 Thessalonians 2; 2 Peter 3:1-13; Revelation 19.*

They are throughout the Bible. We know that he is coming again. There are many prophecies that not only prophesied his first coming; but the way that the prophets prophesied it, (if you remember); punctuation marks have meaning.

If you put a comma in the wrong place, if you ignore a comma or a quotation mark or a colon or a semi-colon or an exclamation point or a question mark, all of these marks tell the reader that something happened just then.

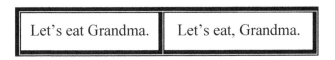

| Let's eat Grandma. | Let's eat, Grandma. |

Punctuation marks matter.

When you research the scriptures and especially if you look at it in the original context in which it was given, you will say, "Hey, wait a minute. The way that has been interpreted and the way it should be interpreted don't connect. That is why it is important for you to know the principles of interpretation and it is important for us to understand the proper way to interpret scripture.

Principles of Interpreting Prophecy

This is where we tie all of the things together. We are bringing this to a close, so we have to tie everything from Class 1 to this particular class and the next two classes.

Guidelines Based Upon the Principles of Scriptural Interpretation

Although prophecy is unique in its nature, the guidelines for its interpretation are to be primarily taken from the principles that are used to interpret the whole of scripture. It is here that the principles that we have previously discussed come into play.

The Context Principle

More misinterpretation of biblical prophecy has occurred because of the lack of the use of this foundational, basic elementary principle.

a.) The first rule of hermeneutics is **"scripture interprets scripture."** It must be applied to prophecy.

b.) Any verse of prophecy must be considered in the light of its biblical, testamental and book context.

c.) Caution must be used in the interpreting a verse of prophecy in the light of its passage context. This is because the prophets (caught up in an ecstatic state) often did not weave together a context with a logical train of thought or a chronological treatment of events.

That first rule has been broken on so many levels that it is absolutely ridiculous. We noted that in the context principle you have the context of the passage. I know people talk about the

"Non-Inspired Version" and all of that, but this is why when it comes down to the various versions of the Bible, I use different versions for different reasons.

I probably have about fifteen or twenty Bibles. Then I have Bible software with practically every version of the Bible that is available.

Every Bible is formatted. The King James Bible unfortunately is formatted by verses, so what the King James Bible writers did is decide to put headings in the verse passages.

One of the problems with headings on a particular passage is that you can see how they are often in paragraph form. Chapters and verses are within the paragraph. The average person who is not taught this stuff wouldn't even pay attention to it. In other Bibles it is formatted into verses. In the King James it is a challenge to use the context principle. That is because now you have to use English principles in order to determine when a subject matter changes.

In English when a subject matter changes or there is a transition from one thought to another thought, there is a new paragraph. That is an indication that there is a transition in thought. You are transitioning from one thought to a totally different thought.

The NIV and some other Bibles put it in a paragraph form to let you know that there is a transition of thought. The other thing it does is that it puts a heading, like "The Healing of a Paralytic" or "The Calling of Matthew." What this does to the unlearned researcher is that it creates a mindset before you even read the passage.

The writer here in his or her attempt to try to help you with the context principle is leading. In a court of law the opposing counsel would say, "I object. Counsel is leading the witness." A lot of these headings — what it does is lead the reader. The reader now comes to the conclusion of the writer, which removes the reader's ability to think for himself or herself.

It is good in one sense that the King James doesn't do that, but in another sense you can read run-on. One sentence runs into another sentence runs into another sentence to another to another (or chapter or verse). Pretty soon you will see that a person is reading a chapter and everything within that chapter, when oftentimes there is a transition of thinking in that chapter.

So if I am reading chapter 1 of one book of the Bible, it could have five or six or seven or eight transitions to the point where now the context changes. If I just extrapolate that verse (which in the King James is easier to do) and then mix it with some other verses, pretty soon I have what they call a "topical sermon." This is not an expository sermon. It is a topical sermon where I want to find out everything about food, for example.

Now unfortunately you can only do that in the Old Testament. That is because once you get into the New Testament, everything is edible according to some of these people.

When you begin to deal with the topical sermon, that is the only time you can take verses out of context, if you would. You will find that if I want to do a series on Adam, then I am going to find out every place in the Bible where Adam is mentioned and I will use that.

You should be able to recognize these types of sermons when you are listening to ministers. These things have been done to us. We don't even know that they are done. With most of us, when you hear "three-point sermon," you will know exactly what is going on. The preacher is going to make three points. And typically those points are going to have some rhythmic flow.

These are popular in Baptist Churches and in Calvinistic, Reformed, Presbyterian and Methodist Churches. With Pentecostals there are no three-point sermons. You will find more of the cut and paste style. You will find individuals pulling scriptures out of the air and making them say whatever they want them to say. Then they put a little dream in there and throw a little prophecy in there. The next thing you know, you have folks running around the building getting "slain in the Spirit."

This is not to make fun of this stuff, but you must be aware of how people have come in and slaughtered the scripture to make it fit their agendas or their denominational flow or thinking.

In considering point C (of the context principle), a prophecy could go back and forth. Similar to the book of *Revelation* (which is a prophetic book), it doesn't follow a chronological order. We here in the West especially, read a book from the beginning to the end. Everything is in chronological order. In some books, when you begin to talk about a novel where you have flows of thought, it differs. When you think about something like *Pilgrim's Progress* and John Bunyan's writings (an allegory), you will have random thoughts going on all at the same time.

Revelation is one of those books where it is not in chronological order. *Daniel* is not in chronological order. When you even look at the Torah, the Torah has verses that are repeats of verses in different places. Then *Deuteronomy* ties it all together.

You have to be able to look at things within contexts. Sometimes the context is not a particular flow or is not in a logical train of thought or a chronological order.

This is where the Spirit comes in. **If you read the Bible like you read a book, you will ignore the work of the Spirit.**

Here are a couple more additions to the context principle application to prophecy:

d.) In dealing with prophecy, the interpreter must work from whole to part and part to whole.

e.) The obscure passages should be interpreted in light of the clear.

As we learned in the context principle, there is the context of the passage. There is the context of the chapter. There is the context of the book. There is the context of the testament and then there is the context of the entire Bible.

If I want to learn about Abel, what is interesting is that YeHoVaH has more to say about Abel (seemingly) in the book of *Hebrews* than he does in the book of *Genesis*. When it comes to the Melek Tzedek, very little is said about Melchizedek in the Torah. You will find more in the *Psalms* and you will even find even more in the book of *Hebrews*.

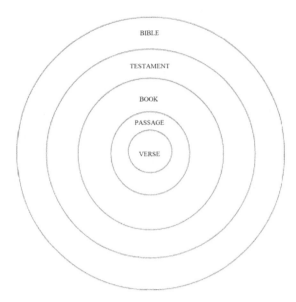

In order to understand Melchizedek, you cannot just deal with the context that is there in the book of *Genesis*. You have to look at the whole.

Now the whole of the Bible helps us to get an understanding of who this fellow Melek Tzedek is. Some people make an argument concerning Adam. I had one fellow who gave an interpretation. I know he meant well, but the interpretation of *Genesis 1* and *2* was if YeHoVaH created two groups of people. One he doesn't name, but the other group he names. So now Adam has children that marry this other group of unnamed people. It looks that way, but that is not the way it is.

One can make an argument (although it would be a shallow argument), that in one place he creates these individuals. In the other place he gives them names.

In order to understand *Genesis 1* and *2*, we see in *Genesis 5* that he gives us a broader stroke of *Genesis 1* and *2* as it relates to the genealogy whereas *Genesis 5* doesn't even mention Abel and Cain. It starts out with Seth.

You have to look at the obscure passages and say, okay. Did YeHoVaH create another race of people that he neglected to tell us about but that he lets us know that he did? It is like, okay. He created these people, but don't pay any attention to it. They are just out here and from time to time they will show up, but you won't know anything about them. They'll just show up. Don't try to understand it.

YeHoVaH says that with all of our getting that we should get what? An understanding. He is not the author of confusion. He is not trying to confuse us. He is not leaving cliff-hangers. He is an intelligent being. He created intelligent people. There are times when we have to use our intelligence as well as our discernment.

I received a letter. The timing of this letter was interesting. The letter is from a person who is asserting themselves as a prophet.

I guess I got a copy of the letter because of our name, House Of Israel. I don't know if he went through the phone book or went through the Internet and sent everyone who has "Israel" or "Judah" or anybody that is associated with the name. I don't know. But I get this letter and it is from Prophet So-and-So. It is to the President of the Ethiopian Crown Council, but it is sent to me. I guess because we are a part of the House of Israel and I am Black, then I "must" be an Ethiopian Jew.

And that is the other thing. Folks say, "Well, yeah. There are other Jews, but they are Ethiopians." So there are Black and White. There are White Jews and all the Black Jews. One fellow asked me when he saw my tzitzits, "Are you an Ethiopian?" Am I an Ethiopian? Why? Because I am part of the House of Israel and because I am of the African persuasion? Therefore I must be a Black Jew.

I am telling you that this way of thinking, this frame of thinking has already been framed and fashioned by the powers that be. We don't even know that they are there, but here is how we think today. We didn't get here by accident. This was by design that you are either a Jew or a Gentile. There are only two groups of people: Jews and Gentiles. If you are not Jewish, you are a Gentile. And if you are not a Gentile, then you are Jewish. If you are Jewish, you are either White or you are Black and if you are Black, you are from Ethiopia.

Now, I didn't come up with this. I didn't come up with it. It was here before I got here. I have to deal with it. I have to live in this culture and try to make sense of it and try to help other people make sense of it.

It is amazing when you deal with Torah-observant people. Torah-observant people have taken on this mindset, even though the term "Gentile" is in the Torah but the term "Jew" is not. YeHoVaH never refers to his people as Jewish. He refers to his people as Israel or Judah (and mainly Israel).

When Paul talked about and wrote "all of Israel," he didn't say all of the Jews would be saved. He said "all of Israel" and we have to understand what that is.

The letter writer says that God promised King David that every generation he would raise up one of the King Solomon's sons to sit on his throne. Wait a minute. That is in the opening of the letter that God promised this. This is the prophet. Then he gives a scripture, *Psalm 89:3-4.*

First of all, YeHoVaH never made such a promise. Oftentimes if you want to cut to the chase — this is why when somebody gives me a book, I want to see what is the general opening. One of the things that I have learned in literature and in English is that when you are writing a letter, you have your opening, your body and your closing. The opening phrase, the opening statement, is generally what the body is going to be sort of built upon, even though there will be transitions of thought. Then it will close by bringing the opening, the body and the close together.

Well, I have read several books and generally in the opening, in the introduction, in the first paragraph of the first chapter you can pretty much get an idea of where this person is going to go (at least for me). I don't know if everybody has an ability to do that, but I do.

Generally in anything that deals with theology, a person is going to state the case and then they are going to make the case. They state the case and then the body is to make the case that was stated.

Now, when I read the opening statement of this letter, I note very much at that particular point that everything that is going to come behind this particular phrase is going to be off because the opening phrase is off. YeHoVaH never made Solomon a promise like that. He made this promise to David.

But the individual takes *Psalms*. This happens all of the time and it is just amazing.

(Psalm 89:1-4) *"I will sing of the mercies of the LORD for ever: with my mouth will I make known thy faithfulness to all generations. For I have said, 'Mercy shall be built up forever: thy faithfulness shalt thou establish in the very heavens.' I have made a covenant with my chosen (David), I have sworn unto David my servant, 'Thy seed will I establish forever, and build up thy throne to all generations. Selah.'"*

Whose seed? David. **There will always be someone of David's household on the throne.** Yeshua is a son of David or he is referred to as a son of David, but this individual now wants to take that from David and then associate it with Solomon. Well, the moment you associate it with Solomon, now you can get into Haile Selassie. You can get into the Ethiopians and the Coptics. You can get into the Rastafarians. You can get into all of these off-brand religious groups that trace their lineage (supposedly) back to Solomon.

Haile Selassie was supposed to have been the descendant of Solomon's encounter with the Queen of Sheba. Generations, many generations pass and this is supposed to now be the lineage of Solomon which is the body of this letter. It is based upon scripture that is misinterpreted. Therefore the body and the case that one is trying to make (to state the case or make the case) is already flawed. This is how we got so many denominations today.

It is amazing that it is all based upon how the Baptists (for example) see John the Baptist. John the Baptist is the "founder" of the Baptist Church. The day of Pentecost was the day that the church was "born." The Pentecostal movement was "established" on the Day of Pentecost. Now we have the "Church of Christ" and the "Church of God in Christ." This is how all of these denominations get their name.

People say that I did the same thing for the House Of Israel. Well, do you know what? The House of Israel is what YeHoVaH is establishing. He established the House of Israel. Man can't do it. We are part of the House of Israel. We are not *the* House of Israel. We are all a part of the House of Israel because we are part of the family, the household, the commonwealth of Israel which is YeHoVaH's house and his people.

It's simple.

The First Mention Principle and Prophecy

Recognizing the value of first mention, the interpreter should be faithful to consult the first mention of the prophetic theme with which he or she is dealing. When we begin to deal with the first mention principle, remember that we noted that the first time a thing is mentioned is not necessarily the first time it shows up in scripture.

We see that David gave tithes (several tenths of everything) to the Melek Tzedek. But we were able to trace this principle all the way back to Cain and Abel when Cain brought the fruit of the ground and Abel brought the firstlings and the fat thereof.

The word "tithe" is not mentioned there, but the principle that evolved into the giving of tithes and offerings is mentioned right there in *Genesis 4* although it doesn't show up until *Genesis 14.*

The Comparative Mention Principle

a.) The interpreter should be diligent to search through scripture for any possible fulfillment of the prophecy under consideration.

There is a particular prophecy that Daniel speaks about. Then Messiah speaks about it. That was the abomination that caused desolation. The abomination that caused desolation appears to have a two-fold fulfillment. There is the one with Antiochus Epiphanes in the days of the Maccabees and then the one where Yeshua comes along and says when you see the abomination that causes desolation. This indicates that this is a future event, although some interpret it as something that has already happened.

b.) In interpreting prophecy, all prophetic passages relating to the same subject must be brought together and compared.

Now you have to do some comparatives. You have to compare these prophecies to see.

The Progressive Mention Principle

a.) When dealing with a prophetic theme, the interpreter must be aware of its progressive development throughout scripture.

b.) The interpreter must not confuse the progressive development of the prophetic theme.

Folks want to come up with progressive revelation. There are some things that the Father speaks and then he builds upon them.

Genesis 1 — He speaks. Then in *Genesis 2* he gives us more of the picture.

In *Genesis 5* he gives us a much broader stroke, so we are now able to look back. Every book of the Bible has a way of connecting; especially all of the prophetic and historical books of the Bible. The major prophets and the minor prophets all have a connection to the Torah.

The Brit Chadasha/New Testament all connects to the Torah. We see Yeshua and his disciples. We see Paul. All are quoting from the Torah.

The Complete Mention Principle

a.) For the interpreter to understand all that the scripture has to say on any given prophetic subject, he or she must bring together all relevant prophetic passages.

b.) Each prophetic passage must be interpreted in light of this whole.

When you begin to talk about what YeHoVaH said he is going to do, there is YeHoVaH doing what he said he was going to do and then there is the reference to what he did. Then there are times when he refers to what he is going to do if we don't pay attention to what he has done.

It is very difficult. Do you know what people like doing? They like to take sound bytes. Much of what I do when I am dealing with people who have biblical questions is this. Oftentimes a person will read a verse and get stuck on a verse. "What does this verse mean?" Well, if you read five or six more verses, you might get the interpretation of it.

The Election Principle

a.) The interpreter must constantly keep in mind the fact that YeHoVaH's elective purposes are the foundation of prophetic revelation.

b.) When interpreting national prophecy, the interpreter must keep in mind YeHoVaH's elective purpose for that specific nation.

YeHoVaH made some promises to a variety of people besides Israel. He gave land to people besides the twelve tribes. And he declared, "This is their land." Interestingly enough, he made promises of blessing. Think about it. Abraham will become the Father of many nations — MANY nations. Now, I don't know why we have a tendency to read our Bible in such narrow views, but if he is going to become the Father of many nations and all nations will be blessed because of him, all nations will be blessed because of him. Doesn't that mean ALL nations and every nation on the planet?

There are several ways you can look at this and possibly even interpret it. In one sense, because Messiah is going to come through the lineage of Abraham, Messiah himself is going to be the fulfillment of this particular prophecy (that those who call upon the name of Yeshua will now become part of Abraham's blessing). All will now become heirs of Abraham, the seed of Abraham.

But the other is the word itself. It is interesting that when you begin to think about the three major religions in the earth — Judaism, Christianity, and Islam; Christianity was initially Messianic. They were called "Christians" in Antioch. That's what we see the interpreters inserting into the Bible. They weren't called "Christians" in Antioch. There was no such thing. They were called "followers of the way" or "Notzirim" (followers of Messiah).

The term "Christian" is a creation of the Catholic Church. The word is *ekklesia* (what they were). They were the called out ones. They were called out of every nation. Why? Because YeHoVaH had scattered his people to every nation. Now he is calling them out. This faith that they respond to is the word of faith; for faith comes by hearing; by hearing the word of YeHoVaH. When the word of YeHoVaH, the true word of YeHoVaH goes forward, people who have somewhat of a connection or whose past is connected are going to recognize this voice. They will say, "Wait a minute. Hold it. This man doesn't preach like all these other people. This Yeshua doesn't sound like all the other Rabbis. This man preaches with authority." There was a distinction.

It was much so that it threatened all of the religious groups in Yeshua's day to the point where they threatened people. Anybody who put their faith in this man will be kicked out of their synagogues. They won't have access to communion.

Yeshua was one who preached with authority. Those who follow him will have that same authority. That is because he gave them that authority. "All authority," he said, was given to him. This authority he shared with those whom he called.

Here is something else. In the Christian Church we used to hear "Gawd does not share his glory." But the fact of the matter is that Yeshua himself said, "The glory you have given me, Father, I now give to them." He gave his glory. He gave this glory that the Father gave him, to his disciples.

Guess what? That glory that the Father gave to Yeshua, that Yeshua gave to his disciples; that glory is now what we operate in. That's authority. That's power. He does share his glory, but not that men may glory; not that men may now begin to build their own kingdoms. The glory that he has given is for the purpose of advancing his Kingdom. It is to call people back to him and not to some denomination.

That is what he is not going to share. He is not going to share his glory so somebody else can go and build up their kingdom and exalt their kingdom like they tried to do in Babel. His glory is given to his people so that his people will bring people into his glory, not into their own glory.

But you have the old folks who say, "God is not going to share his glory with man" (and that is partially true). **He is not building denominations. He is building the household of faith. That is what he is building. He is not building organizations. He is building people.**

When the priests put the name of YeHoVaH on the people (the Aaronic Blessing), what they are saying is that you are now YeHoVaH's property. Act like it. You are now YeHoVaH's sons and YeHoVaH's daughters. Represent him rightly. You are now his ambassadors. You are his spokesperson. You are his mouthpiece.

You are not here to speak your own words. You are not here to do your own thing. You are not here to go your own way. You have been bought with a price. Your life is not your own, so it is not about you building something that you can put your name on. It is about you building people up so that they are ready for this coming of the Messiah, who is coming.

The Covenantal Principle

a.) All prophecy must be considered in the light of its covenantal background.

b.) The interpreter must determine which covenant was the basis for the prophet's ministry.

There were certain things that the prophets — Jeremiah, specifically, Daniel is another, that were called to a generation, to a people who in that calling to a generation, to a people, to a nation, prophesied to the nation. They spoke of those things which were to come. They were dealing with those things that were at that particular moment and warning the people of YeHoVaH of what they were doing and what they were supposed to be doing. It is just as he said, "Jeremiah, I want you to tell my people here is what is going to happen. Let them know they are going to be carried away." He is telling them things before they happen and while they are happening.

This is important when you begin to study prophecy. I am going to tell you something. One of the major things that you want to do when you are reading *Jeremiah* is this. There are some key things you need to know. For instance, at what time in Israel's history was Jeremiah the prophet? Under what kingdom? When you can put the prophet at a particular time, you can now see the timeframe in which this prophet was prophesying. You can see where Israel was at that particular time in prophecy.

Now you have put the prophet into context. So the prophecies that are going to be prophesied by the prophet are during a particular era. They are during a particular time in Israel's history while YeHoVaH is doing certain things to his people, for his people or in the midst of his people.

You need to know. You just don't say, "Oh, the prophet Joel said such and such." When did Joel say this? At what time in history did Joel speak?

If I want to think about it, there were prophetic words that were given during Y2K. Remember Y2K? People were saying "Blah-blah-blah, this is going to happen and that's going to happen." There was a great panic and people were doing all kinds of things. You think there are preppers now? Man, there was some serious prepping going on in Y2K. Remember? "The whole grid is just going to collapse! The computers as we know it are all going to stop!"

There were things that were said specifically to that generation and during that era. Now, if I want to take a prophecy that was prophesied to the Y2K generation and try to apply it to this generation, can you imagine that? It doesn't even compute.

There were prophecies that were prophesied before Israel went into captivity that prophesied the coming of that captivity and what would take place during that captivity. Those prophesies were specific. They were to a time.

Some of you all remember about five or six years ago, the Prayer of Jabez. Man, the whole Christian world was praying the Prayer of Jabez. Now they want God to enlarge their territory. Jabez prayed a prayer and YeHoVaH answered Jabez' prayer. That prayer was associated with whom? Jabez. It was based upon his name.

Unless your name is Jabez, people want to hijack Jabez's prayer. They want to hijack Jabez's blessings.

Here is another one. "Not by power nor might, but by my Spirit says YeHoVaH." This was spoken to a specific time to a specific people for a specific reason of what YeHoVaH was going to do.

You say, "Okay. This was a word of YeHoVaH." Yes, this was a word of YeHoVaH for this particular people and how can I apply that today? You have to be careful that you don't take prophecy out of context. Let me tell you something. When you are seeking tongues instead of the ability to prophecy, you have no choice but to live on old prophecies.

YeHoVaH is speaking to his people today. This is the work of the Holy Spirit. The Holy Spirit is to teach us all things. He is to guide us and to show us things to come. This is why YeHoVaH says, "In that day I am going to pour out my Spirit on all flesh. My Spirit will not just be to the prophets. My Spirit will be on all flesh. And the abilities that the prophets had, my people will have because they will have my Spirit just like my Spirit was with the prophets."

You shall prophecy. You shall speak those things that are not as though they were. You shall receive revelation and prophetic utterance from the Almighty by his Spirit to speak to the things that are in your midst and the things that are in your presence and the things that are to come. You can speak to the nations. That is what prophecy was for. That is what the prophets were given the prophecies for; to speak to the people. But you can't build your prophecies off of the wrong foundation (your prophecy, your prophets).

In order to test the Spirit and in order to operate by the Spirit, you have to know what the word says. You can't be cutting and pasting and taking things and making them say something that the scripture doesn't say. That is critical, but if you are too busy seeking the speaking in tongues instead of coveting to prophecy, then you will not be in a place where you can hear YeHoVaH's voice and speak what YeHoVaH says.

That is the danger of misinterpreting the scriptures. Instead of tarrying for the Holy Spirit to speak on some unknown language, you are seeking the Holy Spirit to be the mouthpiece of YeHoVaH. Those things that he revealed to us in secret, now we can declare boldly from the rooftops.

He wants us to hear. He wants to us know what is his heart and what is his mind. He has given us the mind that he desires us to have, but we are so busy thinking our own thoughts and doing our own things and doing things our own way. That is not what he is calling us to do.

Now people are reading *The Purpose Driven Life*. They want to know what their purpose is. Let me tell you something. **You are not going to find your purpose in a book. You are going to find your purpose sitting in the presence of the Almighty.**

The people who found their purpose wrote it in a book. Now they are selling books and people are buying books. That is that person's prophetic word or that is that person's word from YeHoVaH.

What is yours?

c.) The interpreter must have a thorough knowledge of the covenants in order to be able to discern the covenants referred to in various prophetic passages.

d.) The developmental progression and interrelatedness of the covenants must be recognized when dealing with prophecy.

This is what the schools of the prophets were about. The schools of the prophets were to teach the people the covenants. They could understand the covenants from the Torah. The Torah explained the covenants that were important to YeHoVaH's people.

This New Covenant is the Old Covenant written in us. How do you know what is written? You refer to what is written.

How do you know what he is writing? If you don't know what is written, then you won't properly interpret what he is writing,

We have looked at the covenant principle in this training. We looked at all of the covenants.

e.) All prophecy must be ultimately interpreted in the light of the New Covenant. Old Testament prophecy must be interpreted through the cross. It must not be used to overrule the Everlasting New Covenant.

When we begin to look at these particular covenants, we know that Jeremiah said that there is a New Covenant that YeHoVaH is going to establish. When that New Covenant is established, then we are going to see the Everlasting Covenant come into fruition.

Has the New Covenant been established? That is the question. The New Covenant has been ratified in the blood of Yeshua.

We are going to experience this New Covenant. We are experiencing it. The New Covenant will be firmly established when the Messiah returns. There will come a point in time when this New Covenant is here (and here we can look at the language). The moment you get away from what the scriptures say and you get into sermons, then you begin to believe what the sermon said.

Notice what it says here.

(Jeremiah 31:33-34) "*'But this shall be the covenant that I will make with the house of Israel; After those days,' saith the* LORD, *'I will put my law in their inward parts, and write it in their hearts; and will be their God, and they shall be my people. And* **they shall teach no more** *every man his neighbor, and every man his brother, saying, Know the* LORD: *for they shall all know me, from the least of them unto the greatest of them,' saith the* LORD: *'for I will forgive their iniquity, and I will remember their sin no more.'"*

When the New Covenant is established, there will be no more need for teaching. The fact that we are still teaching, the fact that we are still trying to get the gospel of the Kingdom to the ends of the world is a firm indication that the New Covenant is not fully realized.

This is what the prophet said, so how can someone interpret what the prophet said and make it say something other than what it is saying? "Well, right now this is the age of the church. This is the New Covenant. He has written his law in my heart." This is what the church is saying.

Well, if he has written his law in your heart, why aren't you keeping his law? What law are you talking about?

"No, he wrote a new law."

"Well, what law is that?"

"Love. It's the law of love. Just love everybody."

I tell you that if you don't understand the principles and properly apply these principles, then chances are you are going to be misled. You will follow blind guides. You will end up in a place where the Almighty has not predetermined that you end up.

Many of us have been going down that road for a long time. We do this until by the grace of the Almighty our eyes are opened. Then it is like, "Oh, wait a minute! Hold it. We have been going in the wrong direction." Now many of us are trying to holler and scream at some of our family members and friends and loved ones who are still going in that direction and they think we have lost our minds.

We can actually say (as the song says) "I was blind, but now I see." Seriously. I see. **Now I'm not blind anymore. The scales of religion have fallen off.**

Class 103 Study Summary

Key Points

1. The New/Renewed Covenant with the House of Israel and with the House of Judah is the covenant/prophecy that most people are familiar with. It is a Messianic prophecy.

2. All of Israel is not going to become Jewish. It will become the House of Israel. The New Covenant will consist of all of the tribes together under the House of Israel.

3. The ekklesia/called out ones prophecies deal mainly with that which was to be the fruit of Messiah's sufferings; even the glory of the ekklesia or the called out ones.

4. The ekklesia has been wrongly interpreted to be the "church." In actuality it is the called out ones of the faith.

5. Pentecostals have misinterpreted *Joel 2* to speaking in tongues. As a result, they believe that the "evidence" of the Holy Spirit is speaking in tongues. This is a false interpretation. Now they are tarrying for the Holy Ghost. Scripture reveals that tongues are the least of the gifts.

6. The second coming of Messiah prophecies deal primarily with the Messiah's return to consummate that which he initiated at his first coming. That is what we are looking to.

7. Punctuation did not occur in the Hebrew scriptures the same way it is used in the English translations. It was added during translation. Punctuation is very important in the Bible. When it is misplaced, it can certainly change the meaning of the word.

8. Although prophecy is unique in its nature, the guidelines for its interpretation are to be primarily taken from the principles that are used to interpret the whole of scripture.

Review Exercise

1. In this lesson we have circled back to the hermeneutical principles of biblical interpretation that we spent quite a lot of time on earlier in this course. You should feel equipped to use these principles. If you sense from this review that you might benefit from revisiting those, be sure to go back to those lessons and get a firm grasp on these essentials.

2. On the fourth page of this lesson (under item 3) there are some citations concerning the second coming of Messiah. Be sure to read those carefully and prayerfully. Resolve any potential conflicts through further study. You may find it useful to make a chart showing what information each gives about this important event in *your* future.

3. Make some notes here about how each principle specifically relates to prophecy:

    a. The context principle:

    _____
    _____
    _____
    _____

    b. The first mention principle:

    _____
    _____
    _____
    _____

    c. The comparative mention principle:

    _____
    _____
    _____
    _____

    d. The progressive mention principle:

    _____
    _____
    _____
    _____

e. The complete mention principle:

_____

_____

_____

_____

f. The election principle:

_____

_____

_____

_____

g. The covenantal principle:

_____

_____

_____

_____

4. Do you believe that any prophecy found in the Bible can be satisfactorily interpreted using the Bible? Why or why not?

_____

_____

_____

_____

_____

_____

_____

_____

_____

Rate the following statements
by filling in the most appropriate number.

(1 = I do not agree 10 = I agree completely)

Objectives:

1. I can define the classifications of written Messianic prophecy.

   1. ◯   2. ◯   3. ◯   4. ◯   5. ◯   6. ◯   7. ◯   8. ◯   9. ◯   10. ◯

2. I can explain interpretative principles as they apply to the interpretation of prophecy.

   1. ◯   2. ◯   3. ◯   4. ◯   5. ◯   6. ◯   7. ◯   8. ◯   9. ◯   10. ◯

My Journal

What I learned from this class:

_____

_____

_____

_____

_____

_____

_____

_____

_____

_____

_____

_____

_____

_____

_____

_____

_____

_____

_____

Discipleship Training Class 104

Principles of Interpreting Prophecy (part 2)

Objectives:

As a Discipleship student, at the end of this class you will be able to:

- Define the hermeneutical principles in the successful interpretation of prophecy
- Define the five unique guidelines in the interpretation of prophecy

Can you believe that we are actually coming to the conclusion of two years of Discipleship Training?

We are going to pick up where we left off in the last lesson as we are talking about the interpretation of prophecy. We were about to get into the ethnic division principle. We didn't get into it, so we are going to pick up from there.

The Ethnic Division Principle

When it comes down to the principles for interpreting prophecy or the principles for the interpretation of prophecy, we are now connecting all of the principles that we have learned as we talk about the hermeneutics of the art and science of biblical interpretation or biblical hermeneutics. We looked at all of these principles that we went through over the last 103 lessons.

Now we are seeing how all of these principles not only are utilized in the interpretation of scripture, but especially prophecy. **A lot of scripture is prophecy.** Some of it has already come to pass and some is yet to come to pass. We have to distinguish between those which were spoken of that have come to pass and those that are yet to come to pass.

a.) To properly interpret prophecy, the interpreter must have a thorough knowledge of YeHoVaH's appointed ethnic divisions and their respective places in his purposes.

When we looked at the ethnic division principle, we note that the Father dealt with specifics. He dealt with people in specific regions. He dealt with people in specific areas and language. There were certain things that he spoke about in his word as it related to the twelve tribes of Israel and also as it related to the surrounding nations and as it related to the nations that they were going into. All of these principles are now being pulled together.

b.) In order to distinguish between these divisions, the interpreter should ask himself the following questions:

- Does this verse refer to the united nation, the whole House of Israel?
- Does it refer to the ten tribe House of Israel, the Northern kingdom?
- Does it refer to the two tribe House of Judah, the Southern kingdom?

When it comes down to various prophecies, there were some that were specific for Abraham. There were prophecies that were specific for Isaac and for Jacob and for the twelve tribes and there were some specific for the divided nation. We have to ask these questions.

"United nation" does not refer to that which is in New York City. We are talking about the united nation as it relates to the House of Israel. When we talk about Israel today, Israel has been exiled. It has been spread to the four corners of the earth (if the earth has corners). It has been spread to the nations of the world. And for the most part, we look at Israel as two houses — the House of Israel and the House of Judah.

- When we look at a particular prophecy we have to ask ourselves.
- Does this particular prophecy refer to the whole House of Israel?
- Does it refer to the ten tribe House of Israel, the Northern kingdom?
- Does it refer to the two tribe House of Judah, the Southern kingdom?
- Does it refer to the Gentile nations? (These are the non-Hebrew nations.)
- Does it refer to the ekklesia, chosen out of every nation?

These are questions that we have to ask ourselves as we are looking at prophecy in order to come to somewhat of the right conclusion in our interpretation.

The Chronometrical Principle

a.) It must be recognized that the prophets were not always aware of the time element in their own prophecies. (*1 Peter 1:10-12*)

There were prophecies that where spoken which came to pass during the prophet's lifetime. There were prophecies that were spoken that were to come to pass that have not even come to pass (and here we are at least a thousand years removed).

(1 Peter 1:10-12) *"Of which salvation the prophets have enquired and searched diligently, who prophesied of the grace that should come unto you: Searching what, or what manner of time the Spirit of Christ which was in them did signify, when it testified beforehand the sufferings of Christ, and the glory that should follow. Unto whom it was revealed, that not unto themselves, but unto us they did minister the things, which are now reported unto you by them that have preached the gospel unto you with the Holy Ghost sent down from heaven; which things the angels desire to look into."*

Peter is speaking here. As the chronometrical principle points out, prophets were speaking back then of things that are actually manifesting right now, or in Peter's day. What Peter was saying about some of the things that the prophets were speaking was that they really had no understanding of what they were saying. But these prophecies that they were speaking; the things that they were speaking about were for us.

We certainly know that in Peter and Paul they referred to things that were written for our ensample or for us to note and for us to understand.

b.) The prophets were caught up into YeHoVaH's timeless perspective in which past, present and future were laid out before them. Thus in transcending time, some prophetic passages involve a weaving together of the past, present and future. Often in speaking to their own generations, the prophets would use the past as a stage upon which to foretell the future.

We see this certainly even in Moses' life, in Jeremiah's life, in Daniel and especially those prophets or those individuals who were before the carrying away into Babylon or during the carrying away into Babylon. Whereas even when they returned, Nehemiah and Ezra began to speak of the things that the people did which caused them to go into captivity, some of the things that the people were doing were similar to the things that the people did that caused the captivity in the first place.

There are things that people are doing today, even though the church today does not necessarily consider itself either one of the two Houses of Israel, but a separate entity. The idea of replacement theology removes the two-house prophetic nature of scripture and adds an entirely different element. Then it begins to try to interpret prophecy through that element.

That is where it gets really tricky.

To the reader, the time elements seem to be confused. At times they utilized what is known as "the prophetic perfect tense." This is speaking of future events as though they had already occurred. Therefore the interpreter must move with extreme caution in assigning prophetic passages to specific time fulfillments.

One of the things that you are going to see as a conclusion of these particular studies is one of the reasons why I am very, very careful about dealing with prophecy. Now, there are people who have no issue with dealing with prophecy. I am not saying that I have an issue, but when I began to apply the principles to interpret prophecy, I understand that a prophet could speak as though they are speaking in the present tense about something that is not going to happen until way out into the future.

I also note that many today try to interpret biblical prophecy through current events when looking at the news. There are certain individuals on television. Their whole platform is headlines around the world. They are pulling headlines here and headlines there. It really grieves me, especially when I see people that I know, ministers that I know. They are taking prophecy way out of context to try to apply it to this generation.

It is like, okay. How do you take a thousand-year old prophecy and say that this is the time that this is happening? When the fact is that the surrounding elements — like it really is a united nation prophecy or it is a two-house prophecy that has absolutely nothing to do with America.

I am seeing some real foolishness going on. You can mention certain names who are sensationalizing the scriptures in order to build some kind of name or reputation or following.

I don't know what the motive is behind it, but I do know that it does more damage than it does good.

We have to move with extreme caution when we begin to try to assign prophetic passages to specific time fulfillments.

c.) The interpreter should ask him or herself the following questions in order to distinguish the time element in prophetic fulfillment:

1) Was the prophecy fulfilled during the lifetime of the prophet who was speaking?

That is certainly a legitimate question. There are certain prophecies that were already fulfilled. We do know that there are some prophecies that seem to have more than one element of fulfillment as some would effectively argue. They talk about the prophecy that Daniel spoke about concerning the abomination that causes desolation. Many would say that when Antiochus Epiphanes did what he did during the days of the Maccabees, that it was a fulfillment of Daniel's prophecy. And yet after that Yeshua talks about how when you see the abomination that causes desolation, these are some things that should be done.

Even though that had been completed, it is being spoken of as if it hasn't been fulfilled. We are left with no choice but to accept the fact that this is a two-pronged fulfillment. That is not unusual for prophecies in the Bible.

It is a matter of whether or not you read a hundred miles an hour over it or you take the time to dissect it and look at it to see whether or not this is a two-pronged or a three-pronged fulfillment that the prophecy is prophesying.

2) Was the prophecy fulfilled during the time of the captivity of the House of Israel to Assyria or the House of Judah to Babylon?
3) Was the prophecy fulfilled in the restoration of Judah from Babylon at the close of seventy years of captivity?
4) Was the prophecy fulfilled during the time of Judah in the land after the Babylonian captivity during the intertestamental period?
5) Was the prophecy fulfilled in the New Testament times in relation to the Messiah, the ekklesia or the Hebrew nation?

The intertestament period was that period when you have the apocryphal writings, where you have the books of the Maccabees and other writings that were once part of the 1611 King James Bible and some of the other books that somehow made their way out of those particular works.

It is interesting about a fellow, Rabbi Schneerson. There were those who believed that he was actually the Messiah. During the time when he passed, they held vigils expecting his resurrection. When he didn't resurrect from the grave, there were individuals who got disillusioned and disheartened and many walked away from Orthodox Judaism.

There was a word out awhile ago about this famous Rabbi who predicted that once former Prime Minister Ariel Sharon died, the Messiah would be ushered in or he would be revealed. I have heard individuals say that Schneerson revealed to his inner circle how to be able to determine those who were of Messiah.

You have people who got disillusioned and they walked away from Judaism. They walked away from the Orthodox faith and began to embrace the Messiah. Then you have people today who argue the facts of whether Messiah fulfilled the prophecies of scripture or if he has not fulfilled the prophecies of scripture. Let me tell you something. That is a true argument, to a point.

The reason why many in Judaism don't accept Messiah is because there are certain prophecies that have not yet been fulfilled.

According to the prophets who prophesied, when you take a good look at some of these prophecies (especially Jeremiah's prophecy in *Jeremiah 31*), you can see this two-pronged approach. You can see that there is a first coming and there is a second coming.

The fact is that Messiah has not reestablished Israel as a nation. That is a fulfillment of the prophecy that concerns the Messiah that is going to be fulfilled upon his return.

There are those who can legitimately argue and say, "Well, no. All of the prophecies concerning the Messiah have not been fulfilled." And yet we cannot deny that a great deal of prophecy concerning the coming of Messiah has been fulfilled that is associated with his first coming and the conclusion of those that will be fulfilled at the second coming which he himself predicted and the prophets predicted. But because people look through scripture using a specific lens, they don't see the whole picture. They see part of the picture.

So prophecy today is still being fulfilled.

6) Is the prophecy currently being fulfilled?
7) Is the prophecy to be fulfilled in the final years prior to the second coming of Messiah?
8) Is the prophecy to be fulfilled at the second advent of Messiah?

There are questions that you have to ask. If people can successfully argue and some are successfully arguing to people who don't do their homework. They are not grounded and rooted in the faith. We have to be aware of the fact that there are people who just go and come. There are folks who get disillusioned with that faith. They get disillusioned with this faith. They are like a leaf blowing in the wind.

The moment you challenge them in a particular area and show them some scripture that gets at the heart of their sacred cow they are holding onto, now they have to grab onto some other cow or some other sacred thing.

All of this is because of the understanding of the principles that are involved. If you don't understand the principles that are employed in the interpretation of prophecy, then you will look at prophecy from a skewed view. Therefore you are really at the mercy of those who have a different interpretation.

9) Is the prophecy to find fulfillment in the future ages:

- The Kingdom of YeHoVaH relative to earth?
- The eternal state of the new heaven and new earth?

There are certain things we know. There will come a point where there will be no more weeping. You have to understand that when you begin to look at this whole "no more weeping," it will only be those individuals who are within relationship. Outside of the city (the Bible says) there are going to be dogs. Outside of the city there will be a lot of weeping. There will be gnashing of teeth and there will be all kinds of things. That is because the abominable, the liars and all these whoremongers and people who are doing the detestable things are not going to be allowed in the city. This will happen when we talk about the new heaven and the new earth and the holy city that is coming down.

That is when we begin to look at the chronometrical principle in association with the interpretation of prophecy.

The Breach Principle

The interpreter must recognize that some prophetic passages deal with conditional promises. Because of this, the promise may be fulfilled in the prophet's generation if certain conditions are met.

When we look at the book of *Jonah* based upon what YeHoVaH said concerning Nineveh, Nineveh should have been destroyed. But YeHoVaH chose to recant because of Nineveh's repentance.

That is one of the beautiful things about repentance. We have to understand that repentance does not necessarily undo what has been done. For example if a person is in a state of rage and they murder someone and then they come to their senses. "Oh, what have I done?" There is Godly sorrow. There is true heart-felt repentance. They truly feel badly for what they have done. Yet they have a murder conviction to deal with.

The repentance of the person does not undo what has been done, but it certainly grants the mercy of the Almighty. It may even grant some mercy of the judge when they see that there is legitimate remorse. In some cases a person may even have to go through some kind of therapy. You have people who snap. You have people who do things and mentally they are unstable. I mean, there are a whole lot of things, but still the person whose life has been taken, that life is gone.

A person can repent, but it does not undo what has been done. And yet in the eyes of the Almighty, it can cause his heart to turn toward that person.

This is certainly one of the cases we find in the Bible and that says, "The Father repented that he had made man." He turns his wrath away. And then even today his desire when we are living in such a wicked world and yet the wrath of the Almighty is not coming upon us or upon this world as this world deserves because the Father does not desire that any should perish.

This makes our work that much more important.

We have such an important role in the Kingdom of YeHoVaH. That is because he is withholding his wrath. He is giving us time to get the true gospel message out so that people will turn. They will recognize, "Hey. What I am doing is wrong. How I am living is wrong."

It is amazing just watching how people seem to take the mercy and the withholding of God's wrath for granted. That is really unfortunate.

Peter wrote about this. He said that there are those who are saying, "You guys have been talking about how the Messiah is going to come and you have been talking this stuff now for almost 2,000 years." That is a long time (from his first coming to his second coming). We are looking at almost 2,000 years having past. Since that time people have been saying, "He's coming! He's coming!"

Okay, we have heard it. We have heard it and we still proclaim that he is coming. Do you know that after awhile you can get dull of hearing? It goes in one ear and out the other. After awhile you just start going through the motions. After awhile you get complacent. After awhile the world around you seems to be so desensitized and attracted to where generations now are getting sucked into the world around us. That is because, okay, y'all been talkin' that "Jesus is coming" stuff or that "Yeshua is coming" stuff or that "the Lord is coming" stuff. You have been talking and they have been talking this stuff. The old folks used to say the same thing.

Now you have "twerking" Grandmas and "twerking" Great-Grandmas. The world is a mess.

There is some sad stuff going on out there in the name of Jesus and in the name of Yeshua. It is really, really sad.

Now with the breach principle, if the conditions are not met, the fulfillment of the promise may be postponed to another generation. With this in mind, the prophet ministers to the people; either exhorting them to fulfill the conditions, or pronouncing judgment upon them for having failed to do so.

This is one of the things that we see even when Moses began to share the word of YeHoVaH in *Exodus 20*. He said, "YeHoVaH is a jealous Elohim, visiting the iniquities of the Father to the third and fourth generation." Even scientists today in the medical arena, when they talk about certain hereditary types of diseases, they say that they can skip generations.

This has been scientifically declared. It has been scientifically "proven" that diabetes can hit one or two people in a household of five; while three in the household never even come under the influence or are affected.

There are heart conditions, heart diseases and certain types of traits. There are sickle cell anemia traits and other types of traits that certain people in the family may be affected by and autism and all kinds of other things that are taking place in a family. You have certain people in the family that are affected while other people in the family are not affected, even though everybody is coming from the same parents.

Here it says that if certain conditions are not met, the fulfillment of the promise may be postponed to another generation. With this in mind, the prophet ministers either exhorting them to fulfill the conditions or pronouncing judgment upon them for having failed to do so.

This is one of the things that would do us all good to try to do. I know for some of us it is very tough. How do you put yourself into a different era? I think of myself. I was watching one of the things that I look at from time to time. There are a lot of judge shows on TV. These judges have real cases coming into their courtroom — Judge Mathis and Judge Judy and others. They have real cases that are coming. And being in certain situations where I have gone into courtrooms with people, I have seen people standing before judges.

Judges have to sit and figure this stuff out. Every time I see one of these judge shows I think about Moses out in the wilderness. I think about having to sit there and listen. Then one of the things that hits me was Solomon when he had to deal with these two women who came into his presence. One of them knew full well that the baby wasn't hers. Think about it. You have a person showing up in court laying claim to a child that they know full well is not theirs, but they are there acting as if this child is legitimately theirs.

Imagine being a judge in that situation. You have to try to figure out who is telling the truth. And here it is when we begin to talk about how you are dealing with people. We are trying to put ourselves in those particular situations.

Imagine us (you, me) being children in the wilderness with the children of Israel. You really don't know how you would act unless you are actually in that situation. You would not know unless you were out there in the wilderness day and night and were hungry and not knowing where you were going and all kinds of things.

It took a lot of faith, but we see that there wasn't a lot of faith in the wilderness. There wasn't a lot of faith. They didn't have a jack-leg preacher. They didn't have preachers from every denomination saying, "We have the truth. We have the truth and we have the truth." They had Moses. They had Joshua. They had Aaron.

They had the pillar of fire and the cloud. They had the *shekinah*. They had the Ark and yet even Aaron the high priest died in the wilderness. All of those individuals died out there in the wilderness; all because they lacked faith.

Then the Bible says that these things were written for us. We are those people today.

With all of the things that are going on around us, it is easier than you think to get disillusioned. It is easy to take our eyes of the one who gives the prize to those who finish the course. That is because we are surrounded by people who are complaining and murmuring and they are watering down the faith that was once delivered. They have a belief where all you have to do now is to mentally ascend to a particular thought.

It has become so watered down today. I think today that it is more difficult than it was in their day. As a matter of fact, I am convinced of that because I do declare that right now I am aware that everything I do is being seen and recorded. Even my thoughts, Father knows. There is no pillar of fire that I can look at. There is no cloud. The miracles that were being done in the wilderness aren't as prevalent. They are not happening among us today like Moses performed in the wilderness in the midst of the people.

I think today that it is a more difficult walk of faith than it was in the days of Moses. Even Moses got frustrated with the people of YeHoVaH.

When these elements exist in a passage, the interpreter must be careful to interpret the passage in light of them and that is when conditions are not met and fulfillments of the promise are postponed to another generation.

The interpreter must also recognize that the prophets often viewed future events as mountain peaks close together, with no valleys in between. Thus in a given passage, the prophets group together events whose fulfillments may occur centuries apart.

When you think about what Isaiah prophesied, Isaiah actually prophesied concerning God with us; Immanu-el. He prophesied concerning the Messiah. But Isaiah was long gone when that prophecy came to pass. Because of Isaiah's prophecy, there were people who were actually looking for this King. And then you had foreigners. This is an indictment to Israel. You had foreigners who came from distant lands who did not claim to be part of Israel, but who recognized that a King had been born in the midst of them. They themselves had no idea.

The Messiah-Centered Principle

Since the prophets were men who dealt with human history from the divine perspective and since Messiah is the solution to the dilemma of human history, the message of the prophets concerns him. (*1 Peter 1:10-12*) Although Messiah is the center of the truth communicated by the prophets, the interpreter must discern whether each particular passage relates to the Messiah directly or indirectly.

When the canon process was instituted, the goal was to determine whether or not a particular writing or work was actually inspired and worthy to be dubbed as "scripture." Now you have individuals who are looking at hundreds of writings to see. "Okay, where do we see this particular writing as being inspired?" One of the key focuses was, "Is the Messiah spoken of in this particular writing?"

Now, if that is a primary focus, then there will be some problems. That is because when it comes down to some of the writings in the book — for instance, there are a couple of them that come to mind right away. One of them is *Esther*. Another is *the Song of Solomon*. Both of those books had a difficult time meeting the rod of canon.

There are some writings in the Brit Chadasha or New Testament. There were questions surrounding *Jude* and whether or not *Jude* was inspired. There were questions as to whether *James*, the writing of *James* was inspired (or not). These were questionable writings and there are others.

- Is the Messiah the focus of this writing?

- Do we see the Messiah?
- Does this point to the Messiah?
- Does it refer or relate to what the Messiah is going to do?
- How do we equate this writing as Messianic?

There were some challenges.

The interpreter must be careful not to force Messiah-centric interpretation upon a prophetic passage or even a book for that matter. Passages that do not relate to Messiah should not be interpreted as such.

There are some things that people want to force. They want to make it say something. It is talking about the Messiah. This is one of the challenges even as we see the Ethiopian eunuch in the book of *Acts* when YeHoVaH told Philip to go and join himself with him. The first questions are:

- Who is the prophet talking about?
- Is he speaking of himself?
- Is he speaking of someone else?"

Prophecies containing Messiah-centric elements must be interpreted in the light of clear New Testament historical and doctrinal revelation.

These are key. It is important for us to keep things within their historical and doctrinal perspective. You can't ignore history. I know that when it came down to high school, like many people I was one of those individuals who questioned the relevance of the things that were being taught. "How in the world am I going to use history? And where in the world is geography ever going to play a role in my life?" It was the same with literature.

With certain aspects of math, it is like physics and calculus, come on. All we need to do is multiplication, addition and subtractions. I need to know how much money I am going to get paid. I need to know how much tax they are going to take out of my check and what I will have left. I need to be able to say, "Okay. This is what I've got coming in. This is what I can do with it. This is what I have to live on."

That is basic stuff. When you start getting into calculus and physics and any of the other aspects of that whole mathematical system, unless you are becoming an architect, engineer or something of that nature, it was irrelevant.

Geography was one of those subjects. If you are not planning on traveling anywhere, what are you going to do with geography?

History — Why do I want to know about dead people? That is what history really deals with. It is history. That is history. As a matter of fact, that is ancient history. That is so old. How is that going to help me?

Yet when it comes down to understanding scripture, now I am seeing all of the benefits of those things that I questioned years and years and years ago and I am glad that I didn't totally discount it. Now I am seeing the importance of looking at the historical. I am seeing the importance of understanding the geography. When I see Yeshua and I read the Bible and I understand the world and the structure of the world, I realize that Yeshua at times went outside of Israel.

Well, if I didn't understand geography, I wouldn't know that. I would think that most of everything that Yeshua did was either in Galilee or in Jerusalem. When I began to look at the missionary journeys and where the disciples went and how the gospel began to travel, that required geography. It also encounters history. Now I am beginning to relate and equate the people to whom the gospel went and the forerunners of the missionary work. I am now understanding the role that Italy and Rome and Italians played in the shaping of the gospel as we know it today.

The Moral Principle

The interpreter must recognize that the principles of YeHoVaH are timeless. Thus principles which are applied to one generation are actually applicable to all.

Now you have people who refer to the ten commandments as a "moral code." The moment you begin to give things different names, you have the liberty of redefining it. And once you redefine something, you take it from its original and give it another identity.

People are notorious for that.

One of the things that I had to deal with early on in this Messianic journey is the term "law." Many people are offended. The Torah was somewhat foreign, so people wanted to give it a nice user-friendly pretty name: "God's instructions." And in truth, it is. But in the Bible in the King James, the NIV and the New Literal Translation and all of these other translations that people have, nowhere is it identified as "God's instructions." It is always "law."

The law has a negative connotation in the minds of many people. People didn't want to identify something negative with the Almighty in order to make it palatable for people. YeHoVaH says, "These are my laws. These are my commandments." This is what they are.

We don't have to cloak that. We don't cloak manmade laws. The speed limit — is that the city council's instructions? No. That is the speed limit. They are laws that are here in the city. The police are law enforcers. They are there to enforce the law.

They call them courts of law, not courts of instructions. The judge who sits on the bench is there to define or to measure out the judgments to those who break the law.

I have had to deal with this issue. Now you have "moral codes." Then you have "dietary laws" or "dietary." In some communities, one way to get around having to do the Torah or the law is that you get into diet. Once you begin to refer to these as a diet, or that these are the means by which Father intended man to eat — one of the main arguments in certain communities is that the introduction of meat was a result of YeHoVaH wanting to shorten the lives of men.

I mean, there are all kinds of arguments and positions that people take. But when we begin to look at what is written, we know that the law is what YeHoVaH gave his people so that they could live according to his way of life in his kingdom.

Many prophetic passages are simply inspired preaching (forth-telling) in which the prophet is applying timeless principles to his own generation. We looked at that in the previous lesson. Before the interpreter can apply those principles to his generation, he must correctly discern how the prophet applied them to this own.

In the Torah, especially with the word "remember"; every time you see the word "remember," it is a reminder of something that has been instructed or given. It is a command. "Don't forget."

The Symbolic Principle

a.) Symbols used in types, allegories and parables are also a vital part of prophecy. Since the prophets many times are revealing the unknown in the terminology of the known, symbolism seems to be one of the favorite vehicles of expression.

b.) The interpreter must recognize that in apocalyptic prophecy, fanciful, non-real symbols are often used (e.g. *Daniel 7; Revelation 13*). Many times these symbols are non-real aggregates of real parts. In these special cases, great care must be taken to interpret the parts while interpreting the whole symbol.

It is really amazing when you begin to look at some of these beasts. You begin to talk about these beasts as symbols. You see Ezekiel's wheel within a wheel and what these eyes represent and all of these kinds of things. The next thing you know, people have volumes of books.

It is amazing when you begin to see each generation and how they interpret prophecy in their generation based upon the current technology. You wonder about 500 years ago or 1,000 years ago. When you begin to look at 1,000 years ago, how were they interpreting *Zechariah*? Was it a nuclear holocaust? Nuclear energy had not even been invented yet and yet the prophecy was given.

So 1,000 years ago or 2,000 years ago how they would interpret *Zechariah* would have been based upon the inventions or the technology or what was currently available to them. They would be trying to interpret a prophecy that was given by someone in previous generations.

Now you have everything from microchips to implants. You have all kinds of interpretations of the "mark of the beast." Each person is convincing, especially when they put that twist of "Well, this is what the Lord showed me." They are convincing in their communications and they write books. If they sold hundreds and thousands and thousands of copies of these books, obviously they know what they are talking about, right? They are on the bestseller lists.

c.) In interpreting the symbols in prophecy, the first rule of hermeneutics should be followed: **Let scripture interpret scripture.** The basic qualifications of the symbolic principle must be followed.

You cannot ever, ever, ever, ever, EVER ignore this principle. **You can't ignore this rule.** If you ignore this rule, then nine times out of ten or ten times out of ten you will probably end up being wrong.

I find this amazing. We are going to look at this a little bit later. What I find amazing is prophecy that is given by the Holy Spirit. The Holy Spirit puts words into an individual's being to proclaim or to prophesy. This is a work of the Spirit. If the Spirit is doing the work, what makes people think that they can naturally interpret this? "Well, just give me a few tools to work with and I can figure this out. Give me some books. Let's do some word studies and we can come to the actual interpretation of this prophecy."

So now by natural means individuals are convinced that they have interpreted that which was given by the Spirit. This is when we begin to look at types and allegories and parables. It is very difficult to interpret symbols. That is because again, based on your knowledge and understanding and what you ate, your conclusion is going to be different than someone else's.

The Numerical Principle

While the interpreter must recognize evident numerical significance in prophecy, he or she must be careful not to distort prophecy by forcing extreme numerical significances upon its interpretation.

When it came down to the numerical principle, I purposely did not get into the numerical principle other than a brief skim. Then I moved on because this particular principle has been so abused. I mean, it has been extremely abused. I have read several books. I am always disturbed when people try to see numbers in the scriptures.

The number three means "this." The number four, the number six or the number ten or eleven or twelve means "this." Then over here, this denomination looks at the numerical principle from a different view.

Then there is numerology. You have those who believe that every letter of the Hebrew alphabet has a number. Every letter of every alphabet has a number. The letters of the English alphabet — we have 26 letters from 1 to 26. So A is 1 and Z is number 26. When you begin to look at the English language and you apply these different numbers, based upon the letters you can come up with some stuff.

You can do that with the Hebrew alphabet and the Hebrew language. Now you are into Kabbalah and you are into all kinds of tricky interpretation. This is what people do when they lack the Holy Spirit.

If the Father doesn't give you revelation, you don't have it. All you have is an opinion. You have a conclusion that you have come to from your study. You have a so-called revelation that came by the compilation of reading this book and that book and this work and sitting under this teacher.

Yeah, I am simple. I try to keep it simple because there are a whole lot of complicated teachings out there. Everybody is going to come to their own conclusion because there are no systematic principles of understanding in the discipline not to go beyond what is written. They begin to read into things.

The Holy Spirit gives the prophecy. The Holy Spirit will give the interpretation.

It is amazing. It is absolutely amazing how people (especially in the Messianics), in the Hebrew Roots and all of this, give so much credence to individuals and their writings over decades and centuries. They give credence to sages who not only reject Messiah, but who do not have the Spirit of YeHoVaH.

When it comes down to science and medicine, a person can go to medical school to learn the human body. They can learn all of the intricacies of the human body: how it works, what makes it work, what causes it to malfunction and how to try to fix it. They learn to diagnose and repair malfunctions and how to even begin to rebuild limbs and all kinds of things. But no human being on the planet can make another human being. You can diagnose it. You can see how it works. You can see the intricacies. You can see how the brain functions. You can see how the brain relates to the rest of the body. You can see how every member and organ and tissue and vein and every part of the body works. You can see how it works down to the minutest detail, but you can't make a human being. It can't happen.

The same thing goes with animals. You see silk plants and you see imitations where people can imitate. They can create a replica of something, but YeHoVaH is the original. He makes originals.

When it comes down to what he has given, if the Spirit is what gives us the word, then it is going to take the Spirit to interpret it. This is what spiritual manifestations are when you begin to talk about the need for the Spirit.

Yeshua is the prophet. But if you have people who reject Yeshua as the Prophet, then they have no choice but to listen to sages. Now, don't get me wrong. There are a lot of good works out there. There are a lot of good writings.

But what it boils down to is the conclusion that people come to in their studies. They present some very good studies. I have read some good studies from people. I have read how they have meticulously gone through the Torah and how they have gone through the prophets and how they have associated the Torah and the prophets. And I have read how they have been able to give us some wonderful insights and history and just some wonderful things. But when it comes down to the interpretation of what he has given to us, only he can give us the interpretation of that.

He said in his word, except he watches over the city, the watchers watch in vain. Except he builds a house, the laborers labor in vain. Yeshua said himself, "everybody that came before him were thieves and robbers." Period. He says, "Beware of the leaven. Beware of the teachings. Beware of these things."

Yet people ignore his warnings. They call people "Rabbi." They don't beware of the leaven in teachings. As a matter of fact, they take the leaven and the teachings that he told them to beware of and begin to feed it to people who can't endure sound doctrine. Or they refuse to endure sound doctrine because they are of the mindset that "it can't be this simple."

What is complicated about treating people the way you want to be treated? What is so complicated about it? Father has given us some very simple rules to follow. Why do we have to go and make up thousands more rules to keep the simple ones that he has given us? All we have to do is obey the ones he has given us.

But it is too hard? No. His rules, his law is not burdensome. His law is not grievous. His law is not hard.

What is hard is deciding whether or not we are going to obey it. That is the hard part. Once you make up your mind that you are going to obey him, then it is "easy-peasy." You just have to deal with a world that does not want to obey him.

That world now thinks that you are crazy because you have chosen to obey him.

Is it you who is crazy or is it the world around you that is crazy? I choose to declare that it is the world that is crazy. The only sanity — I am one of the only sane people on the planet. What about you?

I think I am hanging around some sane people.

But an insane world is calling sane people insane while calling the insane people sane. The Bible says that this is going to happen. You call good evil and evil good.

I look at the news. If you want a career, if you want to make a lot of money, all you have to do is something crazy. You just have to go out and find the weirdest thing you can come up with. Have sex with somebody. Make a video and put it on *YouTube*. Now you are on "The View" and "Ellen." If Oprah was still there, you would be on "Oprah."

People are doing crazy stuff. Headline news is how some rich kid got drunk, drag raced and cussed out the police. Now it is headlines around the world.

It is just INSANE.

The Typical Principle

The interpreter must recognize the distinction between the types found mainly in the historical writing and the symbolic typical actions primarily confined to the prophets. Some examples of symbolic typical actions in prophecy are:

- Isaiah walking naked and barefoot for three years (*Isaiah 20:2-4*)
- Jeremiah hiding his girdle by the Euphrates (*Jeremiah 13:1-11*)
- Jeremiah putting a yoke upon his neck (*Jeremiah 27:1-15*)
- Ezekiel's miniature portrayal of Jerusalem's siege (*Ezekiel 4*)
- Ezekiel's laying on his side for over a year (*Ezekiel 4*)

Don't try that. If YeHoVaH says for you to do it, then by all means do it, but don't do that. I don't think that is Father giving you those instructions. These are some specific actions that were given to specific individuals.

It is amazing. I have been in ministries where somebody comes up and they can't see. A prophet sends somebody outside to get some dirt. Bring the dirt, spit in it and make mud and put it in somebody's eyes.

"Did the Holy Spirit tell you to do that?"

"No, I read it in the Bible. That is what Jesus did. If it's good enough for Jesus…"

I was reading a couple of weeks ago about some bishop who has his congregation out in the lawn eating grass. Folks are laying out in the grass, eating the grass because he said they would get healed. There is some stuff out there. If putting mud in somebody's eye or if somebody told me that the Spirit told them to do that, I would at least have an example that they could point to in the scriptures.

As much as I might have an issue with that, Messiah did do that, okay. You might have me on that now, but did the Almighty *tell* you to do that?

I can't argue that, especially if the blind person starts seeing. How are you going to argue with that? You can't and yet there are people out there arguing with legitimate miracles. "Oh, that was staged." "God doesn't do that stuff anymore." "It must be magic. It must be sorcery." It must be something.

Do you know that it is blasphemy when you attribute the work of the Holy Spirit to something else?

People have become so cynical to the truth because of all of the fake that is out there. It is to the point where now they don't believe the truth when it shows up.

This is exactly where the people of Messiah's day had come. Here is the Messiah that they, their Grandparents, their Great-Grandparents, their forefathers had been looking for, for generations. He is right there in the midst of them and they call him a devil.

People today are not very different than they were in the day of Moses. They are certainly not much different than they were in the day of Messiah. Same people but different generations. It is the same spirit at work but in different generations.

These actions must each be interpreted in the light of their specific contexts.

The Parabolic Principle

There are relatively few parables to be found in prophecy. (*Ezekiel 17:1-21* is one example.) Thus care must be used to distinguish them from other similar figures of speech.

In interpreting them, their symbols must be interpreted and caused to directly relate to the fundamental lesson the parable is teaching. The basic qualifications of the parabolic principle must be followed.

It is interesting when we think about the parabolic principle. Yeshua spoke the majority of his teachings in parables. It is amazing when people come up with interpretations of Yeshua's teachings that are different than how he interpreted the teaching. Here is the interpretation. How did you get this interpretation? "Well, the Lord showed me."

Peter gives the interpretation of his vision. Now you have a whole different interpretation.

The Allegorical Principle

As with parables, there are relatively few allegories to be found in prophecy. (*Isaiah 5:1-7* and *Ezekiel 23:1-49* are examples.) They must also be distinguished from other similar figures of speech.

In interpreting them, the extended analogy must be drawn by interpreting the symbols involved so that the intended lessons may be discovered. The basic qualifications of the allegorical principle must be adhered to.

Basic Guidelines in Interpreting Prophecy

Because prophecy is unique in its nature, there are special guidelines to be followed in addition to those applied generally to the whole of scripture.

1.) Prophets were "in the Spirit" when they prophesied. The interpreter must be under the influence of that same Spirit when he/she seeks to interpret that prophetic word inspired by the Spirit.

You can't get it in your natural just because you have all of these books.

2.) YeHoVaH utilized the prophet's own natural frame of reference. The interpreter must put himself into that frame of reference with appropriate studies in the fields of language, culture, geography and history.

That is where geography and history and linguistics and having some basic understanding of the culture in that era come in.

3.) Prophecy involved both **forth-telling** (inspired preaching for the present) and **foretelling** (predicting the future). These are sometimes woven together in a single passage. They require skillful exegesis on the part of the interpreter to correctly divide them. This is not reading into it, but pulling out what is actually there.

4.) Prophecy may be non-systematic in basically two ways:

- Prophecies are not necessarily arranged in a progressive chain of thought. Rather they are a compilation of fragmentary revelation. (In other words, a prophet may prophesy pieces. They prophecy in part. One prophet may prophesy a part. Another prophet may prophesy another part).

- Prophecies are not necessarily arranged as to their chronological order or order of fulfillment. In recognizing this problem, the interpreter would do well to approach carefully the interpretation of prophecy; utilizing the context group of principles.

5.) In dealing with predictive prophecy, the interpreter must ultimately come to grips with the problem of its fulfillment. He or she must answer the questions:

- Who or what was the prophet actually speaking of?

- When is the prophecy actually fulfilled?

As taught earlier in our studies, **hermeneutics is both a science and an art.** The writings of the prophets presents one of the greatest areas of challenge to the applied skill of the interpreter. The reason for this is found in the great variety of elements which compose the prophetic writings.

This often calls for a weaving together of a number of principles in order to arrive at a proper interpretation of the prophetic passage under consideration. This indeed tests the skill of the interpreter. Not every prophetic passage will require the use of exactly the same principles.

Which principles are to be woven together will depend upon the elements involved in the prophecy. Therefore the interpreter should be fully cognizant of the prophetic elements which need interpreting and the principles to be applied.

The next lesson will be the final part of our two-year curriculum.

Class 104 Study Summary

Key Points

1. A lot of scripture is prophecy. Some of it came to pass during the prophets' lifetime. Some of it has not yet come to pass over 2,000 years later.
2. When we look at the ethnic division principle, we see that Father dealt with people using specifics. He dealt with people in specific regions and with specific languages and areas. There were certain things he spoke which related to the twelve tribes of Israel and with their surroundings.
3. In order to distinguish between the different ethnic divisions, the interpreter must ask themselves specific questions. (See A below.)
4. Often in speaking to their own generation, prophets would use the past as a stage upon which to foretell the future.
5. According to the chronometrical principle, the prophets were not always aware of the time element in their own prophesies. Many people mistakenly try to predict biblical prophecy through current events.
6. We have to move with extreme caution when we try to assign prophetic passages to specific time fulfillments. We have to ask important questions. (See B below.)
7. The reason people in Judaism don't accept Messiah is because certain prophecies are not yet fulfilled.
8. Messiah has not reestablished Israel as a nation. That is a fulfillment of a prophecy that concerns the Messiah and that is going to be fulfilled upon his return.
9. The breach principle as it relates to prophecy emphasizes that the interpreter must realize that some prophetic messages deal with conditional promises. Because of this, the promise may (or may not) be fulfilled in the prophet's generation. Its fulfillment may be delayed for generations.
10. The repentance of a person doesn't undo what was done, but it grants the mercy of the Almighty.
11. There is no way to "twerk" for Messiah. That is not something that is done by holy people.
12. When the Bible's canon process was instituted, the goal was to determine whether or not a particular writing or work was inspired and worthy to be dubbed as scripture. This was focus-dependent.
13. The interpreter must not force Messiah-centric interpretation upon a prophetic passage or book. Prophecies with Messiah-centric elements are to be interpreted in the light of clear New Testament historical and doctrinal revelations.
14. It is important to keep things within their historical and doctrinal perspective. You can't ignore history.
15. With the moral principle, the interpreter must recognize that YeHoVaH's principles are timeless. Thus principles that are applicable to one generation are applicable to all.
16. Many prophetic passages are simply inspired preaching (forth-telling) in which the prophet is applying timeless principles to his own generation.
17. Symbols used in types, allegories and parables are a vital part of prophecy. The interpreter must recognize that in apocalyptic prophecy; fanciful, non-real symbols are often used.
18. While the interpreter must recognize evident numerical significance in prophecy, he or she must be careful not to distort prophecy by forcing extreme numerical significances upon its interpretation.
19. People who lack the Holy Spirit use things like numerology to try to interpret things from signs and symbols to the meaning of languages or events.

Class 104 Study Summary (continued)

Key Points

20. The Holy Spirit gives the prophecy. The Holy Spirit will give the interpretation of same.
21. The interpreter must recognize the distinction between the types found mainly in the historical writings and the symbolic typical actions primarily confined to the prophets. There are specific actions that were given to specific individuals.
22. It is blasphemy to attribute the works of the Holy Spirit to something else.
23. Relatively few parables or allegories are found in prophecy, so care must be taken to distinguish them from other similar figures of speech.
24. Prophets were "in the Spirit" when they prophesied. The interpreter must be under the influence of the same Spirit in order to interpret the prophetic word correctly.
25. YeHoVaH utilized the prophet's own natural frame of reference. The interpreter must put themselves into that frame of reference with appropriate studies in the fields of language, culture, geography and history.
26. Prophecy involving foretelling and forth-telling are sometimes woven together in a single passage. These require skillful exegesis by the interpreter to correctly divide them.
27. Prophecies may be non-systematic in that they are not necessarily arranged in a progressive chain of thought or in chronological order or in their order of fulfillment.
28. Hermeneutics is both a science and an art. The writings of the prophets present the greatest challenge to the applied skill of the interpreter.

A. Key Questions to distinguish between ethnic divisions

1. Does the verse refer to the united nation, the whole House of Israel?
2. Does it refer to the ten tribe House of Israel, the Northern kingdom?
3. Does it refer to the two tribe House of Judah, the Southern kingdom?

B. Key Questions to ask when looking at particular prophecies

1. Does this particular prophecy refer to the whole House of Israel?
2. Does it refer to the ten tribe House of Israel, the Northern kingdom?
3. Does it refer to the two tribe House of Judah, the Southern kingdom?
4. Does it refer to the Gentile nations (Non-Hebrew nations)?
5. Does it refer to the ekklesia, chosen out of every nation?

Key Questions to ask when assigning prophecy to specific times

1. Was the prophecy fulfilled during the lifetime of the prophet who was speaking?
2. Was the prophecy fulfilled during the time of the captivity of the House of Israel to Assyria or the House of Judah to Babylon?
3. Was the prophecy fulfilled in the restoration of Judah from Babylon at the close of seventy years of captivity?
4. Was the prophecy fulfilled during the time of Judah in the land after the Babylonian captivity during the intertestamental period?
5. Was the prophecy fulfilled in the New Testament times in relation to the Messiah, ekklesia or the Hebrew nation?
6. Is the prophecy currently being fulfilled?
7. Is the prophecy to be fulfilled in the final years prior to the second coming of Messiah?
8. Is the prophecy to be fulfilled at the second advent of Messiah?
9. Is the prophecy to find fulfillment in the future ages: the Kingdom of YeHoVaH relative to the earth or the eternal state of the new heaven and new earth?

Review Exercise

1. We expanded our application of interpretative principles in this lesson as they relate specifically to prophecy. Continue the chart started in Lesson 103, "Reflections" by making notes:

a. The ethnic division principle:

_____

_____

_____

_____

b. The chronometrical principle:

_____

_____

_____

_____

c. The breach principle:

_____

_____

_____

_____

d. The Messiah-centric principle:

_____

_____

_____

_____

e. The moral principle:

_____

_____

_____

_____

f. The symbolic principle:

_____

_____

_____

_____

g. The numerical principle:

_____
_____
_____
_____

h. The typical principle:

_____
_____
_____
_____

i. The parabolic principle:

_____
_____
_____
_____

j. The allegorical principle:

_____
_____
_____
_____

2. Application of the chronometrical principle poses special concerns for the interpreter of prophecy. Why? Touch upon all nine questions about the time element and fulfillment an interpreter must ask as to the impact each has on one's interpretation.

_____
_____
_____
_____
_____
_____
_____
_____
_____
_____
_____

3. Here is a graphical organizer to consolidate your notes on the guidelines for interpreting prophecy. Insert one guideline into each individual section:

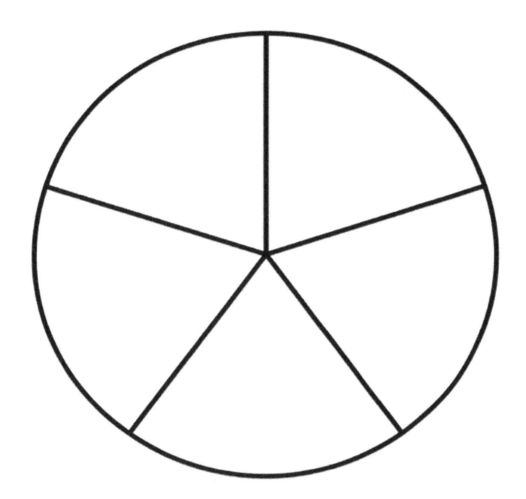

Rate the following statements
by filling in the most appropriate number.

(1 = I do not agree 10 = I agree completely)

Objectives:

1. I can define the hermeneutical principles in the successful interpretation of prophecy.

   1.◯   2.◯   3.◯   4.◯   5.◯   6.◯   7.◯   8.◯   9.◯   10.◯

2. I can define the five unique guidelines in the interpretation of prophecy.

   1.◯   2.◯   3.◯   4.◯   5.◯   6.◯   7.◯   8.◯   9.◯   10.◯

My Journal

What I learned from this class:

_____

_____

_____

_____

_____

_____

_____

_____

_____

_____

_____

_____

_____

Discipleship Training Class 105

The Spirit of Prophecy: A Spiritual Manifestation/Gift

Objectives:

As a Discipleship student, at the end of this class you will be able to:

- Explain the need for the ministration of the Holy Spirit in all of our interpretative work and study
- Describe instances of the filling of the Holy Spirit by persons before *Acts 2*

We are looking at "The Spirit of Prophecy: A Spiritual Manifestation/Gift." In Christian circles it would be considered to be "spiritual gifts." Even in Messianic circles it would be alluded to as spiritual gifts.

Over the last two years I have spent a considerable amount of time laying out the principles of scriptural interpretation. We have looked at terms such as hermeneutics, homiletics, exegesis and a variety of other terms to help aid you in your scriptural studies, research and learning.

If you have taken full advantage of this course, you should be much better equipped in going into the word and confident with the tools that you have been given. You should come to similar conclusions as those who are using the proper tools, when you research the scriptures.

Now as we conclude our basic Discipleship Training, it is only fitting that we conclude with the interpretation of and the principles for properly interpreting prophecy.

Along this journey I have attempted at every turn to point to the importance of the Holy Spirit in scriptural research. The principles, terms and tools I have shared with you only get you so far. Now more than ever it is so important that we be in tune.

It is so important, no matter how many tools we use. We know that there are theologians. There are Ph.D.s. There are Doctors in Theology, Doctors of Divinity and all types of ministries that are coming to different conclusions than what we have come to realize is the true path that the Father has established.

No matter what tools you have, if you try to approach YeHoVaH's word without his Spirit, you are going to end up in a place where I don't believe he desires for you to end up.

It is sad, but highly possible and most probable to have the correct hermeneutical principles, yet fail in scriptural interpretation. You can fail because of a lack of proper union with the one who gave us the scriptures.

You see, the word was given to us by the Spirit of God. YeHoVaH is Spirit, according to *John 4*. When the Spirit came upon the prophets to prophesy; when the Spirit gave instructions to Moses or instructions to the prophets, you cannot interpret what the Spirit has done in a natural manner. The principles and the tools that we are giving people are natural. That is not going to bring you to a spiritual conclusion. It is going to bring you to a natural conclusion. It is going to require the Holy Spirit who gave the word to help us to properly interpret the word so that we come to the right conclusion.

(Revelation 19:9-10) *"And he saith unto me, 'Write, Blessed are they which are called unto the marriage supper of the Lamb.' And he saith unto me, 'These are the true sayings of God.' And I fell at his feet to worship him. And he said unto me, 'See thou do it not: I am thy fellow servant, and of thy brethren that have the testimony of Yeshua: worship God: for the testimony of Yeshua is the spirit of prophecy.'"*

Now, you can be in Messianic circles, Charismatic circles, mainline denominational circles and evangelical circles. One of the least used manifestations or arsenals that the Spirit has given us is the Spirit of Prophecy.

The Spirit of Prophecy is the Holy Spirit's ability to come upon men and women and cause them to speak forth inspired utterances. The Spirit of Prophecy was evident in the Godly line from Adam to Moses and beyond.

Why is this so important? As we get further into this teaching, you are going to see that the way that the Father communicates to us is going to be by his Spirit.

Prophecy is hearing and speaking forth; whether you are foretelling or forth-telling. But **prophecy is the means by which Father communicates.**

How do you hear from him?

When he speaks! We have the same capability of hearing from the Almighty just as Adam did in the cool of the day and just as Abel. We know that YeHoVaH communicated or we see that he communicated, by their response. We know that he spoke to Cain, because we see the conversation.

We know that YeHoVaH spoke to several people. They are human beings just like us. This is the critical part. Besides the priests, the most important subjects in scripture were the prophets. The prophets were YeHoVaH's mouthpiece and to this day, they still are.

In addition to the prophets are the people of YeHoVaH who are given the mandate to take the gospel of the Kingdom to the whole world.

We learned that one aspect of prophecy is foretelling. This aspect of prophecy is in the form of prediction. The prophet speaks for YeHoVaH; communicating his mind for the future. Often both the past and present will be used to deal with the future. Many times the purpose of prophetic prediction is to produce present Godliness.

Then there is forth-telling. This form of prophecy is in the realm of preaching. This is one of the things that I do when I stand here. Even you will do this when you are ministering to people from the word. When you are sharing and you are counseling with people, that is a form of prophecy; especially if you are in tune with the Spirit and not giving people what is coming out of your head, but what is coming out of his mind into your head. These are his thoughts. But oftentimes we have been trained to ignore the thoughts that we have and to give people formulas.

The prophet speaks for YeHoVaH to the people. He is communicating the mind of YeHoVaH for the present. Often the past will be used to deal with the present. This will include such things as exhortation, reproof, warning, edification and comfort.

The Spirit of Prophecy was manifested with Adam, Noah, Abraham and Moses and throughout the scriptures. When the Almighty breathed into Adam, he gave Adam the instructions to name the animals. Adam had never seen any of these before and yet he gave them names. They are what he named them to this day.

Noah was given instruction by the Almighty. Noah, a righteous man, was simply living his life trying to keep from doing the things that the world around him was doing. The Father spoke to Noah and told Noah to build an Ark. For 120 years Noah spoke to a generation very much like the generation we live in today.

"Abraham, leave your Father's house." Abraham lived among people who worshipped idols. But somehow Abraham was able to distinguish the Father's voice from the other voices around him. He followed an invisible entity he had never met.

Moses, in the backside of the desert, was a very powerful man. He ran away from a kingdom to be alone. And here is the thing. You can't get away. You can go to the backside of the desert and hang out with sheep, but the Father knows where you are. He will find you and he will speak to you. He will not allow you to ignore him (like Moses tried to do).

The Spirit of Prophecy manifested corporately during Moses' day when YeHoVaH put the Spirit that was upon Moses onto the seventy. **One of the most powerful passages of scripture is this, the corporate manifestation of YeHoVaH's Spirit.**

*(Numbers 11:25) "And YeHoVaH came down in a cloud, and spake unto him, and took of the spirit that was upon him, and gave it unto the seventy elders: and it came to pass, that, when the spirit rested upon them, **they prophesied**, and did not cease."*

Prior to this, Moses had chosen seventy men (elders). What did they do? You see, this is the evidence of the Spirit in the midst of them. These men, when they were filled; when they received the Spirit of YeHoVaH, they did what? They prophesied.

There were two who were part of the seventy that were not in the group of the seventy and yet…

(Numbers 11:25) "And the LORD came down in a cloud, and spake unto him, and took of the spirit that was upon him, and gave it unto the seventy elders: and it came to pass, that, when the spirit rested upon them, they prophesied, and did not cease."

Here you have these individuals who are prophesying. Unfortunately the scripture does not tell us what they said, so we don't know what they prophesied. But we know that according to the word, they prophesied. I think that is what is important for us to realize. It is not so much what they said.

Now you have people who want to try to have hours and hours of conversation. "Well, what do you think they prophesied?" "What do you think Yeshua wrote in the dirt?" I used to engage in those conversations, but I realized that they are just a big waste of time. After three or four hours of debating and going back and forth, you are no closer to an answer than you were when you started and now three or four hours are gone. For people who have that kind of time, by all means have those discussions.

Here it is. We see that they prophesied.

The Spirit of Prophecy manifested in Saul's day. What I am trying to get us to see here is the importance of the Spirit of Prophesy. We need to see how the Holy Spirit manifested in the people's lives when the Holy Spirit was present. The Holy Spirit would open up the information and the knowledge of the Almighty to come to individuals. During that time when they are under the influence of the Holy Spirit, they are able to speak things that are coming directly from the heavenly realm, from the Almighty.

Here is why this is important. The Bible says that he knows the plans that he has for you. The plans that the Almighty has for you are with him. These individuals, during the time that they are under that inspiration of the Holy Spirit, the Almighty is revealing plans to them. He is revealing to them the plans that are locked up in heaven. So when we see that they prophesied, we don't know what they prophesied. He very well could have been prophesying or releasing to them the plans that he had for their lives and how they were going to accomplish what they had been ordained to accomplish.

For each of them it probably would have been something different, just as it would be something different for you.

It gets better.

*(1 Samuel 19:20) "And Saul sent messengers to take David: and when they saw the company of the prophets prophesying, and Samuel standing as appointed over them, the Spirit of God was upon the messengers of Saul, and **they also prophesied**."*

Saul is after David. Saul is the king. He wants David destroyed. He wants David captured. When you come into the company of spiritual people (especially people who are under the power of the Holy Spirit), you are going to enter into what is being done in the midst of these individuals.

It is no different than when you come into the midst of people who are living ungodly lives. You are going to get caught up in what those individuals are doing. You are either going to be in good communication with people under the influence of the Spirit, or you are going to be in poor communication, evil communication with those individuals who are under the influence of another spirit other than the Holy Spirit. The choice is up to you.

It is your choice and I will tell you something. When you start giving heed to these other spirits, it is going to make it that much more difficult to distinguish the Father's voice in the midst of all of that because you have given it place.

This is one of the main reasons for what Paul was saying. You need to come out from among them. How are you going to be able to clearly hear the voice of the Almighty and distinguish the voice of the Almighty when you are given to all of these other voices?

You need to come out from among them and be separate.

That is a tough thing to do, especially when there is a whole lot of them to come out from among. And when you come out from among them, there is not a whole lot of other people to associate with or to gather with.

*(1 Samuel 19:21) "And when it was told Saul, he sent other messengers, and **they prophesied likewise**. And Saul sent messengers again the third time, and **they prophesied also**."*

Here is the word. Saul sends messengers to take David. They found out where David was. He sent the messengers. "Go get him!" They came with the intent of taking David. They came into the influence of the Spirit. The prophets were prophesying by the Spirit. And just as YeHoVaH took the Spirit that was upon Moses and put it onto the elders and they prophesied, here we see (but it doesn't say this) that it is the same thing. Here is the Spirit now that is on Samuel and the prophets who were prophesying. It now comes upon the messengers of Saul.

What did they do? They prophesied. Somebody came to Saul and said, "Man, those guys got down there where you sent them and instead of taking David, they started doing what they were doing — prophesying."

You have to understand that these men had probably never prophesied until they got in the company of the prophets.

The company you keep is important because the company you keep is going to influence you supernaturally and you don't necessarily realize the supernatural influence. You just find yourself doing things that you would not normally do.

One of the things that they taught when I was in rehabilitation in the drug centers is that there are three things you have to be aware of: people, places and things. When you get into certain places, you start having certain thoughts. When you get around certain people, you start having certain thoughts. This is supernatural stuff that is going on.

The supernatural is real, but you can't see it. All you know is that you come under the influence. You don't even see the influence. The next thing you know it is like, "Man, I wasn't planning on doing that. Where did that come from?"

> **Everything is supernatural, everything.**
> **Everything is spirit, no matter where you are**
> **and no matter where you go. You are always**
> **in the presence of the supernatural.**

You are either going to manifest the Spirit work (the Holy Spirit) or you are going to manifest some other spirit.

Now, I am telling you. You cannot ignore the spiritual arena that we live our lives in twenty-four hours a day, seven days a week.

*(1 Samuel 19:22-24) "Then went he also to Ramah, and came to a great well that is in Sechu: and he asked and said, 'Where are Samuel and David?' And one said, 'Behold, they be at Naioth in Ramah.' And he went thither to Naioth in Ramah: and the Spirit of God was upon him also, and **he went on, and prophesied**, until he came to Naioth in Ramah. And he stripped off his clothes also, and **prophesied before Samuel** in like manner, and lay down naked all that day and all that night. Wherefore they say, 'Is Saul also among the prophets?'"*

Every messenger that Saul sends; when he gets into the presence, they began to prophesy. Now it is Saul himself. Saul is saying, "I am going to go and deal with this matter myself." And Saul, whose motives were not right, came into the company or into the presence. The Bible says that the Spirit of YeHoVaH was upon him.

Is Saul a prophet? That is the question that was being asked.

What we see here is the manifestation of the Holy Spirit. The presence of the Holy Spirit brings the manifestation or the ability to prophesy. We don't see what Saul is prophesying. We don't see what any of the three sets of messengers he sent prophesied, but we know that prophecy is the ability to hear from the Almighty and to speak forth what the Almighty is giving.

In this particular situation, none of these individuals that Saul sent said, "Do you know what? I am going to go down there, and I think I am going to prophesy." That wasn't the plan. They went to capture David. But when they came into the presence of the prophets and the Holy Spirit, **the presence of the Holy Spirit will bring prophecy.**

It doesn't matter how many people are here. When the true Spirit of YeHoVaH is in the presence, then people are going to get ministry. You are going to hear from YeHoVaH, whether it be through the words of the speaker or whether you now in the presence of the Spirit are being communicated to. This is why I say to people, when you come in, bring something to write with.

You need to be in tune, not only to the words that the speaker is saying, but also to what the Spirit is saying to you.

The Father, while you are sitting in the presence, can speak something to you. I hear this so many times. I get phone calls, emails and people telling me about how the word is so strong in the midst of us and how the word is ministering to them and how the Father is revealing things to them. I say to people that what happens is this. I am particularly trying to keep myself in a place where the Spirit of YeHoVaH is not grieved. I try to stay where he can move in the midst of us. If the Spirit is moving in the midst of us, then every last one of us has the place or the ability to hear from YeHoVaH.

The promise of the Holy Spirit would be evidenced by prophesying. If the Holy Spirit is present, the ability to hear from the Almighty is also present.

These are things that I have had to spend a great deal of my ministry on for the last two years, since we have been on Hill Road. We dedicated the place in 2011. We were over on Tyvola Road about a year before we got here. We have been trying hard not only to bring truth; but to unearth, to tear down, to throw down and to destroy some of those faulty foundations where people have been taught things that really don't line up with scripture. In order for the truth to really penetrate, it has to filter its way through all of that stuff.

We are going to see that it is dangerous to be in the presence of the Spirit with all of this other stuff. That is because now things get confusing and people start hearing a mixture. They are hearing part of the Spirit. In one minute Peter says, "You are Messiah, Son of the Living God." The next moment Yeshua is saying, "Get behind me, Satan."

People are open to the spirit realm. But some are not necessarily recognizing, or are in tune with or have decided that they are only going to give access to the Spirit. I am going to tell you something. You can give access to whomever and whatever you want. But you have to be able to recognize when the Holy Spirit is present and what the Holy Spirit is saying.

Long before Shavuot, John the Baptist's Father Zachariah was filled with the Spirit and prophesied. When people hear that the Holy Spirit wasn't given until Shavuot, the Holy Spirit was given at Shavuot, but the Holy Spirit was also given to individuals long before.

As a matter of fact, John's whole family was filled with the Holy Spirit.

🔍 *Luke 1:67-76*

Here the Bible tells us what he prophesied, but it doesn't always let us know. This prophecy is a prophecy that speaks of the things that have been spoken. This prophecy is not speaking so much about the distant future as much as it is saying that what YeHoVaH has said that has now come to pass. This child is going to prepare the way of Messiah.

He is prophesying things that have been spoken. He is bringing it to the present moment and speaking of the very present.

🔍 *Luke 1:77-80*

How could he wax strong in the Spirit? Because the Bible prophesied. I won't get ahead of myself.

Zachariah was a priest whose son was a prophet. Zachariah's whole family was filled with the Spirit.

(Luke 1:15) *"For he shall be great in the sight of YeHoVaH, and shall drink neither wine nor strong drink; and* **he shall be filled with the Holy Ghost, even from his mother's womb.***"*

The word is saying that John is going to be filled with the Spirit even before he is born. We see how that happened.

(Luke 1:41) *"And it came to pass, that, when Elisabeth heard the salutation of Mary, the babe leaped in her womb; and* **Elisabeth was filled with the Holy Ghost***:"*

Zachariah was filled with the Holy Ghost. Elisabeth was filled with the Holy Ghost and at this moment **John was filled even in the womb with the Holy Ghost.** It was long before Shavuot.

You have people who want to say, "The Holy Spirit wasn't given until Shavuot, the day of Pentecost. That is when the church was birthed." No. The Holy Spirit was active from the very day man was made from the dust of the ground. He was active from the very day that YeHoVaH said, "Let there be." The Holy Spirit has been deeply engaged in the lives of people. As we have seen, the Holy Spirit has worked through Adam, Abel, Noah and Abraham. He worked through several of the people in the Tanakh and of course in the Torah.

John was filled with the Spirit from the womb. You can't deny these scriptures. It says this specifically, so there is no guessing. For people to make those lame arguments that nobody was filled with the Holy Spirit prior to Pentecost, it is untrue and yet many still believe that, even when they look at evidence like this.

"Well, the Holy Spirit came upon people before the day of Pentecost and he went." No, they were filled with the Holy Spirit.

We have gone through this. We saw that even in the Old Testament people were filled with the Holy Spirit. It wasn't just the Holy Spirit coming and going; although that was the case too. This is the effect of preaching. People are preaching and teaching and coming up with their own revelations.

They are talking about what "God showed them" and what "God said" and what this means. Then they get into their signs and symbols and all of those things. **They are trying to get into the realm of the spirit without the Holy Spirit.** That is not good.

Look what Elisabeth did. It doesn't say here that she prophesied, but look at what happened.

(Luke 1:42-45) *"And she spake out with a loud voice, and said, 'Blessed art thou among women, and blessed is the fruit of thy womb. And whence is this to me, that* **the mother of my Lord** *should come to me? For, lo, as soon as the voice of thy salutation sounded in mine ears, the babe leaped in my womb for joy. And blessed is she that believed: for there shall be a performance of those things which were told her from the Lord.'"*

Basically she is prophesying. When she was filled with the Holy Spirit, she did exactly what people filled with the Holy Spirit are supposed to do. They speak on behalf of YeHoVaH. She is prophesying a personal prophecy to Mary. It is an exhortation. It is a word of encouragement. It is a word of comfort. She is not talking to just anybody. This is a personal prophecy. It is not for anybody else, but is specifically for Mary. Father has allowed Elisabeth to see that Mary is carrying the very Messiah her husband has supposedly been serving has been looking for and all before them. She is gifted by the Holy Spirit to see that Mary of all people is now the carrier. She is (as Elisabeth says), "the Mother of my Lord."

This is some powerful stuff. She is saying that **what the Father has said to you, believe it**. She is confirming through prophecy.

The promise of the Holy Spirit would be evidenced by prophesying. This is why we have to hit that bad teaching that talks about how "the evidence of the Holy Spirit is speaking in tongues." *That is one of the biggest lies that have been propagated by individuals within the Pentecostal movement.* They have taken the truth and turned it into something else. Now people want to speak in tongues instead of hearing from the Almighty.

I personally believe that is demonic. Am I saying that speaking in tongues is demonic? No. I am talking about the teaching that the "evidence" of the Holy Spirit is speaking in tongues. **This is a teaching that comes from people who don't know what the Bible says.**

We just lay it out from *Genesis* up until this point, what Joel said. He said that when the Spirit comes upon people, what is going to happen? **They are going to prophesy.** In every instance that we have seen up until this point, not one person filled with the Holy Spirit spoke in tongues. Not one of them, but they all prophesied. Why? Because that is the evidence of the presence of the Holy Spirit in one's life.

So where did this stuff come from? It came from individuals who were looking at the book of *Acts* and seeing what people did on the Day of Pentecost. Now they are saying, "Well, see? This is the evidence of the Holy Spirit. They spoke in tongues." They fail to realize that there was interpretation of tongues when they spoke in tongues, because everybody heard it in their own language.

This is the result of ignorant and unlearned individuals trying to interpret an Eastern book from a Western perspective.

(Acts 2:17-18) " 'And it shall come to pass in the last days,' saith God, 'I will pour out of my Spirit upon all flesh: and your sons and your daughters **shall prophesy**, and your young men shall see visions, and your old men shall dream dreams: And on my servants and on my handmaidens I will pour out in those days of my Spirit; **and they shall prophesy**:' "

I have caught a lot of flack. I am not trying to explain somebody else's bad doctrine. Why do they preach that? Ask them.

I am giving you what the scripture says. If you believe what they have preached all this time and you have been seeking to no avail to try to speak in tongues; then you are questioning whether the Holy Spirit is for you or even if you are saved. You question because you haven't spoken in tongues and because you have been chasing a doctrine that people have taught that is being reinforced over and over through denominational teachings. And there are people within those denominations who you trust to know better than you know. I am here to teach and to preach the kind of message that Yeshua preached and that will actually set people free.

The Bible says that the evidence of the Spirit will be prophecy. Your sons and daughters will prophesy. When the Holy Spirit comes (Father says), it will come to pass. How many Pentecostals have gone to the altar to "tarry" for the Holy Spirit so that you can speak forth the utterances of YeHoVaH versus getting some language called tongues?

Then you have people who are talking about how if you don't speak in tongues, you don't have the Holy Ghost.

These are doctrines of demons. That is what it is. Let's call it what it is. I don't care what they say. It is a doctrine of demons. Nowhere in the Bible does it say that the evidence of the Holy Spirit or the evidence that you have been filled with the Spirit is speaking in other tongues. That is a manmade doctrine.

We should covet *zeloo*, (dzay-lo-ō) **G2206** the Holy Spirit and the manifestation of prophecy.

(1 Corinthians 12:31) "But covet earnestly/zeloo the best gifts: and yet show I unto you a more excellent way."

This is one of those places in the Bible where we have been given permission to covet. This word "covet earnestly" is used in another way.

(1 Corinthians 14:1) "Follow after charity, and desire/zeloo spiritual gifts, but rather that ye may prophesy."

Desire and covet. It is the same Greek word: *zeloo*.

G2206 *zeloo* (dzay-lo-o); from **G2205** to have warmth of feeling for or against:--affect, covet (earnestly), (have) desire, (move with) envy, be jealous over, (be) zealous (-ly affect).

It is something that you desire, so desire it to the point where you are zealous about it. You covet it. You are pursuing it.

I am about to get into some things that some people will be challenged by. For too long I have allowed (and we have to not allow) the opinion of other people to stop us from moving in that which the Father has clearly instructed us to move in. I remember when he called me. I was sitting in an Apostolic-Pentecostal Prophetic Church in an audience with all types of excited people. There was preaching and teaching and praise dancing and singing in the Spirit and everything that you would imagine in a Pentecostal circle. For me it was like the Father came in and put this bubble around me. It was just him and me. I was sitting next to my wife yet there was this deafening silence and I heard, "Arthur. I have called you to be an apostle."

I am going to tell you, that was one of the scariest moments in my ministry life. It took me five years to embrace that — FIVE YEARS.

I am here to tell you. I have a son. My son's name is Apostle Arthur Bailey. When this child was in his mother's womb and I am seeking the Father as to what to call him, the Father is still dealing with me on the calling that he has called me to. He told me to give him that name which was designed to help me embrace my own call.

Every time I look at him and every time I call his name, I am reminded of how I had to go to that extreme simply to embrace what the Father spoke to me. Why is that such an issue? I will tell you why it is an issue. It is the opinion of other people. It is what people think and what people are going to say and how people are going to react and what they are going to say about you. All of these other things cause us to acquiesce to them.

We find it in families. Mom and Dad and Grandpa and Grandma and sisters and brothers. We are so consumed with how they feel and how they think to the point where we are afraid to come out of the closet in faith. (I am not talking about some queer closet. I am not talking about some homosexual or other closet where ungodliness is.)

It is amazing that these people, these ungodly people, are heralding things. They are getting onto the rooftops and they are shouting all over the world that we are what we are and you might as well accept it. And if you don't like it, we are going to shove it down your throat. If we have to, we will come and boycott your facility.

Man, if only the saints were that bold!

The saints are Minnie-mousing in some corner. "Oh, no! Don't say that. Jesus is love. We are supposed to love everybody."

You keep loving. To love does not mean that you ignore truth or twist it or compromise.

You have to speak. This kind of speaking will get you the same thing it got Messiah. If you are not willing to pick up your execution stake; and I am not here to offend anybody, but abomination is abomination, period.

I was at the supermarket. There was this fellow next to me. It is amazing once a person gives in to that spirit. Here you have a grown man acting feminine. What kind of spirit is that? Then you have women who want to act like men and cut their hair and wear baggy pants and saggy pants and act like a man. These are perverted. These spirits pervert the character of an individual. That is a perverted spirit.

It is an abomination in his sight and yet this person next to me was under the influence of a different spirit than I am under. And because I am under the Spirit of YeHoVaH, I have a love. I am not going to embarrass this person. As a matter of fact, I let him go before me. I am standing there. I am about to put in an order and he has come there and I am holding up the butcher. He comes back again and I said, "This gentleman — wait on him. I am going to be here awhile."

Then he wanted to invite himself over to my house. I don't know why homosexuals have always seemingly been attracted to me. I don't get it. I am nice. I am sweet. I am not as bad as some people think I am, but at the same time, that is wrong. I am not going to compromise what I believe because of somebody's choice. I am not standing there pointing out his sin to him, but if we engage in a conversation, then chances are if we have any real conversation, we are going to get on the issue of being in right relationship with the Almighty.

Now, that used to be a troubling conversation, but now since the bishops have come out of the closet and the pope has declared these things, and you have archbishops that are pushing this gay agenda, that conversation has been watered down. Now you have openly gay bishops and openly gay pastors and fornicating and adulterating pastors. All kinds of abominable things have come into the so-called "houses of worship."

Now we have to regroup and we have to be able to share with people what the truth is so that they can stand on that truth. And if they are confronted by these entities, they must be able to speak the truth in love and not back down from it.

It is not about compromise. It is about sharing with people. If you care about the things that YeHoVaH cares about, then you know that he cares as much about that person who was standing next to me as he cares about me.

If I mistreat that person because of some twisted perverted view that I might have, then I need to get my twisted, perverted view sanctified so that I can deal with people as people and minister to that person just like I would minister to the homeless person or to the person who is out there doing all types of other abominable things.

This is why it is important to be led by the Spirit and to be under the influence of the Spirit. Otherwise if you come under the influence of traditions and the influence of religion, you will become a person who will do more damage than good. A lot of us have been damaged by religion.

Paul, who wrote most about Spirit manifestations and gifts, indicated that the impartation of spiritual gifts could happen through the laying on of hands.

(Romans 1:11-12) " *For I long to see you, that I may impart unto you some spiritual gift, to the end ye may be established; That is, that I may be comforted together with you by the mutual faith both of you and me.* "

How is Paul going to impart some spiritual gift? Isn't that the work of the Holy Spirit?

He says that there is an impartation that is going to come. We are going to see later that this impartation is going to be from the laying on of one's hands.

When you are in the company of people who are filled with the Spirit, they are going to benefit you mutually as you benefit them. That is because you are going to minister to one another. That is what happens when you come into the body. You minister to one another.

This was demonstrated in *Acts 19.*

(Acts 19:6) *"And when Paul laid his hands upon them, the Holy Ghost came on them; and they spake with tongues, and prophesied."*

Now, what is interesting here is that this is one of those situations where the Pentecostals say, "See there? They spoke in tongues." There was interpretation because the tongues that they spoke in through the prophetic word were understood.

(1 Timothy 5:21-22) *"I charge thee before God, and the Lord Jesus Christ, and the elect angels, that thou observe these things without preferring one before another, doing nothing by partiality. Lay hands suddenly on no man, neither be partaker of other men's sins: keep thyself pure."*

Here is where it gets very interesting. Paul encourages Timothy *not* to lay hands suddenly on anyone. Why? Because through the laying on of hands, there is an impartation. Some of you all have seen when they ordain elders that they lay hands on them. Some people you see, when somebody is sick, you lay hands upon them.

Now, what you don't see is the work of the Spirit. All you see is a physical act. But something supernatural takes place when you lay hands on people for a specific reason. I am not talking about shaking somebody's hand. I am not talking about patting someone on the back. I am talking about you intentionally invoking the Holy Spirit to do a miraculous work by the laying on of your hands. When you are laying hands on someone who is sick and you are praying for their healing, you are expecting a supernatural manifestation to take place. (At least you should be).

Paul is saying, "Timothy, don't lay hands suddenly on no man. Don't do it hastily. Don't rush."

Here you can actually see that what Paul is saying is that you are to be careful. I don't believe he is talking about laying hands on sick people. What I believe he is saying here is don't put people in positions of authority. Don't lay hands on individuals and give them authority over other people.

If you do that and this person is not right, then what you are going to do now is be responsible for the spiritual abuse that comes at the hand of the person that you have ordained or put in a position of authority.

You keep yourself pure. There are people who want the Holy Spirit and whose motives are wrong.

🔎 Acts 8:14-19

What Simon saw is that something supernaturally occurred. Some would argue that they spoke in tongues. Well, it doesn't say that. I can say that they prophesied. It doesn't say that, but we do know that something supernatural happened. Based on all of the evidence we see of what has happened up until this point (both in the Tanakh and in the Brit Chadasha), the primary manifestation of the Holy Spirit is what? It is prophecy, prophesying.

Imagine if you have individuals who see power. They are going to want it. You have people who are sitting. Some of the most prideful, most arrogant times I have ever been a participant in is licensing and ordinations. They want to invite everybody and their Momma. "I am getting ordained. Come and hear me preach!" Come and hear you preach?

You have people who want you to come and hear them preach and they have never really ministered to you. I have seen this and I am looking at this. Then you have people who come in. They are barely in the door and they want to be licensed. They want to be ordained. I want to license and I want to ordain people, but I want to ordain people who are stable; people who are going to do the work of ministry. I want to ordain people whose heart is in the right place and whose motives are for the right purposes. I would ordain people who are going to do the work of ministry. The bottom line is just like when people say, "What school did you go to?" They want to put a value on your education.

What denomination, what church are you a part of? They want to identify what authority are you coming in? What organization are you coming from? Whose name are you coming in?

People want to tell you, "I got my M.D. at Harvard or I got my Ph.D. at Stanford." These names have a tendency to give some form of authority to the person who has that name of that organization behind them.

🔍 *Acts 8:20-21*

Imagine ordaining someone whose heart isn't right. Now, you have jack-legs (as I call them). There are preachers out there who are taking advantage of people within the ministry, not just sexually. They are exercising witchcraft over these individuals in the form of control and manipulation. Their heart is not in the right place.

How do you know when a person's heart is not in the right place? The only way you are going to really know a person whose heart is not in the right place is if you get to know them. You have to know them that labor among you and there are specific instructions.

Think about it. If you are planning on marrying someone and being married to them for the rest of your life, let's say the rest of your life is sixty years. Is it going to hurt you to take a year to get to know this person? That is because once you are married, you are married.

This is a year to get to know the person that you are talking about spending the rest of your life with. Most marriages are ready to be annulled in the first year — seriously. Then to put somebody in ministry. Getting married is one thing because all you are dealing with is your spouse and if there are children. But when you are talking about ministry, you are dealing with households. You are dealing with people who have authority over households in the spirit realm. These are people who are responsible for spiritual guidance and counsel.

The last thing you need is someone whose heart is not in the right place.

The manifestation/gift of prophecy is a body ministry function; while the office of the prophet is a headship function. The manifestation/gift of prophecy is an extension of the Holy Spirit.

To neglect, eliminate or forbid the function of any of the manifestations/gifts given to the body of Messiah by Yeshua is to render the body of Messiah anemic, divided, dysfunctional and immature.

There are too many spiritual people who are immature. It is unfortunate because they have been neglected.

This is why Paul wrote:

(1 Corinthians 14:1) "Follow after charity, and desire/zeloo spiritual gifts, but rather that ye may prophesy."

Desire! Desire to prophesy.

(1 Thessalonians 5:16-18) "Rejoice evermore. Pray without ceasing. In everything give thanks: for this is the will of God in Christ Jesus concerning you."

This is his will for you.

(1 Thessalonians 5:19) "Quench not the Spirit."

I can preach for a day on this one. **Don't quench the Spirit.** How do you know you are not quenching the Spirit? **Here is how you know you are quenching the Spirit.** I can tell you right now how you are quenching the Spirit. That is if you are not in tune. **If you are not actively aware and inquiring, then you have already quenched the Spirit.**

The steps of the righteous are ordered. The Father desires to be with you wherever you go: while you are driving in your car, while you are walking the dog, while you are sitting on the celestial throne in your home, while you are working on that proposal and in that classroom or on that computer.

Whatever you are doing, whether it is washing dishes, emptying the trash, mowing the lawn, shoveling snow or whatever it is, the Father is there because he wants to protect you. He wants to keep you safe. He wants to make you aware; even if you are mowing the lawn and you are about to run over a piece of metal. If that blade hits that metal and it tears a hole in that base of that lawnmower and it hits your leg and takes it off; now you'd have to be amputated because you weren't in tune. I know.

That sounds mean. Or you are mowing your lawn next to a road and a car is passing by. Now, here it is that you are about to run over something that is going to shoot something out of that lawn mower and into that oncoming car and cause injury to the occupants.

The Holy Spirit is saying, "Hey! Wait a minute! Stop! You are about to run over something! Shut it down! Look ahead!" Everything that is in front of us, the Holy Spirit is trying to warn us about. But if we are not in tune with the Spirit, we have already quenched the Spirit. We are just doing our own thing and the next thing you know, here we are.

You are not supposed to be there. We don't have to be there, but there is a good chance that we will end up in a bad place if we are not in tune with the Holy Spirit that is trying to lead us and guide us.

(1 Thessalonians 5:20) *"Despise not prophesyings."*

Don't despise it.

G1848 *exoutheneo;* a variation of **G1847** *exoudeneo,* ex-oo-den-o'-o: and meaning the same: -- contemptible, despise, least esteemed, set at nought.

If you are not esteeming prophecy, then you are despising it. It is that simple.

Prophesying is, "Okay, Father, what are you saying?" This is every day and every moment of the day. Like it says, "Pray without ceasing." Be in constant communion. Be constantly listening because he is constantly trying to show you something.

(1 Thessalonians 5:21-23) *"Prove all things; hold fast that which is good. Abstain from all appearance of evil. And the very Elohim of peace sanctify you wholly; and I pray God your whole spirit and soul and body be preserved blameless unto the coming of our Messiah Yeshua."*

This is what he is saying. **Don't despise. Don't quench the Spirit. Don't despise prophecy.** What is going to happen is that the God of peace is going to sanctify you entirely; your whole spirit, soul, and body. You will be so in tune with the Almighty.

You won't have to be one of those people saying, "I wonder what my purpose is." The Father who has a plan for you knows how to reveal that plan to you. But that means that you have to take time to get into his presence and seek his face intentionally. Then you have to be ready, like Habakkuk was ready. He had his paper and pencil. He was ready to write.

I am writing every day. Stuff comes at me so fast. I am so thankful now that I have this thing on my phone. I can speak into it and I have so many notes on this phone. I am driving down the street. Father is talking to me. I am just — this is going off left and right waiting with notes. I am teachings ahead right now. These are words that the Father is giving me.

These are things, just listening to what the Father is saying. Even being here and doing the teachings. I know the Father desires his people to be blessed and to come into the knowledge of truth so that they and YOU too can walk in the fullness of the calling that he has called you to.

But you have to be willing to set yourself aside and to pull yourself away from people. One of the things that I have had to deal with is that there are a lot of people who have a lot of plans for me. Seriously. There are people who are making plans for me. They are making plans for you too. They have dreams and aspirations and they see how you are going to help them to their destination.

They will exploit and take advantage of the spiritual giftings or the abilities that you have been given. They will have you pursuing and moving on the path to help them fulfill their dream and their calling while at the same time you are neglecting the things that the Father has for you.

I have had people wanting me to do something for them and I have had to flat-out tell them, "No, I can't do that. I can't allow you to manipulate or to exploit the calling on my life. I can't let you do that. I really can't."

There are people who are sitting. I have come to a point now where I have to be careful about who I spend time with. There are folks who have plans. But my plan is to know the Father's plan so that I can be in his plan. The only way I am going to stay in his plan is that I know what that plan is. I can't be running around here thinking, "Okay, I wonder if that is the Lord saying to me…well, maybe God is going to use this to show me…maybe he's speaking…"

Do you or don't you know his voice? Why do you have to guess? Until you know, you are guessing.

The only way you are going to know is if you shut it down, shut people down, steal away and inquire of him that he might show you. Then spend time doing that so that he can consistently reveal to you and bring you confirmation and all the things that you need. He has a plan for you.

But know this. The enemy has a plan for you too. Somebody said that the enemy of "best" is "good." Is that your very best or is that good enough?

(1 Thessalonians 5:24) *"Faithful is he that calleth you, who also will do it."*

Class 105 Study Summary

Key Points

1. No matter what tools you use, if you try to approach the word without the Holy Spirit, you will fail in your scriptural interpretation. The word was given to us by the Spirit of YeHoVaH. We need him to interpret what he gave to us.

2. Prophecy is hearing and speaking forth whether you are foretelling or forth-telling. It is the means by which the Father communicates.

3. YeHoVaH is still speaking to his people today and you can hear from him.

4. One of the most powerful passages of scripture was the corporate manifestation of the Spirit of the Almighty upon the seventy elders. When we are in the presence of a prophet, we and others will prophesy. We don't have to be in a prophet's presence though, to prophesy.

5. When the Spirit of YeHoVaH comes upon us, we will prophesy.

6. The company we keep is important because it will influence us supernaturally, even if we don't realize that influence.

7. John the Baptist (Yochanan) was filled in the womb with the Holy Spirit.

8. People who claim that "God showed them" or that "God said" but who do not have the Holy Spirit get their signs and symbols from other things. They are trying to get into the realm of the spirit without the Holy Spirit and that is not good.

9. "The evidence" of the Holy Spirit is not just speaking in tongues. We don't "tarry" for the Holy Spirit. Tongues is the least of the gifts of the Spirit. Many lies have been propagated by religion and are doctrines of demons. The Bible says that the evidence of the Holy Spirit will be *prophecy*.

10. The impartation of the spiritual gifts can occur from the laying on of hands.

11. The manifestation/gift of prophecy is an extension of the Holy Spirit and a body ministry function while the office of the prophet is a headship function.

12. Don't quench the Spirit. We do this by not actively being aware of and inquiring of the Holy Spirit.

13. The steps of the righteous are ordered by YeHoVaH. He desires to be with us everywhere we go and he wants us to be aware that he is always with us.

14. We are not to despise prophecy. We should desire it as well as the other gifts of the Spirit.

15. The enemy has a plan for you just like the Father has a plan for you. Make sure you are on the Father's plan or by default you will be on the enemy's plan.

Review Exercise

1. In our discussion of desiring to prophecy, can you identify that desire within yourself at this time? Why or why not?

_____

_____

_____

_____

2. How is the company you keep significant in relation to the Holy Spirit in workings in your life?

_____

_____

_____

_____

_____

_____

3. There will be some who will challenge the notion of the filling presence of the Holy Spirit before _Acts 2_. Can you prove that the Holy Spirit was ministering among YeHoVaH's people before Pentecost/Shavuot?

_____

_____

_____

_____

_____

_____

_____

_____

4. Summarize the most important concept or idea that you have been exposed to within this Discipleship Training course and how you believe it will continue to impact your life and the lives of those you come into contact with. Be prayerful and specific.

_____

_____

_____

_____

_____

_____

Rate the following statements
by filling in the most appropriate number.

(1 = I do not agree 10 = I agree completely)

Objectives:

1. I can explain the need for the ministration of the Holy Spirit in all of our interpretative work and study.

   1. ◯ 2. ◯ 3. ◯ 4. ◯ 5. ◯ 6. ◯ 7. ◯ 8. ◯ 9. ◯ 10. ◯

2. I can describe instances of the filling of the Holy Spirit by persons before *Acts 2.*

   1. ◯ 2. ◯ 3. ◯ 4. ◯ 5. ◯ 6. ◯ 7. ◯ 8. ◯ 9. ◯ 10. ◯

My Journal

What I learned from this class:

_____

_____

_____

_____

_____

_____

_____

_____

_____

_____

_____

_____

Congratulations!

You have just completed

Discipleship Training

―――

Workbooks 1-8

Classes 1 – 105

Made in the USA
Middletown, DE
11 January 2022

58383878R00157